Literary Lives

General Editor: **Richard Dutton,** Professor of English, Lancaster University

This series offers stimulating accounts of the literary careers of the most admired and influential English-language authors. Volumes follow the outline of the writers' working lives, not in the spirit of traditional biography, but aiming to trace the professional, publishing and social contexts which shaped their writing.

Published titles include:

Literary Lives
Series Standing Order ISBN 0-333-71486-5 hardcover
Series Standing Order ISBN 0-333-80334-5 paperback
(*outside North America only*)

You can receive future titles in this series as they are published by placing a standing order. Please contact your bookseller or, in case of difficulty, write to us at the address below with your name and address, the title of the series and one of the ISBNs quoted above.

Customer Services Department, Macmillan Distribution Ltd, Houndmills, Basingstoke, Hampshire RG21 6XS, England

Rudyard Kipling

A Literary Life

Phillip Mallett

First published 2003 by
PALGRAVE MACMILLAN
Houndmills, Basingstoke, Hampshire RG21 6XS and
175 Fifth Avenue, New York, N.Y. 10010
Companies and representatives throughout the world

PALGRAVE MACMILLAN is the global academic imprint of the Palgrave
Macmillan division of St. Martin's Press, LLC and of Palgrave Macmillan Ltd.
Macmillan® is a registered trademark in the United States, United Kingdom
and other countries. Palgrave is a registered trademark in the European
Union and other countries.

ISBN 0–333–55720–4 hardback
ISBN 0–333–55721–2 paperback

This book is printed on paper suitable for recycling and made from fully
managed and sustained forest sources.

A catalogue record for this book is available from the British Library.

Library of Congress Cataloging–in–Publication Data
Mallett, Phillip, 1946–
    Rudyard Kipling : a literary life / Phillip Mallett.
        p. cm. — (Literary lives)
    Includes bibliographical references (p.) and index.
    ISBN 0–333–55720–4
        1. Kipling, Rudyard, 1865–1936. 2. Kipling, Rudyard, 1865–1936–
    –Political and social views. 3. Authors, English—19th century—Biography.
    4. Authors, English—20th century—Biography. 5. Journalists—Great
    Britain—Biography. 6. British—India—History. I. Title. II. Literary lives
    (Palgrave Macmillan (Firm))

    PR4856.M24 2003
    828'.809—dc21
    [B]

                                                                2003048286

10   9   8   7   6   5   4   3   2   1
12   11   10   09   08   07   06   05   04   03

Printed and bound in Great Britain by
Antony Rowe Ltd, Chippenham and Eastbourne

In Memoriam
John and Ellen Burrage

Contents

Preface

The narrator of Ian McEwan's *Black Dogs*, seeking to write a biography of his parents-in-law, reflects that 'Turning-points are the inventions of story-tellers and dramatists, a necessary invention when life is reduced to, traduced by, a plot.' This biography is intended, like Kipling's auto-biographical *Something of Myself*, to look at the life of Rudyard Kipling 'from the point of view of his work'. I have wanted to attend to the forces, in particular the places and persons, which shaped his writing, to his dealings with the literary world which he took by storm in 1889–90, but in which he was always an awkward and troubling presence, and to his increasing involvement with politics after he returned to England from America in 1896. My first concern has been with Kipling's public rather than his private life. But I have, necessarily, described turning-points, drawn connections, made inferences, while being mindful of the obvious truth that even for the best-documented lives the evidence is partial: even for one's own.

In *Something of Myself* Kipling gives one sentence to his marriage: 'and then to London to be married in January '92 in the thick of an influenza epidemic, when the undertakers had run out of black horses and the dead had to be content with brown ones'. His biographers however are bound to say more, and I have done so. Victorian critics of the novel liked to speak of its power to tell the truth. But rather than truth, what the novels declare is a community in the process of creating and sharing the values by which it lived: deciding who was good, and who bad, but also how and why characters lived and moved and had their being. The biographers' truth is of a similar kind; a biography is true if the story it tells is informed by the values of the community to which the reader belongs, and by its beliefs about how men and women live their lives – about, for example, the reasons which might lead a young author to marry a woman others found difficult, or charmless. In recent years biography seems to have usurped the role of the nineteenth-century three-decker, as, increasingly, it has come to match it in length. Both (it might be argued) deploy a notion of 'character' which hardly exists in the postmodern novel; both offer a shared understanding of a text which re-presents the world, and in doing so confirms the truth of the text and the reader's existence as an autonomous and knowing subject. To some readers what follows will no doubt seem ideologically suspect, like the Classic Realist Text. It would be possible to write a post-modern biography of Kipling. This is not it, but I have tried not to assume an undue authority over the narrative which follows.

I began this study in the conviction that Kipling is the greatest English writer of the short story. I end it with the same conviction. In writing it I have drawn on papers given at various conferences: at the College of St Paul and St Mary, Cheltenham, on the short story; at the University of Swansea, on the literature of region and nation; at the University of Leiden, on national stereotypes; and at the Jagiellonian University, Krakow, on intertextuality. I am indebted to these institutions, and to those who responded to the papers. My chief scholarly debt, as it must be for every student of Kipling, is to the work of Thomas Pinney, the editor of *Something of Myself*, of *Kipling's India: Uncollected Sketches*, and of *The Letters of Rudyard Kipling*. If anything could have reconciled Kipling to the publication of his letters, it would be the skill and knowledge with which Professor Pinney has carried out his work, and I am glad to acknowledge it here. I have greatly enjoyed conversations about Kipling with Sandra Kemp, Uli Knoepflmacher, Craig Raine and Wendy Vacani, and with that good and gentle man, the late Robin Gilmour: my thanks to them all.

Except where otherwise indicated, quotations from Kipling's prose are from the Macmillan Uniform edition; those from the poetry are from the *Definitive Edition of Rudyard Kipling's Verse*, first published by Hodder and Stoughton in 1940.

1
Childhood and Youth

Rudyard Kipling mistrusted biographers. In *Something of Myself*, written in the last year of his life, he derided recent biographical writing as a form of 'Higher Cannibalism', engaged in 'the exhumation of scarcely cold notorieties . . . with sprightly inferences and "sex"-deductions to suit the mood of the market'.[1] He told his wife that his own book would deal with his life from the point of view of his work. It was to be a literary life, not a personal confession. The title flaunts its reticence, and 'something of myself' has often been taken to mean 'not much of myself'; Kipling's official biographer describes it as 'a reluctant release of what little he wished his readers to know'.[2] There is no mention of his unhappy love-affair with Florence Garrard, which figures so awkwardly in *The Light that Failed*; or of his friendship with Wolcott Balestier, whose sudden death precipitated his marriage to Wolcott's sister, Carrie; or of the quarrel with his brother-in-law Beatty, which persuaded him to abandon the home he and Carrie had made in Vermont, and return to England. He records the birth of his daughter Josephine, but not her name; he is silent about her death in 1899, at the age of six. By closing the narrative in 1907, with his visit to Stockholm to receive the Nobel Prize, he avoids any reference to the death of his parents, or to that of his only son John, at Loos in September 1915, just six weeks after his eighteenth birthday.

But writers do not begin autobiographies without reason. *Something of Myself* is written with the same economy of means and richness of implication as the stories Kipling had been writing for fifty years. Nowhere is this more apparent than in the opening chapter, his portrait of the artist as a young boy. It is not the only account he was to give of his genesis as a writer, but it is one to which his biographers have necessarily paid attention.

1

The chapter is constructed as a fable of exile, from both India and his parents. It opens with Kipling's childhood in Bombay, where his father taught architectural sculpture to Indian students, and his earliest memories, of 'golden and purple fruits at the level of my shoulder' in the market, of night-winds heard through palm or banana leaves, the song of the tree-frogs, and of Arab dhows going out to sea (*SM* 33). Here he lived at peace, and at the centre of the world around him. Or rather, of both worlds: the world of the servants, where he spoke Hindi and ruled as an unquestioned despot, and that of his parents, where he was allowed to play with lumps of wet clay in his Father's studio, and where 'the Mother sang wonderful songs at a black piano' when he and his younger sister Alice – known to her family as Trix – were allowed to join the adults in the dining-room (*SM* 4).

Exile was in the form of his journey to England, shortly before his sixth birthday, to the house of Mrs Holloway in Southsea, where he was to spend the next five years. It was the tradition among Anglo-Indians to send their children 'home' for a time, partly to get an English education and put down roots, and partly, too, to wean them from the influence of servants and ayahs whose devotion was taken on trust, but whose notions of hygiene, religious observance and sexual morality were not. Anglo-Indians worked hard to keep alive the idea of Home, and of the day of their return, and looked down on those who stayed on after their period of duty was over. Kipling and Trix were already at the stage where they had to be reminded to speak English when they joined their parents, and after a third child, John, died at birth in April 1870, it must have seemed prudent to remove them from the rigours of the Indian climate. And so, in October 1871, Rudyard and his sister were left at Lorne Lodge on the south coast, 'a new small house smelling of aridity and emptiness', as the paying guests of Pryse Holloway, his wife Sarah, and their eleven-year-old son Harry (*SM* 5).

For whatever reason – perhaps they could not bear to – Alice and Lockwood had done nothing to prepare their children for the coming separation. Rudyard told the story of these years three times: in his autobiography, in the short story 'Baa Baa, Black Sheep', written in 1888, and again two years later in the novel *The Light that Failed*. Whatever his parents had to say about 'Black Sheep' – and they must have said something – did nothing to change his own view of events, and on the key points the three narratives echo each other closely.[3] In none is there any effort to understand Mrs Holloway – Aunty Rosa, as the children in 'Baa Baa, Black Sheep' are taught to call her, or 'the Woman' as Kipling calls her in the autobiography, the capitals miming his derision – and it has been left to his biographers to consider her side of the story. Her position was hardly an easy one. She had married late, into a well-connected Oxfordshire family, but her husband's career had been undistinguished. He had served for five years in the Royal Navy, and later in the merchant marine, for a time as a whaler, before settling to a position as Chief Officer in the Coastguards in 1855. He and Sarah married in 1859, moving to Southsea soon after his retirement a decade later. Over the years his social status had slipped below that of the rest of his family; that he and his wife needed to take in boarders tells its own story about their financial position.

Even if their circumstances had been more comfortable, Rudyard was not the easiest child to manage. Mrs Holloway had been asked to teach him to read and write, so that he could send letters to his parents, but he was slow and stubborn, whereas Trix, aged three, was quicker and more responsive. On an earlier visit to England, at the time of his sister's birth, he had proved himself a difficult child, clumsy, noisy and demanding, and for that reason if for no other his parents had preferred not to leave the children with relatives. Widowed three years after the Kiplings' arrival, and anxious for her own son – after his father's death he left school, aged fourteen, to work in a bank – Mrs Holloway understandably found Rudyard hard to cope with.

How far, or if at all, he exaggerated the ill-treatment he received at her hands is difficult to determine.[4] He got on well with 'Captain' Holloway, who told him tales of naval battles and whaling adventures; he and Trix were visited by members of their mother's family, who evidently found nothing amiss, and Trix stayed on a further three years after Rudyard had been removed. In later life her memories of these years were ambiguous, allowing that her brother had sometimes deepened grey into black, while supporting his claim that Mrs Holloway had treated him harshly after her husband's death. Kipling's own memories were unyielding. From being the centre of attention, he became the marginalised 'Black Sheep', confronted with 'the full vigour of the Evangelical', and the threat of 'Hell . . . in all its terrors' (*SM* 6). Instead of having servants whom he could order about, he found himself liable to be beaten, and, worse than that, beaten by a woman: a terrible blow to his sense of caste. He was tormented by Harry as well as by Mrs Holloway, and unhappy at his day school. The account in 'Baa Baa, Black Sheep' suggests that at times he felt that Trix had taken sides against him, while the absence of explanation from his parents seemed to suggest that they too had rejected him. When later in life he wrote of the 'horror of desolation, abandonment, and realised worthlessness' that can afflict the young, it was these years he had in mind.[5] Lorne Lodge was always 'the House of Desolation'.

But Kipling was to claim that the experience of these years was not wholly wasted. Punch, in 'Baa Baa, Black Sheep', is first seen demanding 'the story about the Ranee that was turned into a tiger'. The demand is answered, and 'the Hamal [house-boy] made the tiger-noises in twenty different keys'. With Aunty Rosa this joyous storytelling is exchanged for a spelling book – 'a dirty brown book filled with unintelligible dots and marks'. In time, however, Punch learns to read, and thereafter he can pass 'into a land of his own', free from Aunty Rosa, and 'string himself tales of travel and adventure'. Punch has made the passage from listening to reading to telling stories. In the autobiography, Kipling recalls that when he was sent a copy of *Robinson Crusoe* he took to playing the role of the solitary, sitting on the floor of his basement room behind a piece of packing case 'which kept off any other world. Thus fenced about, everything inside the fence was quite real, but mixed with the smell of damp cupboards. If the bit of board fell, I had to begin the magic all over again. . . . The magic, you see, lies in the ring or fence that you take refuge in' (*SM* 8). The same might be said of the ordering power of fiction, or of those other rituals and institutions – the Club, freemasonry, the Family Square – to which Kipling was drawn throughout his life. In his loyalty to these, he stands apart from most of his contemporaries; in his belief that an unfailing allegiance to the craft of writing might be an act of defence against the chaos of the world, he comes closer to them. The passage stands suggestively midway between a Victorian notion of reading as a means of escape, and a frankly modernist aesthetic.

Punch/Kipling has also learned to lie, and is beaten for doing so. He consoles himself by inventing 'horrible punishments' for his tormentors, or 'plotting another line of the tangled web of deception' woven around Aunty Rosa. Even in 1888, when the story was first published, Kipling's readers might have seen in Punch's young imaginings some of the characteristics of the fiction, which so often turns on the desire for revenge. In the autobiography, Kipling claimed that his childhood unhappiness had drained him 'of any capacity for real, personal hate' (*SM* 12); he might more plausibly have written that these were the years which taught him how to hate. But it also taught him 'constant wariness, the habit of observation, and attendance on moods and tempers' (*SM* 11). In *Something of Myself* he repeatedly offers Robert Browning's Fra Lippo Lippi, street-urchin turned monk-artist, his senses sharpened by the need for self-preservation, as a model of the kind of writer he was himself to become: one who 'learns the look of things and none the less / For admonition'. This argues a view of himself as a realist, alert to the ways of the world, rather than as a fantasist, acting out in stories the revenges he could not achieve in real life. What is common to both accounts is the acute sense of audience, and of the need to be effective on a particular group, and to be admitted as part of it.

He was able to let down his guard during occasional escapes to 'The Grange', the home of his aunt Georgiana Burne-Jones, 'the beloved Aunt', where he found kindly adults, children with whom he could be at ease, and a delight in play and make-believe. There too in the evenings he could hang over the stairs listening to 'deep-voiced men laughing together over dinner', 'the loveliest sound in the world' (*SM* 10) – a sentence which comes oddly from a man approaching his seventies, but perhaps suggests why he wrote so many farces, and why the conclusions to these stories, with strong men reduced to tears of helpless laughter, leave most readers feeling uncomfortable.

It was on one these visits, at the end of 1876, that his aunt realised his distress, and wrote to tell his mother of it. Around this time he suffered 'some sort of nervous breakdown', which led him to see 'shadows and things that were not there'. This is associated with the discovery of his extreme short-sightedness, and anticipates the recurring images of blindness in his writing; it links too with his memory of the time a few months later when 'the night got into my head', so that he wandered around the house till daybreak (*SM* 13). This was to happen to him again and again throughout his life, and something like it happens to many of his characters, from Morrowbie Jukes on a manic ride across country in a story written when Kipling was only twenty, to the shell-shocked John Marden in his last collection. It is if anything too easy to see traces of the precocious but wary child at Lorne Lodge in Kipling's stories: few writers give so strongly the impression of having understood the way people speak and behave from the outside, while refusing to be drawn into intimacy with them. But he liked to say that he had two sides to his head, and the image of the night-wandering boy suggests his no less powerful fascination with the haunted and the obsessed. It is in the driving single emotion, or the solitary driven character – Larry Tighe in ' "Love-o'-Women" ', Vickery in 'Mrs Bathurst', Grace Ashcroft in 'The Wish House', Manallace in 'Dayspring Mishandled' – that Kipling often finds his subject. Typically, the obsession is simply a given: it is the fact of it, not the question of where it originated, or how it developed, that excites him. He gave his conscious loyalty to the pack, group or tribe, but his imagination was stirred by loneliness.

The Family Square

In March 1877 Alice Kipling returned to England, putting an end to her son's ordeal, and a year later Lockwood too arrived in Europe, on furlough for eight months. From this time on, Rudyard's parents were to remain key figures in his life; in *Something of Myself* he suggests that they were his most important audience until their deaths, when he was in his mid-forties. There is an element of compensation in this – to idealise his parents was one way to resist the fear that they had betrayed him – but his early work was certainly fostered and prompted by his family. It was his mother who arranged in 1881 for the publication in Lahore of twenty-three of his poems as *Schoolboy Lyrics*, without his knowledge, and to his annoyance; in 1884 he published a collection of parodies, *Echoes*, with his sister; and in 1885 *Quartette*, the Christmas annual of the *Civil and Military Gazette*, consisted of work by all four Kiplings, identified as 'Four Anglo-Indian Writers'. Rudyard was ready to submit his work to the judgement of both parents. When an early story touching on sexual irregularities was 'abolished' by his mother, he accepted her ruling, if not quite without demur, and he frequently sought his father's advice, especially while writing *Kim*, which they 'smoked over' together (*SM* 43, 82). It was his mother, 'with her quick flutter of the hands', who helped him find the line he was looking for in 'The English Flag': 'And what should they know of England who only England know?' (*SM* 54).

There are items on each side of the balance-sheet here. Kipling's allegiance to the 'Family Square', made up of himself and the capitalised Father, Mother and Maiden, is the prototype of his many determined efforts to write of and for a group, often with the over-insistence suggested by the capitals. But his father's craftsmanship became his son's, and many of Rudyard's images for his work are drawn from the practical arts – thus *Rewards and Fairies* was worked in 'three or four overlaid tints and textures', to reveal themselves according to the shifting light of different readers (*SM* 111). And he was always capable of shedding an influence if it did not fit. His mother had written and published some poems, partly influenced by William Morris (there is a half-buried reference to her in one of Morris's poems),[6] and some of Rudyard's earlier verse employs the same Pre-Raphaelite landscapes, broken rhythms, and atmosphere of sexual tension. Whether this came to him from Morris directly, or through his mother, it was a voice and manner he quickly dropped.

John Lockwood Kipling, like his future wife the child of a Methodist minister, was educated at Woodhouse Grove, a Methodist boarding-school near Bradford, leaving at the age of fourteen to take up work in the potteries in Staffordshire, and to study at the School of Art in Stoke. By the time he was twenty-one he was in London, working on the exterior decoration of what was to become the Victoria and Albert Museum. But he kept up his Staffordshire connections, and it was in Burslem that he came into contact with another young Methodist, Frederic Macdonald, and through him with his sister Alice. Lockwood and Alice became engaged at a picnic in 1863 near Lake Rudyard, and married two years later, in March 1865, at St Mary Abbots Church in Kensington. Their decision to marry in the Church of England, rather than in a Methodist chapel, makes it clear that neither of them was much attached to the Methodist faith; nor, unlike many of their contemporaries, were they much troubled by lapsing from it. It was then perhaps as well that ill-health kept Alice's parents from attending the wedding, though Lockwood's mother did so. Most of the guests at the reception were among Alice's friends in the world of art, not that of church or chapel: Dante Gabriel and William Michael Rossetti, Swinburne, Ford Madox Brown. A month later the couple left for Bombay, where Lockwood was to take up a place teaching architectural sculpture at the Sir Jamjetsee Jeheebhoy School of Art and Industry. It was in Bombay that their first son, named after the lake where they had met, was born on 30 December 1865.

The family into which Lockwood had married was a remarkable one. At its head was George Macdonald, a Methodist minister whose faith was tempered by a generous tolerance.[7] His own father had been brought to Methodism by Wesley himself, and when his younger son Fred became President of the Methodist Conference in 1899, the event marked over a century of Macdonald activity within the movement. With an ever-growing family, George and Hannah Macdonald had little leisure and few luxuries;[8] they found enough money to provide for Harry, the eldest son, to go to university, but Fred had to make do with a variety of day schools, while the girls were taught by their mother, helped out with access to their father's library.

Alice was the eldest of the five daughters who survived to maturity. After the family moved to London in 1853, she and her sister Georgiana spent much of their time in and around Pre-Raphaelite circles, among the 'stunners' invited to William Morris's rooms in Red Lion Square and the Prinseps' home at Little Holland House. They owed the connection to their brother Harry, who had been at school with Edward Burne-Jones (still, at that time, plain Jones); like many Victorian young women, they depended largely on their brothers, and on their brothers' friends, for their intellectual stimulus – and, in due course, for their husbands. Georgiana became engaged to Burne-Jones when she was only fifteen, and he all but penniless; he was not much better off when they married four years later, on 9 June 1860, chosen as the anniversary of the death of Dante's Beatrice. As the married sister, Georgie provided the milieu in which another, Agnes, could meet her husband, the painter Edward Poynter. Poynter's classicising is of little interest beside the more idiosyncratic work of Burne-Jones, but he was clearly a man with a career to make, a future President of the Royal Academy and, like Burne-Jones, a future baronet. Soon after Agnes's engagement came that of Louisa, into another Methodist family, the Baldwins. Alfred Baldwin was already a partner in the family's iron foundry, and on the way to making a fortune. He himself went into Parliament; their son, Stanley, served three times as Prime Minister. Despite their differences – Kipling's politics were more abrasive than his cousin's – Rudyard and Stanley remained friendly over the years. Edith, the youngest of the sisters, remained unmarried; after the death of Hannah Macdonald in 1875, she moved in with Alfred and Louisa.[9]

Alice had been engaged at least three times before she met Lockwood (once to the Irish poet William Allingham), she had seen Georgie marry before her, and she was already twenty-six when she met her eventual husband. But whatever fears might have led her into it, her marriage was to be a success. It was not quite a union of opposites, though Alice is always described as witty, and Lockwood as a quiet and unassuming man. 'Witty', in Victorian usage, is often a code word for 'clever' when applied to women, but the word was appropriate for Alice in both senses (when her father called her a flirt, she spelled out 'P-H-L-U-R-T' and asked with affected innocence 'Phlurt. What is that?'). There was more than a touch of asperity in her nature; as her brother Fred put it, she 'knew how to give advice in pungent form'.[10] She never much liked India, but she was determined to turn her time there to advantage. Lockwood, who had a genuine enthusiasm for Indian arts and crafts, found it more congenial.

Theirs was to be a classic Victorian story of hard work and self-help. Lockwood took on pupils to help make ends meet, and both he and Alice wrote for the newspapers, in particular the *Pioneer* in Allahabad. In 1875 he became head of the new Mayo School of Industrial Art in Lahore, as well as Curator of the Museum, the role his son was to give him in *Kim*, where he continued to promote native handicrafts and to oppose what he saw as the damaging tendency towards Europeanisation. The following year he designed and executed seventy banners as part of the Delhi Durbar, the celebrations to mark Victoria's adoption of the title of Empress of India. Alice clearly helped his advancement; her commitment to doing so was one reason for sending the children to England, and Lockwood's promotion persuaded her to delay a planned visit home. It was not too difficult to shine in the small Anglo-Indian community in Lahore, although the rules of precedence were strict, and the Kiplings were low in the social order, but Alice had increasingly famous relatives, and good skills as a hostess. The Viceroy in 1876, Lord Lytton, was known in London circles as the poet 'Owen Meredith', and the Kiplings became personal friends. They repeated their success with Lord Dufferin, Viceroy from 1884 to 1888, who was heard to remark that 'Dullness and Mrs Kipling were never in the same room together'. In 1887 Lockwood was made a Companion of the Order of the Indian Empire; in 1890 he was invited to design the Indian Room at Osborne House, the Queen's home on the Isle of Wight.

He and Alice returned to England in 1893, settling at Tisbury in Wiltshire, where they were taken up by the Wyndhams, at the centre of the group of cultured aristocrats known as 'the Souls'. By then their son's fame was assured; Trix, however, had made an unhappy marriage, which brought her, in 1898, to the first of a series of breakdowns, and Alice spent much of her time over the next decade nursing her daughter.[11] The two came to share an interest in psychic phenomena, including automatic writing; Lockwood was sceptical, Rudyard concerned but curious.[12] Eventually Alice's own health gave way, and she died in November 1910. Lockwood followed her two months later, in January 1911. Trix was intermittently ill until the 1930s; after the death of her husband in 1942, she settled in Edinburgh, where she died in 1948.

The United Services College

Kipling's removal from Lorne Lodge in March 1877 was the beginning of a period of relaxation with his mother and his sister, spent partly in London and partly in Epping Forest, where he and Trix rode ponies and played with their cousin Stanley. There was also time for his mother to encourage his reading – Emerson's *Poems*, stories by Bret Harte, and *Sidonia the Sorceress*, a favourite Pre-Raphaelite text. Then at the end of the year, Rudyard was left with Georgiana and Mary Craik, and their friend Miss Winnard, the three 'Ladies of Warwick Gardens', in a house which he remembered as 'filled with books, peace, kindliness, patience and what today would be called "culture" ' (*SM* 15). The two Misses Craik and Miss Winnard moved on the genteel fringe of the Pre-Raphaelite world. They knew Jean Ingelow and Christina Rossetti; two clay pipes which Carlyle had once smoked hung on the wall, tied with black ribbon. Georgiana was herself a minor novelist, writing on her knee by the fireside. Life in Warwick Gardens was tame after the excitements of hoop-races and pig-killings in Epping Forest, but it allowed Kipling a period of transition before he was sent on to school, and over the next few years he spent a number of holidays there. Trix, too, was later to stay in Warwick Gardens, but for the time being she returned to Southsea. Evidently Alice Kipling still trusted Mrs Holloway; so, presumably, did Trix. But this time there was to be no risk of the children feeling abandoned. Alice remained in Europe until the autumn of 1880, and when in 1878 Lockwood returned on leave, father and son went together to Paris, where Lockwood was to supervise the Indian exhibit at the International Exposition. It was the first time they had seen each other since 1871.

The school Kipling entered in January 1878, shortly after his twelfth birthday, was the United Services College on the North Devon coast near Bideford. The subject of the USC was one on which he could always be drawn throughout his life, perhaps because it was at school that he began to recognise the caste to which he was to belong; school was to Kipling what class has been to other writers. In *Something of Myself* he describes the USC as 'the School before its time', and in a speech to mark the retirement of the headmaster, Cormell Price, in 1894, he claimed 'All that the College – all that Mr Price – has ever arrived at was to make men able to make and keep empires.'[13] Both statements are exaggerated. The College had been set up in 1874 by a group of Army officers, primarily to serve the needs of boys born overseas into Army families. The main objective was to prepare them for the Army entrance examinations at Sandhurst and Woolwich, at a lower cost than the 'crammers' which generally catered for the less able students. To that end its buildings were unpretentious, it accepted a number of problem pupils, and its staff were for the most part undistinguished. As a new foundation, it was less burdened with traditions than some of its competitors – there was no school corps, and no organised fagging – and perhaps its chief advantage to Kipling, though not one he liked to play up in later years, was precisely that it did not knock off the rough edges of its more individualist students.

That it did not do so owed much to the personality of Cormell Price. Price had been at school in Birmingham with two of Kipling's uncles, Burne-Jones and Henry Macdonald, and had become friendly at Oxford with William Morris, where he had helped to paint the Union walls with

Pre-Raphaelite frescoes. Lockwood and Alice could rely on him to protect their ungainly, short-sighted son from the worst rigours of public-school life. Outside the school Rudyard knew Price as 'Uncle Crom', and as a very different man from the Head celebrated in *Stalky & Co.* For one thing, Price, like Morris and Burne-Jones, was opposed to the aggressive imperialism being adopted by Disraeli, and immediately before travelling down to Bideford with his new pupil had been involved with them in the Workmen's Neutrality Demonstration, called in protest against the policy of intervention in the Russo-Turkish war. It was this crisis which brought the word 'jingoism' into the language, from the refrain of the music-hall song: 'We don't want to fight, yet by Jingo! if we do, / We've got the ships, we've got the men, and got the money too.' Price was, very exactly, not a Jingoist. He was in fact something of a Russophile, having spent several years in Russia as a private tutor before becoming a schoolmaster. He was happy to prepare his students for the Army, but unlike Kipling he was not willing to identify the role of the Army with the ambitions of Empire.

Nor was Price as ready with the cane as his counterpart in *Stalky & Co.*, who flogs the boys of Study 5 with 'a certain clarity of outline that stamps the work of the artist'.[14] Beresford, the original of M'Turk in *Stalky*, scoffed at one such story, where the boys wash the blood off their backs after a beating, while Dunsterville, the original of Stalky, records that the worst bullying had stopped before Rudyard arrived. Even so, Kipling remembered his first term as 'horrible', and his first year-and-a-half as 'not pleasant'. But by the end of that time he, Dunsterville and Beresford had become friends. All three were strong personalities, made stronger by their friendship, who needed and thrived upon the school's readiness to tolerate an unusual level of nonconformity. Both in the stories and in his non-fictional recollections, Kipling ascribed this tolerance to Price's far-sightedness; Beresford, less generously, attributed it to his lack of natural authority. But then, Beresford habitually referred to the masters as 'ushers'.

Price's success over twenty years as headmaster at the USC lends support to the more charitable account. Kipling certainly had good reasons to appreciate the kindness and wisdom of 'Uncle Crom'. In many ways his education was unlike that normally offered at an English public school. It owed little to the games ethos which he was later to celebrate, in his 1893 essay on 'An English School', as a means of learning more than could be itemised on the end-of-term bills. The essay, as he acknowledged, was a 'flagrant puff' for the USC, which was running into financial difficulties, but from time to time Kipling seems to have felt the need at least to affect such pieties.[15] More often, and with more conviction, he treats them with the irony to which they are subjected in *Stalky & Co*. But whatever he made of it later, he took little part as a schoolboy in the usual system of cricket and football. Obliged to wear glasses with thick pebble lenses – earning him the nickname 'Giggers', schoolboy slang for giglamps – and physically uncoordinated, he was excused games, though he enjoyed swimming in the sea off the North Devon coast. For all its sly malice, Beresford's description of him as 'the Epicurean Giglamps, the art and literature crank, the anti-sport, anti-athletic highbrow', is nearer the mark than the later Kipling would have wished.[16]

Then, in 1881, when it was clear that he would not be going on to university – his Latin was indifferent, and his mathematics poor – Kipling was excused from formal lessons and given the run of Price's own library, where he read everything he could lay his hands on. In *Stalky & Co*. he wrote rapturously about the privilege:

> There Beetle found a fat arm-chair, a silver ink-stand and unlimited pens and paper. There were scores and scores of ancient dramatists, there were Hakluyt, his *Voyages*; French translations of Muscovite authors called Pushkin and Lermontoff; little tales of a heady and bewildering nature, interspersed with unusual songs – Peacock was that writer's name; . . . an odd theme, purporting to be a translation of something called a 'Rubaiyat', which the Head said was a poem not yet come to its own; there were hundreds of volumes of verse – Crashaw; Dryden; Alexander Smith; L.E.L.; Lydia Sigourney; Fletcher and a *Purple Island*; Donne; Marlowe's *Faust*; . . . *Ossian*; *The Earthly Paradise*; *Atalanta in Calydon*; and Rossetti – to name only a few.

At the same time he was developing an enthusiasm for a number of American authors who were to remain among his favourites, among them Bret Harte, Longfellow and Mark Twain, and in particular Walt Whitman, whom he defended against the criticism of his English and Classics master, William Crofts, later to serve as the model for King in *Stalky & Co*. Kipling acknowledged Crofts's scholarship and sincerity, but it was another master, F. W. Haslam, who paid his pupil the oblique compliment of prophesying that he would die a 'scurrilous journalist', at once recognising his talent, and cautioning him against too easy a reliance on it (*SM* 23). The remark has the kind of cleverness that Kipling always admired.

It was Crofts who introduced Kipling to Horace's *Odes*, which were to become a passion in later years. According to the autobiography, he also introduced him to Browning when he threw a volume of *Men and Women* at his head during class, though Kipling might already have known him as a favourite poet of Alice and Lockwood. Like Browning himself, Kipling delighted in out-of-the-way authors, and was capable of finding something of use to him almost anywhere, but Browning is one of the few writers he seems seriously to have imitated. The dramatic monologues 'The Mary Gloster' and 'McAndrew's Hymn', in *The Seven Seas* (1896), are the most obvious instances, but it is also evident in many of the stories. Some of his early experiments with a disturbed first-person narrator, as in 'The Dream of Duncan Parrenness' and 'The Strange Ride of Morrowbie Jukes', owe as much to Browning as to Poe. Less predictably, his late story 'The Manner of Men' (1930) has a family likeness to 'Cleon' and 'Karshish', both in *Men and Women*. In all three, the speakers – Cleon, Karshish, the two seamen who were once shipwrecked with Paul of Tarsus – try to recount their experiences in secular terms, but sense the need for a different frame of reference, one the reader knows is provided by the Christian story which the speakers refuse to admit. Whether or not the credit should go to Crofts, Browning was the writer the young Kipling most needed to read.

According to *Something of Myself*, 'the tide of writing set in' some time after his second year at the school. The earliest work he was to authorise for publication, a poem called 'The Dusky Crew', was offered to and rejected by the *St Nicholas Magazine* in August 1879:

> Our heads were rough and our hands were black
> With the ink-stain's midnight hue;
> We scouted all, both great and small –
> We were a dusky crew;
> And each boy's hand was against us raised –
> 'Gainst me and the Other Two.

The poem has some autobiographical interest, as evidence of the importance Kipling already attached to his friendship with Dunsterville and Beresford, but as verse it is unremarkable. It was one of several poems – others include a mock-heroic account of a pillow-fight, and a dramatic monologue spoken by a condemned man on the night before his execution – which he contributed to the 'Scribbler', a handwritten magazine produced by the Morris and Burne-Jones children between November 1878 and March 1880. Kipling's poems appear over the name 'Nickson'; Lockwood Kipling used the name 'Nick' for occasional pieces in the *Pioneer*, and the choice of pseudonym perhaps suggests how badly Rudyard wanted to feel himself his father's son. Over the years a shared interest in literature was to be one of the forces holding the family together.

In 1881 Price invited Kipling to revive the school magazine, the *United Services College Chronicle*. Seven issues appeared under his editorship, and he was fond enough of it to send in contributions from India. In his essay on 'An English School' he recorded that it was 'a real printed paper of eight pages, and at first the printer was more thoroughly ignorant of type-setting, and the Editor was more completely ignorant of proof-reading, than any printer and any Editor that ever was' (*SM* 189). The tone of the reminiscence fairly captures the mood and manner of most of the poems he wrote for it: usually facetious, often adapting and parodying the style of Browning, Tennyson and others, and concerned mainly with the trivia of school and study life – food, feuds, the weather. 'There were few atrocities of form and metre that I did not perpetrate', he wrote later, 'and I enjoyed them all' (*SM* 22). The liveliest of the *Chronicle* poems is 'Donec Gratus Eram', a rendering of one of Horace's *Odes* (III, ix) into the Devonshire dialect, written by way of penance after Kipling had offended Crofts by complaining of the absence of rhyme in Latin verse. There are two poems on public themes: a prize poem on a subject set by Price, commemorating Wellington's victory at 'The Battle of Assaye' in 1803, and 'Ave Imperatrix!', written after a shot had been fired at Queen Victoria. The would-be assassin, Robert Maclean, was also a would-be poet, who had been denied permission to dedicate a volume of poems to the Queen. In a letter written at the time Kipling described the school as 'intensely amused' by the event (*Letters*, I.18); in later years he took either the subject or the poem more seriously, and included 'Ave Imperatrix!' in collected editions of his verse.[17]

None of the *Chronicle* poems exhibits much more than competence. They read like the work of a clever boy who happened to exercise his talents in the direction of verse, but might equally have found other uses for his energy. But at the same time Kipling was writing verse of a quite different kind. In July 1880 he had been sent to collect Trix from Lorne Lodge, and had met there a fellow-boarder, Florence Garrard, who was then fifteen years old. He fell in love with her, or convinced himself that he had done so, and seems to have believed himself engaged to her. By 1884, however, if not before, Florence had made it plain that she did not consider herself engaged, and there the matter ended until they met again in 1890. Kipling was then preparing to write the full-length novel which was expected of him, and Florence appears in *The Light that Failed* as Maisie. It is an ungenerous portrait of an intense but loveless woman, ambitious of success as a painter but without the necessary talent, and Florence understandably repudiated it. By the time Kipling sought her out in 1890, she was a student at the Académie Julian in Paris, she had a partner, her fellow-student Mabel Price, and she had no interest in resuming a relationship that for her at least had finished six years before.

The verse that Kipling wrote to or about Florence is mainly interesting as the sign of a road which in the end he was not to take. Before he sailed to India he presented her with a notebook containing 32 poems under the title 'Sundry Phansies'. The elaborately designed title page is rather let down by the note which follows: 'I must apologise for the writing and spelling throughout the book – They are both nearly as bad as the poetry.' Not all the poems were written after the meeting with Florence. The first verse of 'Crossing the Rubicon' was included in a letter to Lockwood in 1879:

> A cry in the silent night,
>   A white face turned to the wall,
> A pang – and then in the minds of men
>   Forgotten – that is all!

This is clearly a more ambitious kind of writing than that undertaken for the *Chronicle*. Some of it is self-consciously derivative, usually of Browning, but more often Kipling seems to be trying out moods and emotions which as yet he knew only through the medium of words. It is the language, and the possible experience, as yet only imagined, that hold his attention, and not the reality of Florence Garrard:

> For each light love leaves some light trace
>   And the heart is seared ere manhood's days,
>   Ere the love that lingers and lights and stays
>   Arrive – and we keep it not.[18]

These poems show Kipling experimenting with different kinds of poetic voice to see which he could believe in, and begin to build on as his own. Andrew Rutherford describes them as private poems, and in a sense they were – certainly not intended for the eyes of his schoolmates, not even those of Beresford and Dunsterville.[19] But he was also willing to send them off in all directions: to his parents, to the Ladies of Warwick Gardens (who upset him by mistaking the 'old, dead king' whom he meant for the God of Love for a dead canary), to his aunt Edith Macdonald, and to Miss Edith Plowden and Mrs John Tavenor Perry, family friends whom he adopted as confidantes.

He also sent a sonnet called 'Two Lives' to the *World*, where it was published in November 1882, earning him a fee of one guinea – enough to treat his Study to an extravagant tea. In his 'Notebook' he described it as 'Not bad – a direct Shakespeare crib which I thought vastly fine when I wrote it.' It is modelled on Shakespeare's sonnet 144, but its theme – a speaker caught between two lives, one strange and valued, the other familiar and despised – suggests something of his real feelings at this time. In a letter to Mrs Tavenor Perry in May 1882 he described himself as 'scribbling away at all sorts of stuff – gas and sewerage and love stories, all in a jumble together' by way of distraction from his problems with Florence (*Letters*, I.23). Physically and intellectually precocious, in love or supposing himself to be so, he was beginning to feel that he was merely marking time at school. Beresford reports that he wanted to go to London; Kipling himself said that he longed to get out of England. In the event, the decision was made for him. During the Easter holidays in 1882 Stephen Wheeler, editor of the *Civil and Military Gazette* in Lahore, agreed to Lockwood Kipling's request to take Rudyard on as his assistant. On 20 September 1882 Kipling sailed from Tilbury docks in the P & O steamer *Brindisi*, bound first for Port Said, thence to Bombay, and then finally by rail to Lahore.

2
Seven Years' Hard: Kipling in India

Kipling's journey to India took him through the Suez Canal, just a few weeks after the defeat of Arabi Pasha at Tel-el-Kebir and the beginning of what the British envisaged as the temporary occupation of Egypt. Their intention was to protect the Canal, which had come under threat from Arabi's supporters, restore the more compliant Khedive to power, and then quietly withdraw. In the event, they were still there seventy years later, until another nationalist leader, Gamal Nasser, compelled them to leave. By one of the ironies of history, the expeditionary force had been sent out by a Liberal government, despite Gladstone's declared policy of non-intervention. In command was Sir Garnet Wolseley, whose exploits in the Zulu wars had made him the nation's leading soldier, while Frederick Roberts, soon to be one of Kipling's heroes, marked time in Madras. These ironies were lost on the young Kipling, but in the four days he had to wait at Port Said he did have time to take in the atmosphere of a base-camp only fifty miles from the scene of battle. Ten years later he was to draw on these impressions for parts of *The Light that Failed*.

He reached Suez on 7 October 1882. It was at Suez, he wrote afterwards, that the first-time traveller had to face 'the black hour of homesickness', but only eleven days later, on 18 October, he landed in Bombay, and at once found himself speaking in the vernacular 'sentences whose meaning I knew not' (*SM* 25).[1] His English years 'fell away, nor ever, I think, came back in full strength'. He felt a sense of return rather than of dislocation, and his arrival in Lahore, after a long journey northwards on the rapidly expanding railway system, was a joyous homecoming, made all the sweeter when Trix came out at the end of 1883 to complete the Family Square.

The elder Kiplings had been in Lahore, the capital of the Punjab, since 1875. Their position cannot have been quite comfortable.

Lockwood's salary was adequate, if modest, but he was not a member of the Indian Civil Service, and in a community where precedent and protocol counted for a good deal they were clearly of minor rank, and sometimes reminded of the fact. There was even an unpleasant rumour that Rudyard was a half-caste. None of this is allowed to disfigure *Something of Myself*, where the emphasis is on the happiness and self-sufficiency of the Family Square. But fifty years later, in the revenge-farce 'Beauty Spots', the victim is a retired Major and his tormentor a young man who has suffered under the same accusation.

Soon after his arrival, Kipling was elected as the youngest member of the Punjab Club, among some seventy white civilians, all 'picked men at their definite work', and each 'talking his own shop'. These men, together with the officers stationed at the fort and in the military cantonment at Mian Mir – altogether only a few hundred in number – were his immediate audience, as the readers of the *Civil & Military Gazette*. From the first, what was impressed upon him was the need for solidarity. The Punjab had been annexed into the Raj as recently as 1849, and still had the character of a frontier province. The Anglo-Indians who lived and worked there were an inward-looking community, suspicious of the government at home, and opposed to talk of progress and reform. They insisted on the absolute superiority of the British, and the essential unchangingness of the Indians. For the most part they preferred to emphasise the 'old' rural India of princes and peasants, and in consequence seriously underestimated the power of the emerging middle-class India of the National Congress. Kipling never directly challenged these ideas, though in his fiction they form only one part of his imaginative vision. But even in *Kim*, the warmest and most generous of his Indian stories, his views on the task of ruling India are shaped by what he heard in the Punjab Club.

In the first half of the nineteenth century that task had been debated in terms of the Evangelical programme to regenerate Indian society by reforming its morality, and the Utilitarian programme to improve its morality by reforming its social structure: hence, on the one hand, the suppression of suttee in the 1820s, the campaign against the Thugs in the 1830s, and the abolition of slavery in 1843, and, on the other, the work done by Macaulay in the 1830s and by Fitzjames Stephen in the 1870s to establish and then to revise the Indian Penal Code. But the principles underpinning both programmes were shaken by the Rebellion of 1857. Increasingly it was argued that the evils of Indian society were not contingent on its history, but the irremediable expression of an inherent Indian character. From the late 1840s, physical anthropologists such as Robert Knox and John Beddoe had advanced the theory of polygenism, arguing against a common origin for the human race and in favour of racial separateness, and these theories lent support to those who held that the peoples native to India were incapable of reform. After 1857, Macaulay's belief, voiced in the House of Commons in 1833, that it would be 'the proudest day in English history' if 'the public mind of India' should be encouraged by its encounter with European knowledge to one day demand European institutions, seemed simply absurd.[2] That route had been tried, and it had failed. There was and would remain, Kipling wrote in 1885 to his cousin Margaret Burne-Jones, an 'immeasurable gulf' between the English and 'the peoples of the land'. British codes might be imposed, but never truly accepted or understood; despite the best efforts of those who governed the country, native life continued 'wholly untouched and unaffected', 'dark and crooked and fantastic'. While it was strategically useful to defer to Indian customs – for example, by tolerating the caste divisions which earlier administrations had sought to override – the government of India could never safely be taken out of British hands: 'if we didn't hold the land in six months it would be one big cock pit of conflicting princelets' (*Letters*, I.98–9). The task facing the British was to rule India, not to reform it.

Fitzjames Stephen made the point with characteristic trenchancy. The British Government in India, he wrote in a letter to *The Times* (1 March 1883), was

> founded not on consent, but on conquest. . . . It represents a belligerent civilisation, and no anomaly can be so striking or so dangerous as its administration by men who, being at the head of a Government founded upon conquest, implying at every point the superiority of the conquering race, of their ideas, their institutions, their opinions, and their principles, and having no justification for its existence except that superiority, shrink from the open, uncompromising, straightforward assertion of it. . . .

Stephen was reacting to a Bill sponsored by Sir Courtenay Ilbert, his successor as Legal Member of the Viceroy's Council. Prior to 1883, Indian judges had jurisdiction over Europeans only in the three Presidencies (Bengal, Madras, and Bombay). The new Bill proposed extending the authority of native magistrates to the other regions of India, removing the privilege Britons had hitherto enjoyed of trial only by judges of their own race. There was a storm of protest, which neither

Lord Ripon, the Viceroy, nor his advisers seem to have anticipated. Initially the *CMG* opposed the Bill, but later changed its ground, arguing that further resistance would be unhelpful. Entering the Punjab Club one evening, Kipling was hissed by fellow members because 'Your dam' rag has ratted over the Bill'. One cannot expect a boy of seventeen to hold out against the views of the older men he has to work, eat and drink with, and it is understandable that the young Kipling was ready to adopt their attitudes as his own. What is striking is that he was never to change them. Even fifty years later, in *Something of Myself*, Kipling chose to summarise the Ilbert Bill in the crudest terms, as obedience to the Liberal principle – the word 'principle' appears in 'scare' quotation marks – that 'Native Judges should try white women', and to suggest, quite unjustly, that the *CMG* changed its stance because its proprietors were angling for their knighthoods (*SM* 31–2). He must have known that the success of Anglo-Indian opposition in getting the Bill watered down caused a good deal of anger among middle-class Indians, and was among the factors which led to the emergence a couple of years later of the National Congress, and a new phase in Indian nationalism. But fairness was never Kipling's strong point. Even in a book to be published after his death, he could not resist one last swipe at the Liberal policies which had so enraged the Punjab Club in the 1880s.

Kipling the journalist

The *Civil & Military Gazette* in Lahore had been founded by James Walker and William Rattigan. It had only a provincial circulation, and the financial success of the enterprise depended largely on the printing-house, which held the contracts for the provincial administration. Walker and Rattigan had also bought into a larger paper, the *Pioneer* of Allahabad, founded by George Allen, to which Kipling was transferred after five years in Lahore. His role at the *CMG*, as he wrote in *Something of Myself*, was to be 'fifty per cent of the "editorial staff" of the one daily paper of the Punjab', a distinction he shared with his editor, Stephen Wheeler. Wheeler was only ten years older than Kipling, but he was already an experienced journalist, and pushed his young assistant hard. In November 1882 Kipling described his working hours as 'from 10 till 4.15 or earlier if I can manage it', and the daily routine as 'intensely interesting' (*Letters*, I.24). The hours were to get longer, and the work more demanding. His immediate duties were to make digests of official publications, and to sift through various local and specialist journals, including Russian newspapers published in French, extracting whatever 'scraps' could be used. In addition he was expected to check correspondence to the paper, and to prepare a column about local events. When Wheeler fell ill, as he often did, it was Kipling's responsibility to make sure the paper continued to appear daily, keeping himself going with an occasional peg of whisky and soda as the office thermometer rose above the hundred mark. He had, as he wrote to Cormell Price, 'about seventy men to bully and hector as I please', and at home he had his own 'man' – in traditional fashion, the son of his father's servant – his own horse, his own cart and groom, and his own office box (*Letters*, 1.28). It must have been exciting enough for a boy only a few months out of school.

In March 1884 he was given his first independent work for the *CMG* when he was sent to report on the Viceroy's visit to Patiala, two hundred miles from Lahore. Here he had at his disposal an elephant and as many horses as he wished, was offered (and refused) a bribe, and had his first glimpse of a world of jewels and 'champagne, treachery, intrigue, princely hospitality'. A 'starlight ride of sixteen miles' on a borrowed horse allowed him to get his story in a day ahead of his rivals, as well as providing material for Chapter 12 of *The Naulahka*, the novel he wrote in collaboration with Wolcott Balestier. His proprietors were suitably impressed, and a year later he was the paper's 'Special Correspondent' for the meeting at Rawalpindi between Lord Dufferin, the new Viceroy, and Abdur Rahman, the new Amir of Afghanistan. In *Something of Myself* Kipling recalls being shot at, 'without malice', by a Pathan sniper after he had ventured into the mouth of the Khyber Pass, but there is no mention of this in the articles he was writing at the time.

This was Kipling's only visit to the North-West Frontier. The last story he wrote before leaving India, 'The Man who would be King', draws on his memories of the mountain landscape and, more deeply, the sense he had at Peshawar, while waiting for the Amir's arrival, of being a despised outsider. Writing in the *CMG*, he applauded the way Peshawar had been 'reservoired, watered, drained and policed', but concluded: 'neither security to life and goods, law, order, discipline, or the best blood of the English wasted on their care, reconcile the calibans of the city of evil countenances to the white stranger within their gates'.[3] In the story, Daniel Dravot usurps a kingdom and intends to rule wisely, only to find himself, like Prospero, confronted by a race of Calibans, 'on whose nature / Nurture can never stick'.

On his return Kipling was sent to Simla, the summer residence of the Viceroy and the Commander-in-Chief, and during the hot season the *de facto* capital of India, to write a series of articles under the heading 'Simla Notes'. His parents too were at Simla, and while Rudyard, not yet twenty, found himself working among people who were near the centre of power, Lockwood and Alice were being taken up by Lord Dufferin. Dufferin was a cultivated man, better liked than his predecessor, and both he and his Vicereine were glad to have the Kiplings on their invitation lists. Trix was now known as a beauty, and in demand at dances and dramatic entertainments: too much in demand perhaps, since Lord Dufferin's son was led to propose to her. It was a mark of the family's success that it was the unhappy Viscount who was asked to leave Simla, and not the young Miss Kipling.

She and her brother were already known as the authors of a volume of verse parodies and imitations, *Echoes, By Two Writers*, published by the *CMG* in Lahore in August 1884, in an edition of 150 copies, with Kipling himself in charge of its production. It received some favourable reviews, though plans for a second edition fell through. In later years the co-authors could not always agree who had written which poems. Kipling laid claim to 32 of them, including four which were also claimed by Trix, but the results were hardly worth battling over, and any one of them might have been written by a dozen other writers even in the small Anglo-Indian community. They were a social rather than a literary achievement; none of them is included in the *Definitive Edition* of Kipling's verse.

Much more significant was the publication in the *CMG* in September 1884 of 'The Gate of the Hundred Sorrows', the earliest of the stories later collected as *Plain Tales from the Hills*, and three days later a poem, 'The Story of Tommy', which in form and subject matter anticipates the *Barrack-Room Ballads*, though it misses the sardonic undercurrents which mark the later work. Effectively, Kipling's career as a major writer dates from these two pieces. By now both the Calcutta *Review* and the Allahabad *Pioneer* were ready to accept his poems. In March 1885 he conceived the idea of an Anglo-Indian novel, 'a two volume business at least', dealing with lower-class Eurasian and native life, and by 30 July had written 237 foolscap pages; provisionally entitled 'Mother Maturin', it was never to be completed, though some of the material found its way into *Kim*.[4] During the second half of 1885, all four Kiplings were at work on *Quartette*, a Christmas supplement to the *CMG*.[5] By the time Rudyard reached his twentieth birthday, on 30 December 1885, the Kipling Family Square could consider itself securely established both at Simla and in the Punjab.

Wheeler did little to encourage his assistant's burgeoning confidence. He kept him to the routine tasks, and Kipling was prompt to challenge any suggestion that he took these lightly, insisting that his early poems and stories were written out of office hours (*Letters*, I.126). But in the summer of 1886 ill-health obliged Wheeler to return to England, and Edward Kay Robinson was transferred from the *Pioneer* to revamp and brighten up the *Gazette*.[6] He quickly recognised that the nearest way to do so was to allow Kipling his head. They soon established an effective and at times furiously productive working relationship, despite an office which was home to three fox-terriers and a tame crow named Obadiah. In the summer of 1887 they bought new type for the paper and changed its format, in part to make room for Kipling's work. In the new layout the right-hand column of the front page was to be used for original contributions, often running over into the first column of the second page. These were known as 'turnovers', and many of Kipling's stories were first published in this form.[7] Only two of the *Plain Tales* had appeared in four years during Wheeler's regime, but under Robinson's more relaxed guidance Kipling was soon writing a new story almost every week.

In *Something of Myself* Kipling writes with affection of Robinson, and with grudging respect of Wheeler. But the hard grind of the journalism had its value. Occasionally it provided the raw material which could later be used as the background to a story. One of the stories Andrew Lang later singled out for special praise, 'The Taking of Lungtungpen', elaborates a brief report in the *CMG* by the simple device of employing a narrator. Writing as a civilian and a journalist, Kipling is limited to routine reflections on the bravery of Private Thomas Atkins; re-told in Mulvaney's stage Irish, the story becomes an illustration of the paradoxical theory that an inexperienced soldier is the best to work with, 'on account of the surpassin' innocence av the choild'. A later and more complex story, 'The Bridge-Builders', draws on an account of the Sutlej Bridge written for the *CMG*. In the article Kipling presents himself as the awed civilian marvelling at the 'hard-headed men of girders and masonry' who can bring to order what 'to the unprofessional eye' looks like chaos. In the story the same material is seen from the perspective of the engineer in charge of the bridge, and gradually opened out into a fable about work and selfhood, and beyond that the relation of Western and Hindu notions of reality.

Kipling's work as a reporter allowed him to discover what India meant to him, and how to write about it. In 'Typhoid at Home', an investigation into the milk supply in Lahore, he adopts the manner of the novelists and reformers who had explored the slums of Manchester and London in the mid-century. The entry into unmappable areas ('high walled clefts', 'dark courtyards'), the assault on the senses ('rainbow hues of putrescence', 'fetid stench'), the claim that what is uncovered breaches the limits of linguistic decency ('unutterable abominations') – these are all familiar from the industrial novels of Disraeli, Dickens and Mrs Gaskell. So too is the governing shape of the narrative: on the one hand, the study of ways to manage an isolable problem by exercising 'efficient and intelligent control'; on the other, the imagination of overwhelming strangeness and danger, with 'the tide of unclean humanity' threatening at any moment to 'burst through its dam of rotten brickwork and filth-smeared wood'. In the journalism the tension between the apparent security of the reporting voice, and a world felt to be unknowable, affords only a baffled recognition of the inevitable outcome, in the form of 'preventable disease leading to death'.[8] But in the early Indian stories the gulf which opens up here becomes one of Kipling's most powerful and unsettling effects. The desire for 'efficient and intelligent control', and the appalled awareness of 'the tide of unclean humanity', mark the boundaries of 'The Strange Ride of Morrowbie Jukes' as well as those of 'Typhoid at Home'.

Kipling used his journalism to explore roles and strategies that he could build on, discard or subvert as a creative writer. Writing in the *CMG* of Anglo-Indian society as it might be seen by a tourist, he adopts the stance of an outsider, impressed above all by the arduousness of Anglo-Indian life. Englishmen in India, comments the tourist, are 'enthusiastic enough about their work – always their work; though, to do them justice, they don't talk about it with a capital W'.[9] This is doubly flattering, both to the Anglo-Indian tradition of affecting to be impressed by nothing, least of all by their own achievements, and to their sense that in India, as not at home, work really was Work. The outsider can say freely what those inside wish to hear, and thus show himself at one with them, and this is no doubt the effect that Kipling wished to achieve.

The Indian verse

Kipling was also exploring his relation to India, and especially to Anglo-India, in his verse for the *CMG*, much of which was an extension of the journalism. Like the rest of Anglo-India he rejoiced when Lord Ripon resigned before his five-year term of office was complete, and he was delighted when his poem, 'Lord Ripon's Reverie', in the form of a parody of Tennyson's 'Locksley Hall', created more of a stir than a leading article written by his rivals at the *Pioneer*. When in 1885 Lady Dufferin, the new Vicereine, set up a fund for the medical education of native women, Kipling supported her campaign with a poem, 'The Song of the Women'. He wrote to his cousin, Margaret Burne-Jones, about his strategy: 'If prose doesn't go home hack out some verses with a lilting refrain that will take and catch the public ear and you have helped to scotch a snake.' Such writing 'mayn't be literature . . . but it may save men and cattle alive and lead to really tangible results' (*Letters*, I.92). The young journalist who had been hissed at the Punjab Club had found a way to put himself right with his severest and most voluble critics, and to align himself with their values.

His readers at the Club were, he recognised, not interested in his 'dreams'. They demanded accuracy when he was writing as a reporter, and the proper level of humour when he was writing verse. In the 'Sundry Phansies' written to or about Florence Garrard he had explored in all seriousness the various poetic idioms his contemporaries thought suitable for the expression of private feeling; two years later, in *Echoes*, he had used parody to begin to distance himself from them, and in the process come closer to choosing his audience—not without some uncertainty, since he sent a copy of *Echoes* to Florence, implicitly submitting himself to her judgement. In the copy he sent to Mrs Tavenor Perry he asked:

> Who is the Public I write for?
> Men 'neath an Indian sky
> Cynical, seedy and dry,
> Are these then the people I write for?
> No, not I.

But increasingly this was the audience he chose to address in his verse. In the summer of 1885 he experimented with a group of six poems in the *CMG* with the collective title 'Bungalow Ballads', determinedly humorous narratives in the approved style of Anglo-Indian *vers de societé*. In 'The Mare's Nest', for example, a wife is deceived into thinking her husband has a mistress, but 'Lilly' turns out to be a racehorse, and all is well. But the poems themselves were unexciting, and the series hardly more than the sum of its parts. In the spring of 1886 he repeated the experiment, with a series of ten 'Departmental Ditties'. It was immediately clear that the shift of focus, from domestic life to official India, had given him the edge he was looking for, and in June 1886 he brought out a collection of twenty-six poems, *Departmental Ditties and Other Verses*, published under his own supervision at the *CMG* press in Lahore.

Kipling's success in these poems depends almost entirely on tone and stance. India, the narrator explains in 'Thrown Away', one of the *Plain Tales*, 'is a place beyond all others where one must not take things too seriously – the mid-day sun always excepted'. The proper view to take of the elaborate hierarchies and cumbersome machinery of government was that these were at once absurd and inevitable: only the young were taken in by them, only the naive expected to change them. The wrong man would always be appointed ('Public Waste'), the rejected man would prove a hero ('Giffen's Debt'), the authorities would always listen to the worst advice ('Pagett, M.P.'). 'The Story of Uriah' is characteristic. It tells how Jack Barrett was transferred to Quetta, leaving his wife at Simla to conduct an affair with the official who arranged the transfer. Within weeks he is dead of fever: 'And Mrs Barrett mourned for him / Five lively months at most.' Kay Robinson comments that the *Departmental Ditties* 'were personal and topical in their origin, and gained tenfold in force for readers who could supply the names and places. . . . Those who had known the real "Jack Barrett", good fellow that he was, and the vile superior and faithless wife who sent him "on duty" to his death, felt the heat of the spirit which inspired Kipling's verse in a way that gave these few lines an imperishable force.'[10]

But this is only part of their effect. The title alludes to II Samuel 11, where David arranges the death of Bathsheba's husband: 'Set ye Uriah in the forefront of the hottest battle, and retire ye from him, that he may be smitten and die.' Jack Barrett's story, the title suggests, is an ancient one, re-told as often as wives are faithless and superiors vile. Those who understand their society will meet it cynically, not take it 'too seriously':

> And, when the Last Great Bugle Call
>   Adown the Hurnai throbs,
> And the last grim joke is entered
> In the big black Book of Jobs,
> And Quetta graveyards give again
>   Their victims to the air,
> I shouldn't like to be the man
>   Who sent Jack Barrett there.

The natural bias of such verse is towards the anecdote in its original sense of a secret or unpublished story, to be disclosed only to the select few who will recognise its significance. Both as a social and as a literary form, the anecdote depends for its success precisely on the refusal to explore complexity. Like the joke, it exists in and for the group; its function is to call into play the values of the one uniquely understanding audience to which it is addressed, which are assumed to need no further justification or commentary. By the act of narration the teller or writer implicitly claims to share those values, and to be ready to confirm them.

The form in which the *Departmental Ditties* were first published was itself a joke. Kipling described it as 'a sort of a book, a lean oblong docket, wire-stitched, to imitate a D.O. Government envelope, printed on one side only, bound in brown paper, and secured with red tape' (*SM* 176). The tape was passed through a slit in the flap of the envelope, which bore the representation of a seal. The docket was addressed 'To / All Heads of Depa . . . / and all Anglo-Indians', and purported to come from one 'Rudyard Kipling Assistant / Department of Public Journalism / Lahore District'. The first edition, of 500 copies, was soon sold out, and a second, containing 31 poems, was published before the end of the year, this time at Calcutta by Thacker, Spink & Co., who later bought the copyright for a modest 500 rupees.[11] This too sold rapidly; as Kipling observed in a letter to Crofts, at the USC, the Anglo-Indian public enjoyed 'reading about what they know and do themselves. Herein I suppose they resemble publics all the world over' (*Letters*, I.138). A third edition, with 41 poems, appeared in 1888, and a fourth, with fifty, in 1890. This was also the first English edition. There had been a brief but favourable notice of the first edition by Andrew Lang in *Longman's Magazine* as early as September 1886, describing the poems as 'quaint', 'amusing' and for the most part 'melancholy', though Kipling perhaps regretted his own ingenuity when Lang was misled by the docket format into supposing they had been issued anonymously.[12]

The fourth edition created its own puzzles by including for the first time a 'Prelude to Departmental Ditties 1885', addressed to the Anglo-Indian audience he had left in March 1889:

> I have written the tale of our life
>   For a sheltered people's mirth,
> In jesting guise – but ye are wise,
>   And ye know what the jest is worth.

This is misleading, since the 'Departmental Ditties' only began to appear in 1886, and were clearly written for Kipling's fellow Anglo-Indians, not for the 'sheltered people' at home. It is also defensive. It might be allowable to make a jest of Anglo-Indian life in 'ditties' to be read only by Anglo-Indians – though Boanerges Blitzen, in 'The Man Who Could Write', finds that to quote 'office scandal' or 'tactless truth' is not, after all, the road to promotion; but it was another matter when these truths and scandals were broadcast in London, where they might be used to bolster arguments about the need for change. By 1890, with the English edition, Kipling had begun to feel protective both of the Anglo-Indian community and of his own role as their laureate. In 'The Galley-Slave', one of the poems added to *Departmental Ditties*, the freed slave looks back with gratitude at his time of service: 'God be thanked! Whate'er comes after, I have lived and toiled with Men!' Kipling too had toiled with Men.

Sir William Hunter, a member of the Governor-General's Council in India from 1881 to 1887, had reviewed the 1888 edition of *Departmental Ditties* in the *Academy* with a mixture of admiration and impatience: 'Making verses, however clever, for the mess-room and the lawn tennis-club cannot be an altogether satisfying lifework.' That last word, from such a source, carried a heavy authority. What, Hunter asked, of that other Anglo-India, made up of men trained by the hard disciplines of heat, solitude, anxiety and ill-health to do 'England's greatest work on earth'? 'Some day a writer will arise – perhaps this young poet is the destined man – who will make that nobler Anglo-Indian world known as it really is.'[13] The 'Prelude' was Kipling's acknowledgement that he was ready for something more than a 'jesting guise'.

Plain tales

By the time Hunter's review appeared, Kipling could claim to have gone some way towards the deeper treatment of Anglo-Indian life. Between November 1886 and June 1887, he had issued 39 stories in the *CMG* under the title 'Plain Tales from the Hills'.[14] In January 1888 he revised and collected 29 of them, and added eleven others, for publication under the same title by Thacker, Spink in Calcutta. Of the eleven, three – 'The Gate of the Hundred Sorrows', 'In the House of Suddhoo', and 'The Story of Muhammad Din' – had appeared in the *CMG*; the remaining eight were now published for the first time. Most of the stories concentrate on Anglo-Indian life, civilian and military, including four which feature Kipling's soldier trio, Mulvaney, Learoyd and Ortheris. Only six of the 40 deal directly with native Indian or Eurasian life, but these include the best stories in the collection.[15]

Kipling revised *Plain Tales* for a number of later editions, particularly for the first English edition, issued by Macmillan in 1890, where most of the changes were designed to make the Indian background more accessible to English readers: thus, 'anna' becomes 'penny', 'this country' becomes 'India', 'you know' becomes 'every household in India knows'. An interpolated paragraph in 'Wressley of the Foreign Office' informs the English reader that India (unlike England) is a place 'where every one knows every one else'. The overall effect of these changes, often simple in themselves, is to shift the relation between narrator and reader. By needing to be explained, such references act as the markers of a world which is remote and strange, to which the narrator does and the reader does not belong. The 'very scenes are strange', wrote Andrew Lang, and the reader is 'baffled by *jhairuns*, and *khitmatgars*, and the rest of it'.[16] Rather than stories of 'out here', written from and addressed to a shared experience, they become tales of 'out there', beyond the reader's range.

In the *CMG* versions, the significant division is not between Anglo-India and Home, but between the Indian world and that of the Anglo-Indians – not least because Indians feature so infrequently, or appear only as part of the mass of humanity. The epigraph to 'In the House of Suddhoo' reads:

> A stone's throw out on either hand
> From that well-ordered road we tread,
>   And all the world is wild and strange.

The pattern in many of Kipling's Indian stories, in *Plain Tales* and in later collections, is to enter this 'wild and strange' world for a few pages, and then return, often with an emphasis that seems designed to foster the doubts it pretends to dismiss, to the 'well-ordered road' – the world of the club and the mess, with their reassuring and familiar rituals. In 1886 Kipling wrote to Kay Robinson that he would happily forgo a career in Fleet Street; Lahore was his 'own place', where he could find 'heat and smells of oil and spices, and puffs of temple incense, and sweat, and darkness, and dirt and lust and cruelty, and, above all, things wonderful and fascinating innumerable' (*Letters*, I.127). But in the stories he was writing at the same time, the narrator is not always so securely in control; even where they most powerfully command our assent, we may not be sure what it is we are assenting to. 'Beyond the Pale' is the story of a secret interracial liaison between the Englishman Trejago and the young Hindu widow Bisesa, which ends with Trejago stabbed in the groin and Bisesa mutilated. The first sentence of the epigraph, identified by Kipling as a Hindu proverb, reads: 'Love heeds not caste nor sleep a broken bed.' The first sentence of the story proper, in the voice of the Anglo-Indian narrator, reads: 'A man should, whatever happens, keep to his own caste, race, and breed.' The disjunction between these two is only the first of the many oppositions in this story of a 'double life': daytime and night-time, English and Indian words, the familiar routines of work and the 'madness' of the affair, all leading towards the opposition of Bisesa's 'roseleaf hands' with the 'funny little gestures' which Trejago finds so appealing, and the nearly healed 'stumps' she holds out to him after their affair has been discovered. What is left at the end is the renewed doubleness of Trejago's existence: outwardly 'a very decent sort of man', who pays his calls regularly, but inwardly a man haunted by his loss, who wakes in the night to wonder what had happened to Bisesa.

The narrator occupies an ambiguous position in this story. It is a tribute to Kipling's extraordinary confidence as a story-teller that we readily believe in the existence of the object-letter – half a bangle, a flower, a pinch of cattle-food and eleven cardamoms – which initiates the liaison. But we sense something odd in the readiness to translate this set of signs, spread out on the lid of Trejago's office-box, while the stumps of Bisesa's arms, thrust out in the moonlight, are the signs of a story the narrator cannot enter. Whether Bisesa confessed the affair, and why, or whether it was discovered, and how, are questions to which we have no answer. The discrepancy between what is so confidently known, and the impossibility of complete knowledge, is finally the most significant of all the oppositions in the story. The narrative voice is drawn towards the sensational on the one level (the mutilation), and the exemplary on the other (the instruction to keep to one's own caste and creed), but neither is adequate to the experience of Trejago and Bisesa. The voice that might have reached their story is heard momentarily in the second sentence of the epigraph – 'I went in search of love and lost myself' – but then silenced by the narrator's insistence on race-separateness.

'Beyond the Pale' is one of a number of stories in which an Englishman loses or comes near to losing his identity, a process sometimes disturbingly figured in the text by the scarred or wounded body of an Indian. Morrowbie Jukes tumbles into a sandpit, where he finds himself trapped among Indians who had recovered after they had been supposed dead, and are now neither living nor dead, including one who bears a scar on his face caused by Jukes; in the sandpit is the body of another Englishman, itself holed by a bullet wound. In 'The Mark of the Beast' (1886), the Englishman, Fleete, 'genial, and inoffensive' but also drunk, grinds out his cigar-butt on an image of Hanuman, the Monkey-god; moments later, a faceless leper embraces him, avenging the insult to the god by turning the Englishman into a beast. Fleete's loss of identity is echoed by a gap in the text, when Strickland and the narrator torture the leper, to make him remove the spell: 'This part is not to be printed.' In 'Bubbling Well Road' (1888) a one-eyed Indian priest who has been branded on the brow presides over a 'black gap' in the ground, into which the narrator nearly falls: 'There were things in the water – black things – and the water was as black as pitch with blue scum atop.' The assumed authority of the narrative voice is repeatedly undermined by the shifts and uncertainties within the stories, and the incompleteness of the explanations they offer.[17] The narrator of 'In the House of Suddhoo' preens himself on his friendship with Suddhoo, and on his understanding of Janoo, the prostitute who is one of Suddhoo's tenants; but as the story unfolds he finds that he is implicated in a chain of events that will conclude in a murder he is powerless to prevent.

Kipling returns to the theme of inter-racial relationships in several of the *Plain Tales*. In 'Kidnapped', Miss Castries has 'what innocent people at Home' call a 'Spanish' complexion (the *CMG* version refers simply to 'they'); the 'opal-tinted onyx at the base of her finger-nails' reveals to the less innocent that she is Eurasian. It follows that marriage between her and Peythroppe of the Indian Civil service would be 'impossible'. The inverted commas are Kipling's, but if they subject the general view to a measure of irony, they do not signify his dissent from it; Miss Castries is the only person in the story to behave with dignity, but nobody doubts that Peythroppe's friends are right to prevent the marriage. 'Lispeth' is the story of a Hill-woman, brought up from childhood by missionaries, who wants to marry an Englishman whose life she has saved. In the *CMG* version, the Chaplain's wife tells her that her hopes are 'wrong and improper', and again the scare quotation marks suggest an irony at the expense of those who assert the racial boundary. Kipling removed them in revision: possibly because he was confident that the irony would be detected by his readers, more probably because he was no longer sure that it ought to be present.

The best of the four soldier tales is 'The Madness of Private Ortheris'. His madness takes the form of homesickness and a longing for the smells of the London streets – 'orange-peel and hasphalt an' gas comin' in over Vaux'all Bridge' – so that Mulvaney has to thrash him with his own belt to prevent him from deserting. Mulvaney, Ortheris and Learoyd were to feature in some eighteen of Kipling's stories, and his touch became increasingly sure. What the early stories suggest is that the three are often drunk, impatient of routine, inclined to theft and occasional outbreaks of violence, but also unfailingly committed to their task as soldiers, though their loyalty is to each other and to the army first, and to the Queen and the Empire second. Their rebellions are temporary, carried out under licence; at the end of the day they not only fall into line, but compel their fellows in the barracks to do so as well. In every sense, they belong to the Army; it is the 'rasp' of his army shirt, and the squeak of his boots, that brings Ortheris to himself. In this story, as in most of the others, the narrator is both a friend and an irrelevance, a journalist who buys their stories for the price of some beer, but who cannot 'come to any conclusion of any kind whatever' about their lives and experience – though the attempt to do so was to produce two fine stories, 'On Greenhow Hill' (1891) and ' "Love-o'-Women" ' (1893).

Of the *Plain Tales* that deal with official Anglo-Indian life, a majority turn on confusions, mistaken identities or missed meetings, suggesting a world where social life is as little under control as the Indian landscape and weather. In his journalism, Kipling warned of chaos and inefficiency if Indians were allowed to govern themselves, but the stories reveal 'the hopelessness and tangle' of life in the Anglo-English community. Some are bitter, others broadly comic, though the laughter is often clouded with anger, as in 'The Arrest of Lieutenant Golightly', who is mistaken for a deserting private after his identity is washed away by the rain. The refusal to look deeper in these stories is justified by the claim that in India, 'where you really see humanity—raw, brown, naked humanity—with nothing between it and the blazing sky', only the foolish and the conceited ponder the final meaning of things. Aurelian McGoggin, who is both conceited and foolish, and has theories, is properly punished by the attack of aphasia which silences him when his colleagues at the Club have been unable to do so. One or two of the stories do push further, to show that what was confidently supposed at home to be a process of initiation, a way of life and work which turned boys into men, might as often be the means of their destruction, as it is for the hero-victim of 'Thrown Away', named simply as 'The Boy', who commits suicide because he supposes that he has disgraced himself.

Taken as a whole, the *Plain Tales* suggest a world where men must be broken in to their work, or break down in the effort to do it. They look to no long-term purpose, since they know or believe that the end of their work will be its own destruction, when an improved India demands to go its own way, and fails in attempting to do so. In the meantime their daily lives will be harsh, their pleasures few, and their attempts to establish any sense of permanency constantly undermined by the physical facts of the landscape; as one of Kipling's ladies at Simla has it, 'we are only little bits of dirt on the hillside – here one day and blown down the *khud* [cliff] the next'.[18]

It is often suggested that the stories of Anglo-Indians at work can be seen as extended metaphors for some more radical trial of the spirit, that the burdens carried by Kipling's subalterns and surveyors are not essentially different from those found in Hardy, Henley or Housman. In such readings, India stands as the sign of the eternal insufficiency of the rational mind, or of the enduringness of the physical world against which human life pales into insignificance, or as a testing ground in which men can prove themselves as men. But to see Kipling's India in this way is to push into the background the political realities of the British presence. Kipling, inconsiderately, keeps more than half an eye on these realities.

One such reality is the line drawn between the white and the non-white races. This line is absolute, if not therefore just, and it is drawn by the whites. At least one of the *Plain Tales*, however, 'The Story of Muhammad Din', suggests that Kipling was not hopelessly bound into such a stance. In this, the shortest of the stories, the unnamed English narrator becomes aware of the existence in his household of young Muhammad Din. His servant Imam Din, the boy's father, begs an old polo ball for him to play with, which the child uses as the centrepiece of a design in the garden – the ball, 'six shrivelled old marigold flowers in a circle round it', outside the circle a square of broken brick and glass, and so on. When the narrator inadvertently tramples over one such design, he is genuinely sorry, and leaves out odds and ends Muhammad can use. When the boy falls ill, he calls a doctor, but too late: 'They have no stamina, these brats,' says the doctor. The story ends: 'A week later, though I would have given much to have avoided it, I met on the road to the Mussulman burying-ground Imam Din, accompanied by one other friend, carrying in his arms, wrapped in a white cloth, all that was left of little Muhammad Din.'

This is a moving story, as that eloquent final sentence testifies. But it also hints at parable. The narrator's courtesy to Muhammad – checking his horse 'that my salutation might not be slurred over or given unseemly' – comes from a position of superiority: the adult on a horse, the child in the dust. The relation between the two suggests in miniature a familiar view of that between the Anglo-Indian and the Indian communities. The narrator has no wish to destroy the child's handiwork, yet his tolerance of it, as after all 'only the play of a baby', mimics conventional Anglo-Indian views of Indian art and architecture, as his patronage of this play, by dropping 'a gaily-spotted sea-shell' for Muhammad to use, echoes the conviction that Anglo-Indians could guide native Indians to a better understanding of their own culture – as indeed the Curator of the Wonder-House at Lahore, modelled on Lockwood Kipling, helps the Lama in *Kim*.

But the narrator, well-intentioned though he is, fails in his role as pseudo-parent: Muhammad dies. Wrapped in its white cloth, the child's body is not the image of an inherently unknowable India, but of the inadequacy of the narrator's uncritical assumption that he can indeed tell 'the story of Muhammad Din'. The authority he takes for granted is called into question by the epigraph: 'Who is the happy man? He that sees, in his own house at home, little children crowned with dust, leaping and falling and crying.' Neither Imam Din nor the narrator is 'in his own house at home'; each is denied the pleasure of children; they are linked by a sorrow they cannot share. Yet the boundary between them appears to be impassable. Only in the fiction, in the wider view which encompasses and goes beyond that of the narrator, is there any possibility of reaching across it. In the best of the *Plain Tales* – in this story, in 'Lispeth', and perhaps in 'Beyond the Pale' – Kipling is patrolling the boundary not merely to defend it, but also to discover its weak point, and push against it.

Allahabad and the *Pioneer*

Plain Tales was published in January 1888. Two months earlier, Kipling's employers had decided to move him from Lahore to Allahabad, 900 miles to the south-east, to work on the *CMG*'s sister paper, the *Pioneer*, and to edit its magazine supplement, *The Week's News*. Since the move was likely to be permanent, he arranged to transfer from Lodge Hope and Perseverance in Lahore, where he had been admitted as a Freemason in April 1886, to Lodge Independence with Philanthropy in Allahabad. Outside the Lodge, his encounters with the local community in Lahore had been mainly with the lower classes – the servants, the printworkers at the *CMG*, or those he met on his various night-wanderings through the liquor shops and the gambling and opium dens of the city. Freemasonry had opened another world to him when he needed it, allowing him to meet middle-class Muslims, Hindus, Sikhs and Jews away from the usual constraints of Anglo-Indian society (*SM* 32–3). It had also offered him a measure of intellectual stability, in a region and at a time of many conflicting creeds. In a story written after the death of his son John at Loos in 1915, 'In the Interests of the

Brethren', another bereaved man and fellow-Mason tells the narrator that 'All Ritual is fortifying.' Kipling certainly thought so.

The move to Allahabad provided new opportunities, not least because the *Pioneer* had a home as well as an Indian audience. Rather than buy in stories each week, Kipling offered to provide his own, and thus found himself with both a larger audience to address, and a larger scale to work to – 'no mere twelve-hundred Plain Tales jammed into rigid frames, but three- or five-thousand-word cartoons once a week' (*SM* 43). He continued to produce material at an astonishing rate: stories and articles for the *CMG*, poems and stories for the *Pioneer*, including most of those which eventually made up *Soldiers Three* and *Wee Willie Winkie*, as well as several travel pieces, beginning with a series of articles about a month-long visit to the native states of Rajputana (Rajasthan), on the edge of the Bikaner desert.[19] These were published in unauthorised editions in 1891 as *Letters of Marque*; Kipling managed to suppress this edition, before issuing them in a revised form in *From Sea to Sea* in 1899.

Letters of marque are documents providing the bearer with a licence to plunder, and in keeping with his title Kipling describes himself as 'the Englishman', out to enjoy a 'perfect month of loaferdom'. This adopted role provides some comic moments at Kipling's expense, but it also allows him to displace his own bewilderment on to India itself. Indian history is represented as impossibly baffling. Its cities and palaces 'breathe of plot and counter-plot, league and intrigue'; its temples are carved in 'friezes of wearying profusion'; even the hills are of a 'mad geological formation . . . tumbled strata that seem to obey no law'. But the dominant mood is relaxed, and there are moments of sheer delight, as in a description of dawn outside Boondi: 'The stars had no fire in them and the fish had stopped jumping, when the black water of the lake paled and grew grey. . . . The grey light moved on the face of the waters till, with no interval, a blood-red glare shot up from the horizon and, inky black against the intense red, a giant crane floated out towards the sun.' Kipling had read his Ruskin, and he had a painter's eye for light and colour.

The central episode in the series is the Englishman's visit to the ruined city of Chitor (Letters X and XI). As he climbs the Tower of Victory, built by Kumbha Rana in the fifteenth century, he finds himself growing uneasy at the sense of 'close-packed horrors' and ancient treacheries, of walls 'worn smooth by naked men', and of the 'shadow-land of lewd monstrosities' suggested by the Hindu carvings. Then, clambering down steps cut out of the rock, he slips, and comes to the edge of 'a dull blue tank, sunk between walls of timeless masonry':

In a slabbed-in recess, water was pouring through a shapeless stone gargoyle, into a trough; which trough again dripped into the tank. Almost under the little trickle of water, was the loathsome Emblem of Creation, and there were flowers and rice around it. Water was trickling from a score of places in the cut face of the hill; oozing between the edges of the steps and welling up between the stone slabs of the terrace. Trees sprouted in the sides of the tank and hid its surroundings. It seemed as though the descent had led the Englishman, firstly, two thousand years away from his own century, and secondly, into a trap, or that the Gau-Mukh would continue to pour water until the tank rose and swamped him, or that some of the stone slabs would fall and crush him flat.

In a moment of panic, he flees across the rocks (it feels 'as though he were treading on the soft, oiled skin of a Hindu'), back into his own time and culture. In *Plain Tales* Kipling had written jauntily of the wild, strange India lying a stone's throw from the well-ordered road, but here he found himself, like Morrowbie Jukes, in a place terrifyingly remote from his moral map, at once eroticized and pathologized: 'there was something uncanny about it all. It was not exactly a feeling of danger or pain, but an apprehension of great evil.' Chitor is the image of an India resistant to inspection and plunder by 'the Englishman'.[20]

No sooner had Kipling arrived in Allahabad than he was on the road again, this time to Calcutta, a visit which confirmed his low opinion of Indian self-government. In a series of articles under the title *City of Dreadful Night*, he wrote that Calcutta smelled of 'the essence of corruption', yet the Municipal Board was 'choked with the names of natives – men of the breed born and raised off this surfeited muck-heap', who quoted John Stuart Mill on the plurality of votes instead of working to improve the drainage. He was still more disturbed to find British women in the slums and brothels; that 'the widow of a soldier of the Queen' should have 'stooped to this common foulness' was an offence against the whole White race. With its Indian politicians discussing the niceties of representative government, and European women working as prostitutes, Calcutta confused the simplicities of White ruler and Black native. The true People of India, on this evidence, were the Eurasians: 'Wanted, therefore, a writer from among the Eurasians, who shall write so that men shall be pleased to read a story of Eurasian life; then outsiders will be interested in the People of India, and will admit that the race has possibilities.' This sentence was as close as Kipling himself was to come to such an admission.

Kipling was becoming unsettled. In May he was ordered back briefly to Lahore to look after the *CMG* while Robinson was on holiday, and found it desperately dull: 'same men, same talk, same billiards – all *connu* and triply *connu*' (*Letters*, I.171). When he rejoined Trix and his mother at Simla in the summer, there were signs of tension between them: 'it is owned that I am no longer ownable and only a visitor in the land. The Mother says that is so and the Sister too and their eyes see far' (*Letters*, I.205). The Sister meanwhile was also shaping a new life for herself, becoming engaged to John Fleming, an officer in the Survey Department, whom both Kipling and his father disliked. The ties which bound the Family Square were loosening. Before the summer was out, Kipling was thinking of a return to England.

But his position in Allahabad was about to improve. Kipling had adopted a Mrs Isabella Burton as a confidante and quasi-Muse; as 'the wittiest woman in India' she was the original dedicatee of the *Plain Tales*, and in her 'curiously cynical way' had helped suggest 'half a hundred ideas and some stories' (*Letters*, I.144, 164). In April 1888, however, Mrs Burton left India, and Kipling turned instead to an American woman only seven years his senior, Mrs Edmonia Hill, known as Ted, whose husband Alex was a meteorologist for the Indian government. On his return from Simla, Kipling became a house-guest of the Hills in Allahabad, which remained his base, except for a month or two when Mrs Hill was seriously unwell, until he, and they, left India in March 1889. From the outset he consulted her about his work, soliciting her advice on how to handle 'a *causerie intime* between two girls at Simla', describing how he drew out a love-sick lieutenant in search of new material, and discussing the pros and cons of writing to order: 'It's nice to dance in fetters. "Give us sentiment, give us fun, but . . . keep within 404 lines." Those are my riding-orders' (*Letters*, I.158, 193). But he also found he could talk freely to her about his childhood (it was in the Hills' house that he wrote 'Baa Baa, Black Sheep', getting into 'a towering rage' as he did so),[21] and about his unsuccessful courtship of a woman he refers to in his letters as 'My Lady'. How far the affair existed outside the letters, or whether 'My Lady' was a projection of the necessarily unattainable Mrs Hill, is open to question; if the letters are a clue, Kipling was more interested in the role of unhappy lover than in the woman who supposedly inspired his feelings. Mrs Hill noted that he was susceptible to pretty women, but there is no firm evidence that his sexual life had moved much beyond the kind of infatuation he had had for Florence Garrard.[22]

Real or not, Kipling's love affairs did not get in the way of his writing. His work for the *Pioneer* produced most of the stories eventually collected as *Soldiers Three* and *Wee Willie Winkie*. Initially, however, they were gathered into six smaller collections as part of a new venture, the Indian Railway Library series. Emile Moreau, the senior partner in A. H. Wheeler & Co., offered Kipling a contract for six paper-bound volumes, with covers designed by Lockwood, for $1000, plus a royalty of $20 per thousand copies after the first 1500.[23] There had never been a full-time professional writer in the small Anglo-Indian community, but Kipling came close to being one. Taken together, the Railway Library volumes read like an imaginative map of India; the advertisement for the series describes them as 'illustrations of the four main features of Anglo-Indian life, viz., the Military, Domestic, Native and Social'.

They also suggest that Kipling was continuing to experiment as a writer, and in particular looking to see how a group of stories could be more than the sum of its parts, perhaps with the idea of working up to a novel. 'The Story of the Gadsbys', the centrepiece of what was to become *Soldiers Three*, is a novella of sorts, in nine sections. It is the story of a marriage, recounted entirely in dialogue though with some rather laboured asides; so far as it has a plot and dénouement, it leads towards Gadsby's reluctant decision to leave his regiment and return home, at the expense, Kipling suggests, of his virility, since even a good marriage 'hampers a man's work' and 'cripples his sword-arm'. Admitting to Mrs Hill that parts of the story were 'a little strained and brutal', he offered a classic defence of literary realism: 'There are certain moods and phases of thought that must be faced boldly and set down unflinchingly so that those who read may know and see the worst that can happen, and in this very knowledge, be strong enough to turn it aside' (*Letters*, I.222). The claim to a moral intention hardly disguises the misogynistic tone; the Envoi, in keeping with the mood of the whole, includes one of Kipling's most-quoted lines: 'He travels the fastest who travels alone.'

'Soldiers Three', the opening group of stories, is similarly uneven. The best is 'Black Jack', which frames Mulvaney's account of one near-murderous dispute in barracks within the narrator's account of another. Ortheris and Learoyd have a minor part in the outer story, but they also hint at a more understanding audience for the inner one than the civilian narrator can provide, for all his goodwill towards the three. The point is made more ponderously in 'In the Matter of a Private': 'There is nobody to speak for Thomas except people who have theories to work off on him; and nobody understands Thomas except Thomas, and he does not always know what is the matter with himself.' 'With the Main Guard' includes an account of hand-to-hand fighting in which Kipling tries to do justice to both the brutality of battle and the devilry of the professional soldier, but as often in the early stories falls into over-emphasis. When a discussion of fighting techniques is closed with the words, ' "Each does ut his own way, like makin' love, " said Mulvaney quietly,' the sentence itself is not quiet, but all too evidently intended to shock. It becomes a kind of test case for the reader, requiring him to assent or else to accept that the story is beyond his understanding. Kipling was always to be tempted by these literary shibboleths.[24] They are effective when they signal a barrier which the narrator too is struggling to overcome; when they seem to celebrate Kipling's passage across the barrier, and the reader's inability to follow, they invite Orwell's comment that Kipling could be 'aesthetically insensitive' and 'morally disgusting'.[25]

The third group of stories in *Soldiers Three*, 'In Black and White', presents native Indian life through Indian voices, usually in conversation with the silent Sahib-narrator. Like 'The Story of the Gadsbys', these read like experiments. 'At Twenty-Two' is the story of a mining accident, which makes an explicit connection to Zola's *Germinal*; 'In Flood Time' is an Indian version of the Hero and Leander story, in which the lover is saved by holding on to the corpse of his rival as the flood carries him down the river. The most successful story is the one which most acknowledges its own limits, 'On the City Wall'. This is unusual in dealing with the Indian middle class, and with it a different kind of challenge to British supremacy than that faced in 1857. Wali Dad belongs to the new class, and is perfectly clear that the Sahibs will never allow him to rise very far; as he points out to the narrator, the measure of the barrier between the whites and the native Indians is that neither group will ever speak to the other about its women. But by the end of the story Wali Dad has been stripped of his Western education; nostrils distended and eyes fixed, he throws himself into a rioting crowd chanting 'Ya Hasan! Ya Husein!' – living proof that while foolish liberals may believe the native is capable of administering the country, the paradoxical reality is that although India will always be inaccessible to the Western mind, only the Sahib can be trusted to govern. In January 1889 Kipling reported so unsympathetically on a meeting of the Indian National Congress that a Captain Hearsey, who held more liberal views, arrived at his office with a horsewhip; the Captain was jailed, and a libel action begun against the *Pioneer*. The controversy may well have helped suggest to Kipling, and to his employers, that it was time to leave India. Kipling was never to get beyond Wali Dad in his view of Indian politicians.

Like *Soldiers Three*, *Wee Willie Winkie* comprises three groups of stories. 'Under the Deodars' is a composite portrait of life at Simla.
Although Simla was effectively the seat of government during the summer months, Kipling turns his attention on the minor players, their
lives alternating between long periods dispersed across the continent
and the claustrophobic routines of the season. Here are intrigues and
liaisons dangereuses, the fear of scandal and the delight in gossip, acted
out in a world which is never private for very long and where moments
of intimacy, more furtive than impassioned, are snatched in the middle
of the soirées and social functions of any small town. The best of the
stories, 'A Wayside Comedy', is set outside Simla, at a small hill-station,
where the extra-marital passions of four people who can no longer bear
to be together have thrust them into a life in which they are not
allowed to be apart. Henry James was to describe Kipling as an English
Balzac; reading this story, which is crafted with the same surgical preci-
sion as *Madame Bovary*, he might equally have called him the English
Flaubert.

Andrew Lang recommended 'Under the Deodars' to those who wanted to see 'the misery, the seamy, sorry side of irregular love affairs',[26]
and in his Preface Kipling felt the need to remind his readers that India
was not entirely made up of 'men and women playing tennis with the
Seventh Commandment'. Two stories seem designed to redress the balance. In 'A Second-Rate Woman' the eponymous heroine, nicknamed
the Dowd by Mrs Hauksbee, saves the life of a child with diphtheria; in
'Only a Subaltern', young Bobby Wicks dies that his men might live.
The former is the more successful, though it ends on a false note, with
an unconvincing gush of tears and kisses from the penitent Mrs
Hauksbee. 'Only a Subaltern', however, hardly strikes a true one – certainly not when the least admirable of Bobby Wicks's men is called on
to draw the moral: 'Hangel! *Bloomin'* Hangel! That's wot 'e is!' To a contemporary reader, the story tries too hard, and becomes mawkish;
Charles Carrington, writing in 1955, argued that it, or stories like it,
moulded that generation of young Englishmen who in 1914 came forward in their thousands to sacrifice themselves in the image Kipling
had created – among them, one has to remind oneself, the young John
Kipling.[27] When W. B. Yeats asked himself, in 'The Man and the Echo',
'Did that play of mine send out / Certain men the English shot?', he
risked sounding vainglorious. Asked of Kipling, the question has a different resonance.

The four stories in 'Wee Willie Winkie' all deal with children; 'Baa
Baa, Black Sheep' was written for this volume. In the preface to the

Railway Library edition, Kipling wrote apologetically that 'it is hard to draw babies correctly', a judgement sadly confirmed by both 'His Majesty the King' and the title story, in each of which the child hero struggles to win signs of affection from his parents.[28] In his stories for children Kipling rarely talked down to his audience; that here he is so condescending about them suggests that the anger he could not admit to feeling towards his parents was displaced into an overstated sympathy with clearly fictional children.

He is more successful in 'The Drums of the Fore and Aft', which tells how two Cockney drummer boys, drunk on the battlefield, help an inexperienced battalion to stand and fight. This was soon one of the most widely praised of Kipling's stories; Henry James confessed to having 'wept profusely' over it.[29] It is perhaps an unexpected success, which has impressed its admirers rather because than in spite of its brutality. Almost alone among the major writers of his time, Kipling claimed to understand and share the values of those who wielded power outside the literary world: the soldiers, builders and administrators, whether of bridges or empires. These were themes the men of letters were accustomed to treat with caution. In 1891, in an introduction to a volume of Kipling's stories, James described him as 'the most complete man of genius' he had known, but also hinted his doubts. Kipling knew too much to leave any 'dimnesses'; there was instead 'a universal loudness', in which James missed 'the voice, as it were, of the civilised man'. 'Civilised man' might admit the need for the politico-military establishment, but was also expected to keep at a distance from it – or at least to drop an 'as it were' into its loudness. Kipling declined to do so. Instead, in stories like 'The Drums of the Fore and Aft', he made plain his belief that the civilities of English life depended on the employment overseas of an army consisting of 'either blackguards or gentlemen, or, best of all, blackguards commanded by gentlemen, to do butcher's work with efficiency and despatch'. This was unpleasant, and it cast a disturbing light on the portrayal of the Soldiers Three, but it was also exciting. It was not just the brilliance of the battle-scenes, but the half-formulated sense of something dangerous in Kipling's position, that thrilled readers like Lang, James and Gosse.

The fifth of the Railway Library volumes, 'The Phantom Rickshaw and Other Stories', includes two early stories, the title piece and 'The Strange Ride of Morrowbie Jukes', first published in 1885. In revising them, Kipling added an introductory frame, so that what had been first-person narratives are presented as edited documents which Kipling-as-editor refuses either to endorse or to repudiate. Both are exercises in what Patrick Brantlinger terms 'Imperial Gothic': stories which combine the ideology of imperialism, often underpinned by a quasi-scientific social and racial Darwinism, with a fascination with those forces of the occult which the advance of civilisation was supposed to have overthrown.[30] To take part in the imperial adventure was to lay claim to personal and racial integrity, but in a number of stories from the 1880s to the outbreak of the Great War – Rider Haggard's *She*, Stevenson's *Dr Jekyll and Mr Hyde*, Bram Stoker's *Dracula*, Wells's *The War of the Worlds* – what is at issue is the threat of individual regression, or worse, of a national descent into barbarism. In its revised form, 'The Phantom Rickshaw' opens with an account of the 'Knowability' of Anglo-India, where every one knows and is known by every one else. Beyond this reassuring interdependence, however, lies 'the Dark World', which enters through 'a crack in Pansay's head' and presses him to death. This 'crack', like the pit Morrowbie Jukes tumbles into, operates like a fault-line in the narrative. To move from the editorial frame into the stories told by Pansay and Jukes is to cross from the known world into what Conrad's Marlow, borrowing the phrase from Kipling, was to call the 'dark places of the earth'. Like 'The Mark of the Beast', 'Bubbling Well Road' and 'The Return of Imray', these stories embody a fear of the loss of a unified self and the wider fear of the loss of empire. What they do not attempt is to explore the connection between the private and the public anxieties. That task would be left to Conrad.

Kipling speaks of 'the dark places of the earth' in 'The Man who would be King', the longest and most ambitious story he was to write before leaving India. It tells of Daniel Dravot and Peachey Carnehan, self-confessed 'loafers' who set off to exploit their military skill, and their Martini rifles, in Kafiristan, where they intend to become kings and make their fortunes. Their weapons and expertise help them on the way to success, their power to kill at a distance half-persuading the natives to accept them as gods, but their real triumph comes when their knowledge of freemasonry enables them to recognise ancient symbols venerated by the local priests. This seems to confirm their divine status, but it also proves their undoing. To ease the burden of kingship, Dravot decides to take a wife. Terrified of a match with a god, the girl bites him, and when he bleeds the imposture is discovered. Dravot is killed, but Carnehan survives crucifixion long enough to return to tell their story to the narrator, a newspaperman whose duties echo Kipling's own.

This is a complex story. Dravot's ambition to make a 'damned fine Nation' of his subjects ends in failure, but there is no suggestion that his aims are inherently fraudulent. Initially, the decision to set the main narrative within the frame of the journalist's encounter with the two men raises the possibility of an ironic or subversive relation between their story and the larger movement of British imperialism, one which will direct attention to the reality behind the fine phrases of official policy. At their first meeting, the narrator and Carnehan talk 'the politics of loaferdom', characterised by its readiness to see things 'from the underside where the lath and plaster is not smoothed off'. This sense of a view from the underside is continued when the narrator returns to his office to await some soon-to-be-forgotten news of a king or a courtier, a courtesan or a constitution. Official India is foolish enough to take these matters solemnly, and speaks of duty and responsibility; the loafers do not, and speak frankly of 'loot'.

But as Carnehan tells his story, the loafer's view is dropped. The implicit charge against Dravot is not that he claimed the right to rule, but that he failed to live up to it. Because his is a *lumpen* version of the imperial ideal, he so far forgets himself as to marry a native, despite Carnehan's warning that to do so will undermine their position. But Carnehan remains loyal, and because the only moral relation taken seriously in the story is that between the two white men, Dravot can atone by admitting his flaws to his friend, and offering magnanimously to die alone. In learning that he wants to 'make' a nation, Dravot has himself been made. Whereas in the outside world kings who are barely distinguishable from courtiers and courtesans die with irritating dilatoriness while newspapers await the announcement, Dravot is real and charged with significance, and he dies with heroic dignity. He is not condemned for his ambition – this becomes his virtue, the capacity to dream big showing him to be a big man – so much as admired for the moral growth which has made him, if only temporarily, 'a veritable King'. This is one effect of the hymn sung near the end of the story by the now deranged Carnehan:

> The Son of Man goes forth to war,
>   A golden crown to gain;
> His blood-red banner streams afar –
>   Who follows in his train?

The answer is that Carnehan does, a disciple bearing the stigmata of his crucifixion, helped on his long journey by the voice of his dead friend.

The fable of a man who allows himself to be worshipped as a god, and is lured to his death by the dream of unlimited power, is bound to suggest Conrad's *Heart of Darkness*, written ten years later, and his critique of colonialism as a system of plunder thinly disguised as the work of benevolent government. Kipling, Conrad wrote to Cunninghame Graham, 'has the wisdom of the passing generations. . . . He squints with the rest of his excellent sort. It is a beautiful squint; it is an useful squint.'[31] The obliquity of Kipling's vision, its one-eyed insistence, obliges him to relegate to the margins of the story what Conrad draws to the centre: the avarice, the desire for personal glory, the intoxication of power. In 'The Man who would be King' the economic motivation for conquest is hidden behind – Kipling might have said, has been refined into – a moral justification, that 'the dark places of the earth' provide an opportunity for heroism and adventure denied to those who stay at home. The people of Kafiristan exist so that Daniel Dravot can struggle to become a king; when he has reached his moral limits, their function is to kill him, so that his death can vindicate his tragic status. What might have been an indictment of the imperial adventure is offered as a defence of it.[32] Appropriately, perhaps, in Kipling's last story before leaving to try his strength as a writer in London, India is seen as a testing-ground in which white men can discover what degree of greatness is in them.

3
The Conquest of London

Towards the end of 1888, Kipling took stock of his position. *Departmental Ditties* had sold well, and been favourably if briefly noticed by Andrew Lang in London. He now sold the copyright for the third and subsequent editions to Thacker, Spink of Calcutta, who had published the second edition. The arrangement for *Plain Tales* had been that he and Thacker, Spink would share the profits equally, but only after they had taken a commission of 25 per cent from sales. Kipling came to resent the size of the commission, but the Indian edition sold quickly; even though the copies sent to England had scarcely sold at all, he still anticipated royalties of £300 a year (*Letters*, I.286). A. H. Wheeler & Co. had given him £200 and a small royalty for the copyright to the six volumes in the Railway Library series. The *Pioneer* was willing to pay for a set of travel pieces he intended to write about his voyage home; the *CMG* was eager for more stories. He had, he told Margaret Mackail, 'mixed with fighters and statesmen, administrators and women who control them all. . . . I've tried to get to know folk from the barrack room and the brothel, to the Ballroom and the Viceroy's Council and I have in a little measure succeeded' (*Letters*, I.288).[1] In short, he had, or thought he had, money, experience and confidence enough to begin his assault on the literary world in London; and in any case he was wearied of India. On 9 March he left Calcutta with Alex and Edmonia Hill for Rangoon on the first stage of a journey which was to take them via Singapore, Hong Kong and Japan to America. Apart from a brief, interrupted visit in 1891, he was not to see India again.

Kipling's travel letters for the *Pioneer*, collected as *From Sea to Sea*, vary in mood from buoyancy to something like panic. It was pleasant to be free of work and responsibility, but disturbing to feel the life he had left behind him in India fading into unimportance. Some of his comments merely answer to what his *Pioneer* audience expected to hear, while others are counterpointed by the calmer perspective of Alex Hill, who appears as 'the Professor', but this is not enough to hide periods of disquiet, reflected in an almost physical hostility to the Chinese: 'Do you know those horrible sponges full of worms that grow in warm seas? You break off a piece of it and the worms break too. Canton was that sponge. . . . Watch the yellow faces that glare at you . . . and you will be afraid, as I was afraid.'[2] He admitted seeing the city 'through the medium of a fevered imagination', and a letter written in January 1890 suggests that he did indeed have some kind of breakdown at this time (*Letters*, II.9). This can be seen as the reaction to a long spell of intense work, but it was also the sign of an ontological crisis. When, in the sixth of his *Pioneer* letters, he wrote 'I want to go Home', he was referring to India; but the purpose of the voyage was to take him 'Home' to London. He was no longer a Sahib, but a young man in a large world heading towards an uncertain future in a country he had last seen as a schoolboy.

He felt less threatened by the Japanese, whom he happily infantilised, in the confidence that Japan lacked the 'last touch of firmness in her character which would enable her to play with the whole round world'. Firmness of character remained the prerogative of the British. His views do little credit to his prescience, since Japan was to defeat China in 1894 and Russia in 1905. But even in Japan he was disturbed by the self-sufficiency with which the Chinese went about their business. The Chinese were 'natives', but like the British they stood apart, moving among the Japanese with the look of adults among children. Instead of deference, they exhibited a confidence that belonged properly to Sahibs. Perhaps the British had conquered the wrong country; if they had ruled China instead of India, they would 'long ago have been expelled from, or have reaped the reward of, the richest land on the face of the earth'.[3]

He was also led to ponder the scale of the empire, imagining a future federation of self-governing colonies, bound to each other and to England by treaty: 'one great iron band girdling the earth', ready to resist any challenge. This aggressive–defensive dream shaped his first response to America, as he noted with satisfaction that San Francisco harbour could be 'silenced by two gun boats from Hong Kong with safety, comfort and despatch'.[4] The words were intended for the *Pioneer*, but together with his other travel pieces from America they were soon available in a pirated edition under a title borrowed from Dickens, *American Notes*. This was appropriate, since Kipling's dislikes half-consciously echoed those Dickens had expressed fifty years earlier. He complained about American accents, the habit of spitting, an over-weening self-esteem, lawlessness, and the importunity of journalists – though this last did not deter him from arriving, unannounced, to interview Mark Twain. The publicity given to his remarks caused him some embarrassment, but for the time his role as the English writer abroad helped to restore his self-confidence.

In between fearing America as a possible enemy, or as the site of Irish plots against British interests, Kipling enthused at the prospect of a future alliance of nations: 'Sixty million people, chiefly of English instincts, who are trained from youth to believe that nothing is impossible, don't go slinking through the centuries like Russian peasantry.' Cocksure and lawless he might be, but the 'Anglo-American-German-Jew' was the Man of the Future, and a friend worth having. Which of the different versions of America predominated depended on where Kipling was, and whom he met. Salmon-fishing in Portland, he looked at America and saw that it was good; in the Yellowstone National Park on the Fourth of July, the displays of self-congratulation struck him as absurd; in the Chicago stockyards, where a woman with scarlet lips and red shoes gazed at the slaughter 'with hard, bold eyes, and was not ashamed', he was appalled, and turned away to get 'peace and rest'.[5]

He found these in the home of Mrs Hill's parents in Pennsylvania, where her father, the Reverend Taylor, was President of Beaver College, a Methodist foundation for women. He found more besides. The 'American maiden', he wrote, having been taught self-respect, and that her fate was in her own hands, was better prepared than her English counterpart to be 'a companion, in the fullest sense of the word, of the man she weds', and to help him through difficult times.[6] If this was a tribute to Mrs Hill, it was also addressed to her younger sister, Caroline Taylor, who was to join Mrs Hill and Kipling on the voyage to England. On 9 October 1889, five days after they landed at Liverpool, Mrs Hill recorded in her diary: 'Carrie engaged to R. K.'

The biographers have been mistrustful of this engagement. It was over by the following January, and Kipling's few surviving letters to Caroline are strained. What he wanted from the relationship is unclear. The letters suggest that he felt much more warmly towards Mrs Hill, and it is hard to resist the suspicion that he wooed Caroline as a surro-gate for her sister; or perhaps he was looking for a 'companion' to sup-port him when he reached London. Whether it was Kipling or Caroline who decided to end the engagement, and why, is equally uncertain. In December he wrote to reassure her of his faith in 'a personal God to whom we are personally responsible for wrong doing', but admitting his inability to believe in eternal punishment or reward, or in the divinity of Christ (*Letters*, II.378). This falls far short of the Methodist position, and might not have been enough to satisfy Caroline, or her parents. Perhaps he anticipated as much. It is also possible, however, that his chance meeting (so he claimed) with Florence Garrard at about this time convinced him that marriage to Caroline would be a mistake.

There is, predictably, no mention of his engagement in *Something of Myself*, but there is one significant passage. Soon after his arrival he moved into a flat in Villiers Street, overlooking the Thames. Trapped indoors by the fog, he gazed for five days at the reflection of his own face 'in the jet-black mirror of the window-panes':

> When the fog thinned, I looked out and saw a man standing opposite the pub where the barmaid lived. Of a sudden his breast turned dull red like a robin's, and he crumpled, having cut his throat. In a few minutes – seconds it seemed – a hand-ambulance arrived and took up the body. A pot-boy with a bucket of steaming water sluiced the blood off into the gutter, and what little crowd had collected went its way. (*SM* 52)

This striking image of isolation and despair seen in a black mirror chimes with letters he sent to the Hills in January and February 1890, explaining that his head had 'given out', and that he was forbidden work (*Letters*, II.7, 9), but whether this breakdown – the 'smash', as he called it – brought about the end of the engagement, or was a reaction to it, is unclear, though the two were surely connected. Whatever the sequence of events, Caroline Taylor dropped from the picture. He continued to correspond with Mrs Hill until the end of his life.

Life in London

Soon after his arrival in England, Kipling wrote to John Addington Symonds that he was 'come to London to start that queer experience known as a literary career'. The letter suggests both his uncertainty and his ambition. Properly respectful towards the older man, one of several writers he invited to keep watch over his performance, 'that you may warn me when I slide from decent work', it is not simply deferential. Acknowledging Symonds's admiration for *Soldiers Three*, Kipling attributes his success to the fact that he loved his characters as he created them, 'very much, I take it, as you loved a man called Benvenuto Cellini and in your translation showed that love – so that he became

alive and swaggered and brawled and beat his way across the pages'
(*Letters*, I.348). As he must have been aware, that string of verbs applies
as well to Mulvaney, Learoyd and Ortheris as to Cellini in Symonds's
translation of the autobiography. The compliment is neatly turned to
allow Kipling to represent himself both as a brother artist and as a new-
comer eager to receive the advice of his seniors. If he was to succeed in
London, he would need allies.

One early call was on Mowbray Morris, editor of *Macmillan's Magazine*.
Macmillan's had a reputation for conservatism (Morris was about to
refuse Hardy's *Tess of the d'Urbervilles* as 'too succulent'), and Kipling was
asked to tone down 'The Incarnation of Krishna Mulvaney' before it was
published in December. But Morris immediately accepted two poems,
'The Ballad of the King's Mercy' and 'The Ballad of East and West', and
Kipling was assured that work for *Macmillan's* would bring him £300 a
year (*Letters*, I.356). Meanwhile, Stephen Wheeler, his former chief at the
CMG, had brought *Soldiers Three* to the attention of Sidney Low, editor of
the *St James's Gazette*. Low was sufficiently impressed to offer a retainer,
which Kipling declined, providing instead a 'grim and fantastic yarn'
about 'a young man who . . . wrote himself out in a desire to accumulate
money'.[7] It was an appropriate subject. McClure's literary syndicate in
America wanted him to write an adventure story for the young,
Longman's Magazine agreed to take a story called 'For One Night Only',
James Payn asked for short stories for the *Cornhill*. Within months if not
weeks it seemed that everybody wanted his work.

Kipling's excitement at his success was tempered by his mistrust of
the London literary scene, where he was invited to dine by people who
with equal politeness applauded his talent and disparaged his politics.
London, he wrote to Mrs Hill, was 'a vile place'. He complained about
the weather, the folly of English liberals regarding India, and about the
'long-haired literati of the Savile Club' (*Letters*, I.358), whom he stigmatised in 'In Partibus' (November 1889):

> But I consort with long-haired things
>   In velvet collar-rolls
> Who talk about the Aims of Art
>   And 'theories' and 'goals',
> And moo and coo with womenfolk
>   About their blessed souls.

This, unsurprisingly, was one of the pieces sent off to the *CMG* in India.
But he was happy with his work on 'The Courting of Dinah Shadd', the

best of the stories about Mulvaney, and one of six stories in *Life's Handicap* (1891) written for *Macmillan's*. He had also been meditating a series of soldier poems, and in February 1890 'Danny Deever', the first of what were to become the *Barrack-Room Ballads*, appeared in the *Scots Observer* to instant acclaim. As well as writing new material, he was busy reworking the old. At Andrew Lang's recommendation, Sampson Low, Marston & Co., offered to take over the Railway Library volumes. Kipling negotiated a contract, and a lightly revised edition of *Soldiers Three* appeared early in 1890, followed by further volumes from the series, with 7000 copies for the English market and 3000 for India. In addition, there was a fourth, enlarged edition of *Departmental Ditties*. The first English edition of *Plain Tales from the Hills* came out in June 1890. A year earlier, the copies sent to England had attracted no interest; the 1890 edition had to be reprinted twice before the end of the year. The Kipling boom had begun.

Kipling's success was so marked that it comes as a shock to realise that it was exactly contemporary with the writing of *New Grub Street* (1891), George Gissing's bitter account of literary life in late Victorian London. Yet the world of Kipling's triumphs is recognisably the same as that in which the novelist Edwin Reardon meets his defeat. In both cases the key fact in the background is the astonishing rise in the amount of fiction being produced. Figures from the *Publishers' Circular* suggest that there were in excess of one thousand adult novels being published annually, but this represents only part of the total market. Both the number of newspapers published in the British Isles, and the number of weekly, monthly and quarterly magazines, passed the 2000 mark in the 1890s, and a high proportion of these included some fiction, while others were wholly devoted to it.[8] As the number of outlets increased so did the variety of formats. Some magazines issued full-length novels in serial form, others like *Black and White* included one or more complete short stories, and others again a sequence of short stories built around a central character, such as the Sherlock Holmes stories in the *Strand Magazine*. The stories Kipling collected in *The Day's Work* (1898) had previously appeared between 1893 and 1897 in thirteen different journals: *Illustrated London News*, *Century Magazine*, *Bombay Gazette*, *The Idler*, *McClure's Magazine*, *Pearson's Magazine*, *Graphic*, *Pocket Magazine*, *Gentlewoman*, *Ladies' Home Journal*, *Scribner's Magazine*, *Pall Mall Gazette* and *Cosmopolitan*. As a rule, it was the first periodical publication that earned most money, though a number of writers – George Moore was one, and Kipling another – hoped that when the stories were published in volume form they would exhibit an underlying unity and coherence.

The reasons behind the growth of the fiction market were many and complex. In part it was fuelled by advances in printing technology, including the use of cylindrical presses fed by paper in a continuous web, low-cost paper made from wood-pulp rather than rags, and the development of the Linotype process. It was also driven by the emergence of new readers following the Education Act of 1870, and of writing consciously designed to meet the needs of a semi-literate audience. The decades either side of 1900 saw the rise of the halfpenny evening and daily papers, including the *Daily Mail*, *Daily Express* and *Daily Mirror*. Parallel to their rise was a decline in the prestige of the older periodicals, beginning to be shouldered aside by brasher competitors like the *Graphic* or the re-vamped *Illustrated London News*, with livelier illustrations and a more adventurous range of fiction. The mass market, with its increased opportunities for advertising, made it possible to recoup the high capital investment required by the new technologies. While some of the family firms, including Macmillan's, continued to prosper, others were outmanoeuvred by a new generation of publishers, 'thrusting' men as the idiom of the day had it, such as Andrew Chatto of Chatto and Windus, George Newnes, founder of the *Strand Magazine* (1891) as well as *Tit-Bits* (1881) – a paper which over the years rejected work by Conrad, Joyce and Virginia Woolf – or William Heinemann, an admirer and friend of Kipling.

The expansion of the market brought about a new relationship between author and publisher. The Society of Authors, founded by Walter Besant in 1884, sought to address the key question of the defence of literary property. Literature, according to Gissing's Jasper Milvain, had become a trade; genius might succeed by 'cosmic force', but 'your successful man of letters is a skilful tradesman'. Unhappily, many men of letters, whether geniuses or not, were poor tradesmen. Gissing and Hardy both paid for the publication of their first novels; both, like Kipling, sold the copyright in their work, to their long-term disadvantage. The Society of Authors insisted that the author should never pay, and urged the adoption of a royalty system as both clearer and fairer than the many alternatives, such as profit-sharing after the publisher's expenses had been met (as Kipling discovered, these were not always open to inspection), or purchase of the copyright either outright or for a fixed term of years.[9]

Under Besant's direction the Society became a powerful pressure-group, leading to the foundation in 1895 of a Publishers' Association as a counter-measure. Relations between the two organisations were often acrimonious, and in the space between them there was room for a new player, the professional literary agent. In exchange for a percentage of an author's earnings, the agent would bring author and publisher to each other's attention, taking on the role that readers like Andrew Lang had filled more casually, but would go beyond that to protect the author's financial interest. Prompted by Besant, Kipling engaged Alexander P. Watt as his agent in 1889, and a year later joined the Society of Authors. He was pleased enough with Watt to recommend him to Olive Schreiner in 1891, on the grounds that 'he . . . saves me all my troubles in fighting with publishers and wasting time in bargaining' (*Letters*, II.43). Watt was in fact just about to engage in one such battle, helping to suppress the unauthorised publication in London of two volumes of Kipling's journalism from the *Pioneer* days, as well as *The Smith Administration*, a collection of stories under the A. H. Wheeler imprint in Allahabad. Kipling was more than a literary tradesman, but he was acutely conscious that what he wrote was his property, and determined to get a good return on it.

From its inception the Society of Authors campaigned for an adequate copyright law. This was an issue in which Kipling was to become publicly involved. Watt had sold the serial rights to a number of his stories to the American company Harper and Brothers for publication in *Harper's Weekly*. In 1890 Harper brought out *The Courting of Dinah Shadd and Other Stories*, an unauthorised collection of five stories they had previously published together with 'The Incarnation of Krishna Mulvaney', which they had not. By way of acknowledgement they sent Kipling a fee of £10, which he promptly returned. He objected that Harper had acquired only the serial rights, and that their action had pre-empted his plans to revise the stories before publishing them in an authorised book version. To W. E. Henley he wrote in a fury at 'the grotesque Yahoodom of nipping pieces off a half-presented foetus', his sense of injury made all the more intense by the fact that only a year earlier Harper had loftily dismissed the chance to publish *Plain Tales* (*Letters*, II.23). In the absence of an international copyright agreement there was little he could do, but he took his quarrel with Harper to the pages of the *Athenaeum* (*Letters*, II.25–6). Two weeks later, the *Athenaeum* published a reply from Besant, Hardy and William Black, pointing out that Harper had in fact behaved better rather than worse than other American publishers, who might have paid him nothing. Still indignant, Kipling responded with a poem, 'The Rhyme of the Three Captains', in which he presented himself as the skipper of a brig robbed by a privateer, and with a cumbersome pun:

We are paid in the coin of the white man's trade – the bezant is
hard, ay, and black.

Harper offered a compromise, by withdrawing 'The Incarnation of
Krishna Mulvaney' and replacing it with 'The Record of Badalia
Herodsfoot', which had already appeared in *Harper's Weekly*, and
Kipling had to be content. The issue was in any case coming to a conclusion. In 1891 the long campaign to persuade America to sign up to
an international copyright agreement was finally achieved by the
Chace Act, extended and made more effective in 1909. Later, Kipling
admitted that it might have been wiser to have held his peace, and
leave these issues to Watt. His disagreement with his fellow-authors was
quickly resolved; Hardy was one of the sponsors for Kipling's election to
the Savile Club a few months later.

The Family Balestier

During his dispute with Harper, Kipling had access to advice from a different quarter. Wolcott Balestier, four years Kipling's senior, had arrived
in England from America in 1888, after trying his hand in various directions, including biography, fiction and journalism. He was now the
London agent for the publisher John W. Lovell, and at the same time
setting up a company with William Heinemann to market English fiction on the continent. Lovell had been one of the most piratical of
American publishers, but with the Chace Act on the horizon he was
seeking to repair his relations with English authors, and Balestier
approached Kipling on his behalf. In a matter of weeks Kipling was on
close terms with both Balestier and his sisters, Caroline and Josephine.
    Balestier was evidently a man of great charm. Edmund Gosse and
Henry James were enchanted by him; James described him as 'the
admirably acute & intelligent young Balestier, who has been of much
business use to me, & a great comfort thereby – besides my liking him
so'.[10] Kipling trusted him enough to allow Lovell to publish an
'Authorized Edition' of his work in America, though his consent was
given with a restatement of his hostility to the business habits of
American publishers (*Letters*, II.31). Balestier's experience of the
American market helps to explain the complex publishing history of
The Light that Failed, the novel Kipling began writing in 1890. Two versions of the story were deposited in the Library of Congress in
November 1890 for copyright purposes: one in fourteen chapters with
an unhappy ending, and another with twelve chapters and a happy

ending, which was then published in *Lippincott's Monthly Magazine* in January 1891. A third version, in fifteen chapters and again with an unhappy ending, was published by Macmillan in March 1891 as the first English edition, with a prefatory note that this was the story 'as it was originally conceived by the Writer'.[11] This was neither so cynical nor so unusual as it might seem; at just this time, Thomas Hardy was preparing a bowdlerised version of *Tess* for publication in the *Graphic*, before restoring the novel 'as originally conceived' for publication in volume form. Kipling and Balestier also agreed to collaborate on an adventure novel, *The Naulahka: A Story of East and West*, written between the summer of 1890 and the following spring, with Rudyard responsible for the Indian scenes and Wolcott for the American ones. Despite his agreement with Watt, Kipling authorised Balestier to deal with it 'absolutely as if it were your own' (*Letters*, II.42).

By the time *The Naulahka* was published in book form, in April 1892, Wolcott had been dead for four months, and Kipling was three months into his marriage to Carrie Balestier. The relation between Kipling's friendship with Balestier and his marriage to his sister has aroused speculation. In brief, the argument has been that Kipling was uncertain about his own sexuality, was drawn to Balestier, and married Carrie in part as the nearest alternative, and in part in an attempt to hide his feelings from himself.[12] There are two orders of question here. So far as the claim concerns motives of which Kipling himself was unconscious, it is unanswerable, though since most studies of male–male relationships refuse to make a simple opposition between straight and gay, it might be argued that uncertainty is the normal condition. The further claim, that Kipling and Balestier were aware of a same-sex desire, and that either or both wished to give it expression, is less convincing. Kipling disparaged introspection; not to inquire too closely into motives was itself part of manliness. It is possible that his feelings for Balestier lay close to the border between the homosocial and the homoerotic, even that he was in love with him, but in an era which valorised the idea of 'comradeship' there was no need for either of them to fear that there was anything unconventional in their friendship. They had good reason to value each other's company. In literary terms 1890 was Kipling's year, but for much of it he was emotionally on edge and in poor physical health; Balestier was confident, restless and, like Kipling, an outsider in the London literary world. Kipling had previously collaborated with his own family on poems and stories; now that he was made welcome by the Balestier family, he was happy to do so again. The friendship between Kipling and Balestier was perhaps a little warmer than that between Thomas Hardy and Horace Moule, probably a little calmer than that between Edmund Gosse and Hamo Thorneycroft, but it was not, to themselves or to those who knew them, out of the ordinary.

Nor is it odd that Kipling should have been attracted to Carrie. He was not good at being on his own. He had already been through his 'smash' and the break-up with Caroline Taylor. In May 1890 he had visited Florence Garrard in Paris, re-awakening old wounds. In September Alex Hill died suddenly; Kipling had been at least half in love with Mrs Hill, and the fact that she was now a young widow must have unsettled him. In October he was ill again, and ordered abroad to Italy for a month to recover. Carrie, meanwhile, was supportive and eagerly involved in the progress of his work. She too had been taken up by the literary world, by the Gosses in particular, and had felt patronised by it, but she was at ease with Kipling. Their courtship was not without its difficulties. Hardy remembered Carrie as 'an attractive and thoughtful young woman',[13] and James recognised her strength in times of crisis, but otherwise few people outside her family warmed to her. She had courage and determination, but not charm, and her managerial skills were sometimes all too visible. Gosse, Henley and James had already lost Robert Louis Stevenson to one strong-minded American woman, and they were not keen to lose Kipling to another. Nor was Alice Kipling. In May 1890 she and Lockwood returned from India for eighteen months (Lockwood had been invited to supervise the design of the 'Indian Room' at Osborne, the Queen's home on the Isle of Wight), and she observed the relationship between her son and her future daughter-in-law without enthusiasm.[14] Lockwood thought Carrie 'a good man spoiled'.

Kipling found himself pulled in different directions. His health, after a second winter in England, was still poor. He had achieved everything in London that he had hoped; he had published or was soon to publish a novel, a volume of short stories and a book of poems, in addition to stories and poems to be collected later; and he was tired. In the *Century Magazine* Edmund Gosse warned of the danger of 'this precocious fecundity', and suggested that it would be in Kipling's best interest to 'be deprived of pens and ink for a few years and be buried again somewhere in the far East'.[15] The doctors offered the same advice. Kipling was persuaded. In May 1891 he and his uncle Fred made a visit to America to see the eldest of the Macdonald children, Harry, who had written to say he was ill; he died before they arrived, and Kipling abruptly turned back to avoid the reporters waiting to interview him. But in August 1891 he set off again, on a voyage which was to take him to Cape Town, New Zealand, Australia and Ceylon, and then by train through the south of India up to Lahore.[16]

His spirits soon revived. At the Cape Naval Station in South Africa he made a new friend, Captain Edward Bayly, the beginning of a fascination with the Royal Navy. He also met and liked Olive Schreiner, whose position on South African affairs was soon to be very different from his own, and later twice found himself a fellow-passenger with General William Booth, founder of the Salvation Army, for whom he conceived 'great respect and admiration' (*SM* 62). He was delighted with New Zealand, with Auckland in particular; less so with Australia, where he sounded a warning note about the threat from China. But then, days after his arrival in Lahore, he received a telegram announcing Wolcott Balestier's death from typhus while on a visit to Dresden. He immediately returned to England, arriving on 10 January 1892.

According to Gosse, the telegram was from Carrie and read: 'WOLCOTT DEAD. COME BACK TO ME.'[17] If that is correct, the last two words must be taken either as a sign that Kipling and Carrie already planned to marry, or as a virtual proposal. On 11 January, the day after his return, Kipling took out a special marriage licence, and a week later he and Carrie were married at All Souls, Langham Place. London was in the grip of influenza, and the only guests besides Kipling's cousin and best man, Ambrose Poynter, were Henry James, William Heinemann, and the Gosse family.

There were various literary matters to settle. Kipling revised his poem 'The Long Trail' to make it a poem for Carrie, changing 'dear lad' to 'dear lass', and made the final selection for *Barrack-Room Ballads*, sent to Methuen for publication in March; from now on Methuen were to publish most of his verse. The arrangements for publishing *The Naulahka* were entrusted to Watt. On 2 February Kipling and Carrie left London for Liverpool, and the following day set sail for New York. They were in England again in the summers of 1894 and 1895, but it was not to be their home until September 1896.

The Light that Failed

Kipling's first novel tells the story of Dick Heldar, a war artist who returns to London from the campaign in the Sudan to seek the fame and fortune he believes is his due. His initial success is interrupted by a chance encounter with a childhood sweetheart, herself determined to make her name as an artist, who demands his support but rejects his love, and then by the onset of blindness as a consequence of an earlier battle wound. In the final chapters of the novel, he makes his way to the Egyptian desert, where he is killed by a sniper's bullet.

The Light that Failed has satisfied few of its readers, but like many first novels it has the urgency which comes from the presence of powerful but inchoate feeling. The heroine, Maisie, is clearly based on Florence Garrard, and most of the work was written in a concentrated burst after Kipling's visit to her studio in Paris in May 1890 in an attempt to revive their engagement. Florence recognised the intended portrait, but criticised it as distorted. In the epigraph to Chapter 7, the speaker complains that his love 'Bade me gather her blue roses'; Florence wrote in the fly-leaf of a copy of the novel that Dick, with his usual 'obliquity of vision', had failed to observe that she was not exacting the impossible of him, 'but *he* of me'.[18] Her reaction is wholly understandable. Dick is accorded throughout a sympathy he does little to earn; his view that it is mere perversity which prevents Maisie from loving him is left unquestioned. The novel generally adopts his conviction that art must be a representation of the external world, the world of 'tobacco and blood', and that it must be closely based on actual experience. Maisie, as a woman, has been denied access to that world, and therefore her art must be nugatory. This simplistic position is contradicted by Dick's own 'Melancolia', which is drawn from his imaginative life – as he puts it, 'I can do it now because I have it inside me' – but Maisie is not allowed to aim at an equivalent success.

The sexual politics of the novel are its most disagreeable aspect. This is not to suggest that Kipling has nothing to offer in this area. There is little effort made to understand Maisie, but there are moments when the self-dislike induced by Dick's relentless pursuit of her anticipates Sue Bridehead's distress in Hardy's *Jude the Obscure*, written four years later. The red-haired impressionist with whom Maisie shares a flat is not allowed the dignity of a name, but she too intermittently eludes the moral scheme which condemns her. Her portrait of Dick, hungry with longing for Maisie, is powerful enough for him to recognise its truth and be humiliated by it; that she loves as well as despises him suggests a complexity for the most part missing in the presentation of the female characters. Nonetheless, the treatment of sexuality in the novel is confused and ugly. In the effort to transform personal hurt into impersonal art, Kipling is impelled to generalise, and the novel is punctuated with assertions that women waste men's time, spoil their work, and demand sympathy when they ought to give it. The only woman it is safe to love is the sea, described as an 'unregenerate old hag' who draws men on 'to scuffle, swear, gamble, and love light loves'. Lip-smacking fantasies of erotic pleasure underscore the note of sexual panic: naked Zanzibari girls dancing 'furiously' by the light of kerosene lamps, endless love-making in the hold of a ship with a 'Negroid-Jewess-Cuban; with morals to match' – a phrase as silly as it is brutal. To love deeply, in this novel, is to be humiliated, and to deserve humiliation.

Countering the love between men and women is 'the austere love that springs up between men who have tugged at the same oar'. However, this love manifests itself in a mixture of horse-play and ten-derness, more mawkish than austere. When Dick suffers a panic attack brought on by his blindness, Torpenhow wrestles him back into bed, holds his hand as he falls asleep, and then kisses him, 'as men do some-times kiss a wounded comrade in the hour of death'. In his delirium Dick even addresses Torpenhow as 'Maisie'. Kipling is embarrassingly insistent on the manliness of their affection – Torpenhow's voice is deep, his grip tight, his hand 'a large and hairy paw' – but the love Kipling/Dick is looking for is essentially maternal; the story ends with Torpenhow on his knees, holding Dick's body in his arms, in a presumably unintended parody of the Pietà.

Kipling is only too deeply engaged in all this, even if the reader is not. Dick's childhood is a reworking of Kipling's miserable years at Southsea, with the difference that Dick really is the orphan Kipling had some-times felt himself to be; his wretchedness as his sight begins to fail recalls Kipling's own, before his extreme short-sightedness was discov-ered and his mother came home to rescue him. As if fearing that the novel could be construed as a covert attack on her, Kipling prefaced the Macmillan edition with a dedicatory poem, 'Mother o' Mine':

> If I were damned of body and soul,
> I know whose prayers would make me whole,
>   *Mother o' mine, O mother o' mine!*

It requires considerable wrenching to make Alice Kipling fit this picture of unwearying maternal devotion. But there was little in the novel to cheer Carrie either. The Macmillan edition was the first to include what is now Chapter 8, celebrating the 'go-fever' that, as she noted, also afflicted Kipling. She might well have wondered, when he set off alone in August 1891, how far he shared the fear expressed in the novel that a woman's love could only spoil a man's work.

The other main area of interest in *The Light that Failed* is the debate about art. In a fit of contempt Dick makes two versions of a picture, one to suit the taste of the public, the other for his own satisfaction, very much as Kipling was to do with the serial and volume versions of the novel. When Torpenhow rounds on him, Dick replies with an epigram: 'Only the free are bond, and only the bond are free.' Good work, he instructs Maisie, does not belong to the person who does it: 'It's put into him or her from the outside.' The artist's responsibility is to master the materials, to work without trickery or shirking, and to wait on what Kipling called his 'Daemon'.[19] Kipling took these ideas seriously, but as it appears in the novel the notion that the artist owes a duty to his art rather than to the public is merely arrogant. As J. M. Barrie recognised, Dick's contempt for those who 'talk about Art and the state of their souls' is shared by his creator. Both assume that because they have knocked about the world, they have little more to learn; both are without sympathy for the mass of humanity. This, in Barrie's view, is fatal to the novel. Without it, Kipling is left 'a rare workman with a contempt for the best material'.[20]

The realism typified by Dick's work as a war artist raises some more general questions. The artillerymen who admire his picture of a field-battery going into action discuss it as if it were a single frame from a piece of cinematic film, picking out the clues which tell them what must have just happened and what must happen next.[21] There is an obvious analogy with many of Kipling's own stories, which similarly compress a phase of life into a vividly rendered moment. But by the 1890s realism had become a difficult issue. Dick's commitment to truthful representation is criticised as 'brutal and coarse'. The same charges had been levelled at Kipling. Reading *Plain Tales*, wrote Oscar Wilde

> one feels as if one were seated under a palm-tree reading life by superb flashes of vulgarity. The jaded, second-rate Anglo-Indians are in exquisite incongruity with their surroundings. The mere lack of style in the story-teller gives an odd journalistic realism to what he tells us.

The version of the essay published in *Intentions* in 1891 added the suggestion that Kipling had 'seen marvellous things through keyholes', a remark that is itself flashy and vulgar. Nonetheless, Wilde's point about the impact made by Kipling's work was well taken. His essay was one of a number which located Kipling at the meeting-point of two kinds of literature, evoking simultaneously an exotic world of palm trees and lightning, and the domestic terrain of keyholes and journalistic realism. Andrew Lang welcomed *Plain Tales* as the opening up of 'an unbroken field of romance', to which he himself was about to add with *The*

World's Desire, a novel about Odysseus's final voyage written in collaboration with Rider Haggard. The *Spectator* applauded *Soldiers Three* as 'realistic in the best sense'; the qualification is a barely coded way of insisting that while Kipling dealt with the actualities of barrack-room life, he was still 'sound and manly' in tone, unlike the 'so-called realists' of France. Humphry Ward contrived to have it both ways, and congratulated Kipling on the discovery of Tommy Atkins as 'a hero of realistic romance'. Kipling's Indian stories helped to focus the debate between the defenders of realism and the advocates of a revived school of romance, and took an added interest from it.[22]

Realism was the dominant mode of Victorian fiction, but until the 1880s the requirement to be realistic had been subordinated to the principle that the author should offer moral instruction, even if only obliquely through the extension of the reader's capacity for sympathy. None of the major novelists would seriously have dissented from the claim made by Trollope in his *Autobiography*, though they might have made it less blandly: 'I have ever thought of myself as a preacher of sermons, and my pulpit as one which I could make both salutary and agreeable to my audience.'[23] Characters were to be lifelike, but they were also to be agreeable; or if not, they were to be kept at a due distance from the reader. The action was to follow the laws of probability, but it was also to lead towards a conclusion in which all loose ends were tied, the good duly rewarded, and the bad either reformed or punished. The realists of the later nineteenth century refused to offer these satisfactions. Instead, like Dick Heldar, they insisted that what was ugly in life should remain so in art. Clara Hewitt disfigured by the vitriol thrown in her face in Gissing's *The Nether World* (1889), Sarah Tucker vomiting outside a public house in Moore's *Esther Waters* (1894), Arabella Donn throwing a pig's pizzle at Jude in *Jude the Obscure* (1895), were all examples of a new realism which was true to life at the expense of offering pleasure, and certainly at the expense of offering pleasurable companions.

The new realists also seemed to challenge the sense that life was providentially arranged, by employing the plot conventions which in mid-Victorian fiction had nudged the story towards a happy ending to emphasise instead the futility of human effort. The unlooked-for inheritance in *The Nether World*, the return home in *Esther Waters*, the concluding marriage in *Jude the Obscure*, are used to frustrate rather than reward the reader. The measure of the artist's integrity was the strength to face facts unflinchingly, not a timid regard for the blushes of a young person; artistic honesty was not to be equated with moral advocacy. It was in these terms that Kipling had defended 'The Story of the Gadsbys'. Increasingly, fidelity to the discipline and technique of writing was to be more important than deference to the precepts of Mrs Grundy.

The literary reviews in the 1880s and 1890s were dominated by disputes about the limits of realism.[24] Much of the animus against Zola was directed less at the novels than at the theory underpinning them, and in particular at his faith in the scientific methods of observation and experimentation. Naturalism, according to Zola in *Le Roman Expérimental* (1880), was simply 'la formule de la science moderne appliquée à la littérature'. Modern science studied human nature as it was shaped by the laws of heredity and by the environment; the naturalist novel continued these studies in fictional form. What disturbed Zola's opponents was the explicit determinism of his position, and the apparent denial of human freedom. Kipling's early readers might similarly have been dismayed at the way conditions of life in India – the heat, stress of work, and isolation from other Europeans – appear to undermine individual autonomy. In fact, however, the naturalistic assumptions of the Indian stories and poems were regularly set aside precisely on the grounds that the world Kipling was writing about was unfamiliar to his English readers; if life under Indian skies followed different laws, that was only another aspect of its general strangeness. Paradoxically, the association of Kipling with the exotic literature of Lang, Pierre Loti and Rider Haggard licensed a realism which might otherwise have attracted more displeasure.

Barrack-Room Ballads and Other Verses

The impetus for the *Barrack-Room Ballads* came from the music hall. In the 1860s and 1870s the theatre-going public had divided along increasingly sharp lines. New theatres were built to suit the taste of the middle class, with decorous orchestral stalls replacing the unruly pit of an earlier period. Inevitably, the new levels of comfort led to higher charges. Priced out of the legitimate theatre, the lower classes were left to find their entertainment in the music halls, at the height of their popularity during Kipling's years in London.[25] Here too the trajectory over the period was from the rowdy to the respectable, with a tendency for performers to avoid controversy in favour of a cheery fatalism and an acceptance of social inequality – a stereotype of the Cockney still current late into the twentieth century. But the transformation from a class to a mass culture was never complete, and there was a wide variety of personae, style and repertoire among the acknowledged stars, ranging from the risqué Marie Lloyd to the elegant Vesta Tilley, who married a Conservative politician, and as Lady de Frece was presented at court in 1923. Gatti's, one of the best known halls, was a few steps from Kipling's rooms in Villiers Street, and he soon found he preferred 'the smoke, the roar, and the good-fellowship' of the halls to dinner parties with the intelligentsia (*SM* 49).

But there was more at issue than his impatience with literary society. The music hall introduced him to performers whose success was based on an easy rapport with their public. In the give-and-take atmosphere of the halls, Kipling began to imagine a way in which the artist might speak for as well as to the audience. The result was the series of soldier poems which appeared between February and July 1890 in Henley's *Scots Observer*. Their publication in *Barrack-Room Ballads and Other Verses* in March 1892 made Kipling the most popular and most frequently quoted poet of his time.

He had already begun to experiment with Cockney dialect through the character of Ortheris, one of the Soldiers Three.[26] In a story like 'His Private Honour', much of it given in Ortheris's own words, the Cockney rhythms – the elisions and glottal stops, the 'so I sez' and 'Jock, 'e sez' – attest that Kipling had at least listened to the stories a man like Ortheris might tell. Peter Keating comments that Kipling was the first major Victorian writer who was not afraid of the working classes, and it is difficult to think of another who could have written without irony of a Cockney's 'honour'.[27] Gissing, for example, rather because than in spite of the fact that he knew working-class life and poverty at first hand, was always offended by what he transcribed. In *New Grub Street*, published a year before the *Ballads*, he remarks that 'the accent of the London poor . . . brands as with hereditary baseness', and in his novels those who use it are entrapped in a nether world, their mores and habits of thought as alien and indelible as their speech patterns.[28] Even in Kipling's stories, where the treatment of the Cockney speaker is more sympathetic, the difference between Ortheris's speech and the language of the narrator echoes the gulf between the man the story is about, and the audience to whom it was addressed.

But Kipling had long understood the power of the anecdote to bring together those who understand the point of the story, and know where to laugh or cry. Now he saw that the music-hall song served a similar function, and began to draw on it for the *Barrack-Room Ballads*. Here he could present the experience of the common soldier as it was told both by and to the common soldier, as in 'Tommy':

I went into a public-'ouse to get a pint o' beer,
The publican 'e up an sez, 'We serve no red-coats here.'
The girls be'ind the bar they laughed and giggled fit to die,
I outs into the street again and to myself sez I:
        O it's Tommy this, an' Tommy that, an' 'Tommy go away';
        But it's 'Thank you, Mister Atkins,' when the band begins to
            play –
        The band begins to play, my boys, the band begins to play.
        O it's 'Thank you, Mister Atkins,' when the band begins to
            play.

The soldiers in the *Barrack-Room Ballads* address their own lives, on their own terms; the voice heard in them has the authority of a class, rather than of a single individual.

It is also a potentially dissident voice. It was easy to admire the soldier abroad, but the soldier at home had always been mistrusted. In an attempt to improve morale and efficiency, Edward Cardwell's reforms of the 1870s had ended the purchase of commissions, abolished peace-time flogging, and introduced short-service enlistment, typically six years overseas and six in the reserve. Army life no longer resembled penal servitude, but pay was still poor, and there was a perennial crisis of recruitment. The *Barrack-Room Ballads* offer a portrait intended to be both realistic and sympathetic, of men who

    . . . aren't no thin red 'eroes, nor we aren't no blackguards too,
    But single men in barracks, most remarkable like you.
                                  'Tommy'

Kipling's Tommy Atkins enjoys the violence of a street brawl fought out with belts as much as he does fighting under orders ('Belts'); when he is arrested for 'Mad drunk and resisting the Guard', the problems of a hangover are balanced by the satisfaction that comes from knowing he 'socked it them hard!' He is patriotically proud of 'the Widow at Windsor', but his sense of race is casual and unsystematic. To be shipped 'somewheres east of Suez' is to find relief from English weather and English morality, in a land 'Where there aren't no Ten Command-ments an' a man can raise a thirst' ('Mandalay'); the 'Fuzzy-Wuzzy' is 'a pore benighted 'eathen but a first-class fightin' man', who was defeated by superior weaponry rather than superior morale. Kipling's soldier knows little and cares less for the grand aims of Empire; the speakers in 'Snarleyow' and 'The Widow's Party' remember the blood and gore, but not the name of the battle or 'the end of all the show'. The aim of the fighting is to extend the power of 'The Widow at Windsor' from 'the Pole to the Tropics', but it is the 'poor beggars in red' who pay the price.

The finest of the *Ballads*, 'Danny Deever', tells of a soldier hanged for shooting a comrade. It uses the question-and-answer pattern of traditional ballads like 'Lord Randall', and like them offers no explanation about motive. It also displays Kipling's tact in the handling of dialect. Aspirates and some final consonants are dropped, but there is no attempt to transliterate Cockney diphthongs and vowel sounds, and rarely more than one change to the word. In the word which resonates through the poem, Kipling drops the final 'g' but retains the aspirate:

> An' they're hangin' Danny Deever in the mornin'.

The interwoven iambics and anapaests make this is a metrically subtle poem as well as an emotionally powerful one, but Kipling's experiments with Cockney have been frequently criticised. E. M. Forster doubted his accuracy as a mimic of Tommy Atkins, while George Orwell thought the attempt both patronising and facetious: to which one might reply that Orwell was an Etonian who worried that his accent might give him away when he pretended to be down and out, and Forster knew working men in a very different way from Kipling.[29] There are undoubtedly uneasy moments, but so there are whenever the educated writer represents the uneducated, and has to speak on their behalf. Hardy faced much the same problem in the treatment of the Wessex dialect, a comparison which arguably works in Kipling's favour. Rather than condescending, the handling of demotic speech in Kipling's soldier stories and the *Barrack-Room Ballads* is an attempt to extend the literary franchise to the supposedly inarticulate.[30]

The point can be made in a more general way. In 'The English Flag' Kipling asked the question: 'And what should they know of England who only England know?' His prolonged attempt to tell the English who they were, and who they had been and might be, was contemporary with another exploration of matters English, in the form of the *New* (later *Oxford*) *English Dictionary*, completed in 1928. In his introductory essay James Murray discussed the shifting relation between standard English and those forms which the *OED* acknowledged, and yet at the same time pushed towards the margins, labelled as archaic, colloquial, dialect, vulgar, and so on. 'The circle of the English language,' he concluded, 'has a well-defined centre but no discernible circumference.'[31] Kipling's aim was to explore the experiences these supposedly aberrant forms arose from, or carried within them. No writer was more interested in frontiers, or, to use Murray's terms, in what lay on the circumference, but in the soldier stories and poems Kipling's imagination is essentially centripetal, readmitting into the circle of Englishness those whom the barriers of region or class had relegated to the margins, and pushed into silence. Kipling, at his best, gave them back their voice.

Life's Handicap

The *Barrack-Room Ballads* were a huge success, reviewed some fifty times in a matter of months, and more or less continuously in print since their first publication. Their success was not without its problems. 'Cleared!', an attack on the Commission which exonerated Charles Parnell from complicity in the Phoenix Park murders of 1882, was rejected by *The Times*: wisely enough, since it was *The Times* which had published what it claimed were Parnell's letters, but which the Commission found to be forgeries. One of Parnell's fiercest opponents was George Saintsbury of the *Saturday Review*, who agreed with Kipling that since Parnell had been suspected he was to all intents and purposes guilty; he and Kipling became lifelong friends. Kipling had intended to keep clear of the various literary 'sets', but once 'Cleared!' had been published by Henley in the *Scots Observer*, he was inevitably associated with 'Henley's regatta'.

His main outlet in the London years continued to be the short story, though his agent, Alexander Watt, urged him to write a novel: ' "Hurry up on your novel" sez he "and become rich" ' (*Letters*, I.370). But it was clear from *The Light that Failed* that the novel was not a form that played to his strengths. In September 1896, it was more than politeness that led him on to reflect to Mrs Humphry Ward on the problems of the 'really truly long story'. He could 'think them by scores', but it was beyond him 'to work out the full frieze':

> It is just the difference between the deep-sea steamer with twelve hundred people aboard . . . and the coastwise boat with a mixed cargo of 'notions'. And so when the liner sees fit to salute the coaster in passing that small boat is mightily encouraged.[32]

But the tide had turned away from the 'really truly long story'. In 1894 Mudie's and W. H. Smith's, the most powerful of the circulating libraries, abruptly abandoned the three-decker as no longer profitable. There were many who welcomed the change. Publishers such as Cassell and Co., whose authors included Robert Louis Stevenson and Rider Haggard, were already developing the market for one-volume novels, especially of the adventure and romance variety. Despite Watt's advice, it was ceasing to be necessary 'to work out the full frieze' in order to be acknowledged as a writer.

The demise of the three-decker, which was so obviously to Kipling's advantage, was accomplished by the fiat of Mudie and W. H. Smith. It is more difficult to account for the rise of the short story, which had become, as Henry James put it, 'an object of almost extravagant dissertation'.[33] Serious attention to the short story as a form came late in England. The shorter fictional pieces of the mid-century, including those by Dickens, Trollope and Mrs Gaskell, can usually be read as if they were stray chapters from longer works. Mrs Gaskell's 'Lizzie Leigh', for example, might have come from one of her own industrial novels. Dickens remarked on the difficulty of constructing his Christmas stories within the 'narrow space' available to him, but 'A Christmas Carol' and 'The Chimes' were substantial tales of around 30,000 words. Trollope wrote forty-plus short stories, but while they were commercially successful he did not think them worth a mention in his *Autobiography* .

In 1884 the American critic Brander Matthews argued in the *Saturday Review* that the British had yet to realise the possibilities of the Short-story, distinguished by the capital letter and the hyphen from stories which simply happened to be short. Edgar Allan Poe had laid the basis for an American philosophy of the form as early as 1842, in his review of Hawthorne's *Twice-Told Tales*. Poe's main argument, that in the short story as in the lyric poem every word must contribute to the single effect aimed at, was restated in numerous later discussions, including Matthews's own *The Philosophy of the Short-story* in 1901. Rather than an inferior kind of fiction, the short story could be seen as a more concentrated and exacting form than the novel, for the reader as for the writer.

While Matthews pointed to what had been achieved by American writers, his compatriot Henry James was looking to Europe, in particular to Russia and France. In an essay on Maupassant for the *Fortnightly Review* in 1888, he noted that 'the short story is but scantily relished in England', where a more leisurely kind of fiction was preferred, and the novelist's idea was 'apt to resemble those old-fashioned carriages which require a wide court to turn round'.[34] This is a disparaging version of Kipling's image of the novel as 'deep-sea steamer', and helps to suggest why the short story was now coming into its own. Kipling had spoken of his own work as a 'coastwise boat with a mixed cargo of "notions"', and it was this heterogeneity that James seized upon in the short story form when in an introduction to an American edition of Kipling's stories, *Mine Own People*, he applauded the younger writer for 'seeing so many chances of touching life in a thousand places, taking it up in innumerable pieces, each a specimen and illustration'.[35]

James's hint, that the artist could no longer expect to see life steadily and see it whole, foreshadows Kipling's fondness for titles with plural forms – *Traffics and Discoveries*, *Debits and Credits*, *Limits and Renewals* – with the implicit suggestion that no one story, for all the despatch and authority with which it is written, can be taken as definitive. It also anticipated an aspect of the short-story form that other writers were to comment on: G. K. Chesterton, for example, in 1906: 'Our modern attraction to the short story is not an accident of form; it is a sign of real fleetingness and fragility; it means that existence is only an impression, and, perhaps, only an illusion. . . . We have no instinct of anything ultimate and enduring beyond the episode.'[36]

This argument has a good deal of force. One of the literary forms that prepared the way for the emergence of the short story, and for a time flourished along with it, was the psychological sketch, usually almost plotless, and often presented as a prose poem.[37] This originated in France with Baudelaire, but it was appropriated by Walter Pater in his *Imaginary Portraits* (1887), and taken up by Wilde and others associated with the Decadent movement. In this context Chesterton's words, that 'existence is only an impression', inevitably recall Pater's Conclusion to *The Renaissance* (1873):

> Experience, already reduced to a swarm of impressions, is ringed round for each one of us by that thick wall of personality through which no real voice has ever pierced on its way to us . . . those impressions of the individual mind to which, for each one of us, experience dwindles down, are in perpetual flight.

A number of the short-story collections of the 1890s, such as Hubert Crackanthorpe's *Wreckage* (1893) and George Egerton's *Keynotes* (1895), were concerned to analyse the fleeting impressions of the isolated individual mind, as were many of the stories published individually in the two main organs of 1890s aestheticism, *The Yellow Book* (1894–97) and its even shorter-lived rival *The Savoy* (1896). Neither published work by Kipling. There are more affinities between his writing and the Aesthetic movement than he would have been willing to admit – though he admired Beardsley's work, and made a point of calling on him – but he kept his stories away from its magazines, and himself at more than arm's length from its leading personalities.

The writers for *The Yellow Book* were self-consciously seeking to do something new: 'new' became the vogue word of the 1890s. Kipling's stories by contrast appeared traditional in form, developments of the yarn, the joke or the anecdote. Their novelty, for the English readers he needed to attract in 1889 and 1890, was mainly a matter of their content, their covers opening up, as H. G. Wells put it, 'like window shutters to reveal the dusty sun-glare and blazing colours of the East'.[38] Unlike the majority of pieces in *The Yellow Book*, Kipling's early stories were strongly plotted, concerned with men and women in extreme situations, in which they and the values which give order to their lives are put to the test. What they explore is the way in which individual identity is created, or at least sustained, by the presence of society and its institutions. To that extent they seem written in resistance to Pater's sense of experience broken down to a series of transient and uniquely personal impressions. Learoyd's loneliness in 'On Greenhow Hill', or Holden's in 'Without Benefit of Clergy', both in *Life's Handicap* (1891), are all the more painful when seen against the need for and the possibility of participation in the shared experience of the community.

Life's Handicap was itself something of a mixed cargo, including stories written before Kipling left India alongside others written after his arrival in England. Unsurprisingly, the best stories were also the most recent. 'On Greenhow Hill' is the finest of Kipling's stories of the Soldiers Three, and one of the most telling examples of his use of a 'frame' around the central story. As the three men lie in wait for a deserter who has been sniping at the camp, Learoyd recalls his days in the mining areas of Yorkshire, his love for 'Liza Roantree, her death from consumption, and his decision to join the army in order to escape a life in which he had lost interest. Despite the bond which holds the three men together, this is essentially a study in isolation. Learoyd's personal history is effectively at an end when Liza's ill-health forces her to leave the area, followed soon after by the Methodist preacher for whom he has come to feel an unwilling respect; 'and I were left alone on Greenhow Hill'. (The iambics invite a half-memory of 'La Belle Dame Sans Merci', with the knight 'Alone and palely loitering' on 'the cold hillside'.) While Learoyd meditates on his loss, and on the social pressures which drove him to enlist, Ortheris is intent on shooting the deserter. He remains coldly indifferent as Learoyd tells his tale:

Private Stanley Ortheris was engaged on his business. A speck of white crawled up the watercourse.

'See that beggar? . . . Got 'im.'

Nothing in his experience on the London streets has prepared him to respond to a story of lost love, and it is this lack of response which Kipling seizes on as the clue to his nature. Murderous, unloved and ungrieving, Ortheris watches 'with the smile of the artist who looks on the completed work' as seven hundred yards away the deserter tumbles face down into a clump of blue gentians, and a raven flaps out of the woods to investigate. Kipling too was clearly satisfied with his work: 'Got 'im' applies as much to his presentation of Ortheris as to the deserter killed by Ortheris's bullet.

In 1891, when *Life's Handicap* was published, Joseph Conrad was still at sea, but there is a Conradian aspect to several of these stories. 'The Head of the District' and 'At the End of the Passage' were both published in magazine form in 1890, the year of Conrad's journey up the Congo, and they benefit from being read side by side. The latter is the story of a group of Anglo-Indians, 'lonely folk who understood the dread meaning of loneliness', who gather when they can at the home of one of their number, Hummil, to talk and play cards, less out of regard for each other than to stave off the horror of being alone – by which they, and Kipling, mean being denied the company of fellow Europeans. It is this, rather than the heat and the overwork, which destroys Hummil. In his waking hours he sees a spectral double of himself; in his sleep, he endures a recurring nightmare in which he is chased by a 'blind face that cries and can't wipe its eyes'. Eventually he is found lying in his bed, his hands still clenched by his side, literally terrified to death.

In 'The Head of the District', a few months earlier, Kipling had described the dying Yardely-Orde, Deputy Commissioner of the Kot-Kumharsen district, giving his last audience to the men of the Khusru Kheyl:

'I speak now true talk, for I am as it were already dead, my children – for though ye be strong men, ye are children.'
'And thou art our father and mother,' broke in Khoda Dad Khan with an oath.

Yardley-Orde is Kipling's ideal Anglo-Indian: a benevolent despot, respected and loved by those he both commands and serves. His achievement will of course be betrayed, in this case by the folly of a government which appoints a Bengali to succeed him, foreshadowing (as Kipling saw it) the deeper folly of Indian self-rule. But by engaging himself in the tasks nearest at hand Yardley-Orde, and others like him, can attain a moral integrity denied to the theorists and politicians. In spite of the vastness of time and space, the first figured in the complexities of Indian history and customs, the second in the immensity of the Indian landscape, they bring order and stability to the world around them, and in doing so achieve it within themselves.

In Conrad's 'Heart of Darkness', first published in 1899, Marlow explains that he values work because it offers 'the chance to find yourself. Your own reality – for yourself, not for others.' But moments later, he redefines it as an absurd series of 'monkey tricks': 'When you have to attend to . . . the mere incidents of the surface, the reality – the reality, I tell you – fades. The inner truth is hidden – luckily, luckily.'[39] It is in this dual vision that Kipling resembles Conrad. Taken together, 'At the End of the Passage' and 'The Head of the District' suggest that the stoicism and commitment to duty of the Anglo-Indian is a mask, worn to keep at bay the sense of desolation. In an effort to stay awake, Hummil places a spur in his bed. Intended literally, the act invites interpretation; he must either spur himself on, or fall into the terror that kills him. Like Marlow's, the work done by the Yardely-Ordes is both real and illusory: both an exercise of responsibility, and a means to escape 'the inner truth', the horror of emptiness. No less than Conrad, Kipling saw the vulnerability of the self in isolation.[40]

Unlike Conrad, however, Kipling was unwilling to recognise that the imperialist pursued his own selfhood at the expense of the native peoples, who in political terms became a subject race, and in literary and moral terms were defined as the 'Other' which had to be faced – or faced down. Benita Parry observes that imperialism is an encounter between peoples, and asks 'what of the moral integrity of those men on whom Europe was carrying out its great experiment in affirming the exhilaration of existentialism?'[41] It is a question to which Kipling offers no answer.

But it is not one that was asked of him in 1891. Only Francis Adams, in the *Fortnightly Review*, noted that the Indian population was viewed 'merely as a huge mass of raw, brown, naked humanity', to be manipulated in one way or another by the British in authority over them.[42] There were discerning essays on Kipling's work during the year, and some hints of the kinds of criticism his work was increasingly to suffer – reservations about the journalistic abruptness of his prose, misgivings about his view of life as a grim practical joke – but the reviewers were for the most part too dazed by his success to do more than pick out isolated aspects of his work. Like Scott and Dickens before him, Kipling was experienced as a phenomenon before he was judged as a writer.

4
Citizens of America

On 3 February 1892 the Kiplings sailed from Liverpool on the SS *Teutonic*. Their plan was to escort Carrie's mother and sister home and then make a honeymoon tour to the Far East, covering the costs of the trip with a series of travel letters for *The Times*, which would also be syndicated around the world by Alex Watt. They arrived in New York eight days later in a flood of winter sunshine, and then moved on to Brattleboro in Vermont, ending their journey with a midnight sleigh ride to the home of Carrie's brother Beatty and his wife Mai, wrapped up against the cold in blankets and buffalo robes. Kipling already knew something of the landscape through the stories of Sarah Orne Jewett and Mary Wilkins Freeman. Now he was enchanted by it, though the abandoned farms on the hill-sides testified to the harshness of an 'iron-bound life . . . in a lean land', for the women perhaps still more than for the men. The presence on the horizon of Mount Monadnock seemed a good omen; he knew the name from his reading of Emerson, and had come to associate it with 'everything that was helpful, healing, and full of quiet'.[1]

Neither his delight in the landscape nor the knowledge that his letters were to be published in the American press could deter him from another attack on New York as 'the shiftless outcome of squalid barbarism and reckless extravagance'.[2] Victorian Englishmen liked to prophesy that America was rushing headlong into general lawlessness, and Kipling was no exception. But Vermont was not New York, and soon after his arrival he told William Carey at the *Century Magazine* that when he and Carrie returned from their tour they would become 'settled down citizens of the United States' (*Letters*, II.52). With this in mind they negotiated with Beatty for a ten-acre plot on which to build a house, finding the $750 he demanded – too much, Carrie thought – from an advance on *The Naulahka*. The Balestiers were prone to feuds, and Beatty and Carrie, the one affable and improvident, the other tense and wary, found it difficult to get on, but at first all went well, and Kipling was happy to begin laying the foundations for a new Family Square.

The Naulahka was serialised in the *Century Magazine* from November 1891 to July 1892, and published in volume form in April 1892. Kingsley Amis and Angus Wilson have spoken up for it, but whatever fun Kipling and Wolcott had in the writing, the result is a rather mechanical stab at the adventure story. The central characters are Nick Tarvin and Kate Sheriff, from the town of Topaz in Colorado. Tarvin has more than his share of the energy Kipling had admired in Wolcott, and is impatient to develop the town. To this end he plans to steal a priceless Indian necklace with which to bribe the wife of a railway magnate, so that she in return will persuade her husband to bring the railway to Topaz. Neither Tarvin nor Kipling seem much troubled by a plan involving theft, corruption and uxoriousness, but it makes a nonsense of the contrast made in the novel between western straightforwardness and the complexity and intrigue of Indian society. Kate, meanwhile, resists Tarvin's proposal of marriage in order to train as a nurse; she too is bound for India, where she hopes to ease the plight of Indian women. Like his, her plans are thwarted, partly by the obduracy of Indian customs and belief, and partly by the growing recognition that she cannot understand or help other women until she herself takes on a woman's proper role, as a wife and mother.

Hero and heroine return to America to marry, but the novel ends with a note of ambiguity. Kate realises 'a woman's complete contentment with the fact that there was a man in the world to do things for her', but there is a hint that she has still to face the sense of 'defeat, remorse, and the torture of an over well-trained conscience'. This brief concession to the moral urgencies of what the 1890s knew as 'the woman question' sits uneasily in the framework of an adventure story. When William Heinemann urged him to write a 'woman-book', Kipling agreed to keep the idea 'under advisement at the back of my head', but wisely took it no further (*Letters*, II.57); the domestic novel was not his territory, and in any case he had been too little time in England to sympathise with feminist arguments developed over half a century of campaigning. Unsurprisingly, *The Naulahka* is most successful when it is most simple, in its contrasting evocations of a small frontier town in America, and the overtly exotic world of India.

In April 1892, as *The Naulahka* was coming out in volume form, Kipling and Carrie sailed for Japan on the next leg of their tour. Kipling was pleased to find that as the granddaughter of a former legal adviser to the Mikado Carrie was treated as an honoured guest; less pleased at what he saw as the westernisation of the country. They spent most of their time in and around Yokohama where, as Kipling put it in his poem 'Buddha at Kamakura', they could 'feel the Soul of all the east' about them. But on 9 June their plans were disrupted by the failure of their bank, the New Oriental Banking Corporation, just hours after Kipling had drawn a mere £10 of the £2000 he had in his account. In the autobiography, he records 'an instant Committee of Ways and Means, which advanced our understanding of each other more than a cycle of solvent matrimony' (*SM* 65). With their money gone, and with Carrie into the third month of her pregnancy, they decided to return to Vermont.

In the event, their situation was less alarming than it appeared. Thomas Cook and Son gave them a refund on their tickets, the Canadian Pacific Railway allowed them free travel, and they eventually recovered their money. But in the crisis Carrie justified what Kipling had written three years earlier, that an American wife could be a real companion to her husband, and she increasingly took over as the manager of their affairs. It was she who handled the accounts, organised their travel and accommodation, dealt with the servants – not, as a rule, very successfully – and guarded her husband's privacy. Her second daughter, Elsie, remembered later that her mother 'introduced into everything she did . . . a sense of strain and worry amounting sometimes to hysteria', and others too found her fretful and officious.[3] Whether or not Kipling did so, he was content to entrust the problems of daily life to her care.

On their return to Vermont, they moved temporarily into a farm cottage, installing a second-hand stove to keep them warm through the coming winter, while Kipling began to extend his literary contacts in America. He already had dealings with the *Century* (Edmund Gosse was the magazine's London agent), and Mary Dodge, perhaps forgetting that she had rejected his schoolboy poem 'The Dusky Crew', had asked him to contribute stories for children to *St Nicholas Magazine*. He now sent her a number of tales, beginning with 'Toomai of the Elephants', which were later to go into *The Jungle Books* or the *Just So Stories*. Remembering the part reading had played in his own childhood, Kipling took his task seriously; he told Mrs Dodge that he would 'sooner make a fair book of stories for children than a new religion' (*Letters*, II.63). There is something more here than an extreme instance of the late Victorian investment in ideas of childhood innocence, Peter Panism run riot. In exploring the traffic between the openness and curiosity of the child's world, and the inflexibility of the adult one, Kipling's children's stories also ask what is won, and what lost, in the attempt to secure a foothold in the social order: not quite a religious question, but one of the recurrent themes of Kipling's fiction.

He himself was about to become a father. On 29 December, the day before his twenty-seventh birthday, Carrie gave birth to Josephine. Kipling was at once an engagingly besotted parent. In 1895 he warned his cousin Stanley Baldwin that a 'woman isn't well before her child comes bodily but it's her spirits and mind that are all on edge afterwards' (*Letters*, II.182), which suggests that Carrie suffered some form of post-natal depression, but at the time he was confident enough to add an end-of-year postscript to her diary, thanking God for the happiest year of his life.

He had good reason to feel happy. His poem 'The Gipsy Trail' had just come out in the *Century* –

> Follow the cross of the gipsy trail
> Over the world and back!

– but in fact he was beginning to feel settled. His financial position was again secure. With regular royalty payments for work already published – *Barrack-Room Ballads* was now in its sixth edition – and new work charged at a rate of $100 per thousand words and rising, his income in 1894 alone was close to £200,000 in present-day terms. He and Carrie chose a Balestier family friend, Herbert Marshall, as architect for their new home, to be built into the hill looking out across the river valley, and named 'Naulakha' by way of tribute to Wolcott. Beatty was appointed foreman on the site, and for a time the steady flow of payments for work done, all meticulously noted by Carrie, helped keep him solvent. By August 1893 the work was completed and they moved in; or rather, Carrie and Josephine did. Lockwood had come to visit in June, celebrating his retirement and the pension he had been granted through Rudyard's influence with Lord Dufferin, while Alice was left to settle their accommodation in Wiltshire. Now father and son escaped on a trip to Canada and New England.

Kipling might reasonably have thought himself entitled to a holiday, since he had just seen through the press a collection of stories, *Many Inventions*, published in May 1893. This was essentially a product of his London years, since ten of the fourteen stories had been previously published in periodicals, the earliest as far back as February 1890. In

keeping with the title, it was the most varied volume he had yet published, including a satire on the moral sickness of London in the form
of a letter home from a Muslim visitor ('One View of the Question'),
his one slum story ('The Record of Badalia Herodsfoot'), a farce
('Brugglesmith'), and a fable about the power and responsibility of the
artist ('The Children of the Zodiac'). 'In the Rukh' features an adult
Mowgli, now a forest ranger and about to marry, and a pale imitation of
what he was to become in the *Jungle Books*.

The most successful story is ' "Love-o'-Women" ', which continues
Kipling's experiments with the vernacular. Writing to Mark Twain
about his series 'Old Times on the Mississippi', William Dean Howells
advised him not to write 'at' an audience, but to 'yarn it off as if
into my sympathetic ear'.[4] Kipling follows this advice in ' "Love-o'-
Women" ', which sets the story of Larry Tighe, a gentleman-ranker,
within the frame of the murder of one soldier by another in a barracks
in India. The frame story is given in the voice of Kipling-as-narrator,
with typically brilliant attention to visual detail, but without the exas-
perating knowingness of some of the earlier tales. Here the reader is
asked to cross several cultural boundaries, from within each of which
events appear in a different light. The Court which tries Sergeant
Raines for murder understands little of what has happened; the narrator knows enough to recognise that the evidence given by Ortheris is
deliberately misleading; Mulvaney, with his greater experience, sees
beyond the narrator, but even he stops short of any claim to full
understanding: 'I can't say fwhat I mean to say bekaze I don't know
how . . .'.

His attempt to say what he means leads him into the story of Larry
Tighe, who repeatedly and deliberately risks his life during a military
campaign. Unknown to Mulvaney, Tighe is in the final stages of loco-
motor ataxia brought on by syphilis; he walks unsteadily, with 'his right
leg swingin' like a lame camel', and his body 'shrivelled like beef-rations
in a hot sun'. Despite himself he survives the campaign, and returns to
be confronted by the woman he has betrayed. His last words before he
dies in her arms are a quotation: ' "I'm dyin', Aigypt – dyin', " he sez.'
Given in the voice of the main narrator, Tighe's view of himself as a
latter-day Antony destroyed by love would be either sentimental or
absurd; stripped of its grandeur by Mulvaney's brogue, it can be read
equally well as a piece of self-mockery, or a defiant last assertion of his
status as a gentleman. Filtered through a confessedly imperfect narrator,
who yarns it off as he 'came across ut – here an' there in little pieces',
the story eludes our final judgement.

'The Disturber of Traffic' has a similarly elaborate frame, and another narrator whose story is 'delivered in pieces', this time on a lighthouse on a foggy night, interrupted by fog-horns and the 'sharp tap of restless night-birds' against the glass. The fog serves as an appropriate background to the murkiness of the inner story. This concerns Dowse, a lighthouse-keeper in the Flores Straits near Timor, where his sole companion is a half man, half sea-gipsy named Challong. Dowse gradually becomes so obsessed by the 'streaks' made in the water by the tides that he tries to exclude shipping from the Straits, which he covers with buoys marking non-existent wrecks. With its oblique reference to Prospero and Caliban on their island, the story hints obscurely at the role of the artist: the lighthouse-keeper is tasked with showing others the way through the tides; the artist too is expected to guide and enlighten. In the late story 'Unprofessional' (1930), Kipling uses the tides as a metaphor for those forces in the universe – whether spiritual or astrological is left unclear – beyond the control of the human mind. If this is how we should read the tides here, Dowse is fighting to ward off an unwanted glimpse into the hidden nature of things. This also seems to be the thrust of the epigraph, a prayer for a veil to be drawn between mankind and 'the wheel and drift of things',

> Lest we should hear too clear, too clear,
> And unto madness see!

Dowse is eventually cured 'by working hard and not looking over the side more than he could help', in line with Kipling's habitual mistrust of introspection, but he remains oppressed by the fear that he has caused others to lose their lives. Angus Wilson understandably describes the story as 'a horrible and purposely puzzling tale';[5] if, as he suggests, it should be read as a parable about art and creativity, its conclusion seems to be that the insight of the artist is a burden rather than a privilege, and brings with it a responsibility that cannot be set aside.

The nature of creativity is also explored in ' "The Finest Story in the World" '. Charlie Mears, a bank clerk with literary ambitions, unwittingly reveals to the narrator a range of metempsychotical experience – in his previous lives he has been a Greek galley slave and a Viking adventurer – but when he falls in love with a shop girl the door closes on his memories. The story makes some play with Hindu notions of reincarnation, as the principle on which 'the half-memory falsely called imagination' is based, but the underlying concern is with an ideal literary immediacy. Charlie's attempts at poetry are weakly derivative, but

the stories which emerge unedited from his memory come 'from experience', 'in a tone of command', with 'absolute assurance'. The narrator
wants to write with equal authority, but he is warned by a Hindu
acquaintance that the perfect concordance of deed and word is unattainable: 'it would mean that all this world would end now—
instanto—fall down on your head'. No story can be told with 'absolute
certainty'; all stories are corrupted in the telling. This particular story is
too uneven to support such grandiose ideas, but at a simpler level it
challenges conventional notions of the literary, and suggests Kipling's
increasing self-consciousness as a writer. It also caught the attention, a
few years later, of T. S. Eliot, another bank clerk with an interest in reincarnation, who drew on Charlie's memories in the 'Death by Water' section of *The Waste Land*.

The 'Naulakha' years

Over the next three years in 'Naulakha' Kipling wrote two volumes of
the *Jungle Books*, *Captains Courageous*, *The Seven Seas* and most of the
stories to be published in *The Day's Work* (1898): by any standards a
remarkable and diverse achievement. At the same time, he continued to
extend his knowledge of American writers. He joined the American
Association of Authors, sought out the dialect poet James Riley and the
rural novelist Hamlin Garland, and renewed his acquaintance with
Mark Twain. He even got on friendly terms with Howells, who in 1890
had written loftily that Kipling's work had little to interest an American
readership, but gradually came round far enough to consider him 'in
some sort American'.[6] But while Kipling's admiration for American literature was genuine, the country provided him with little new material.
Even *Captains Courageous* is more a tribute to his interest in life at sea
than to America, and that aside there is not much beyond 'A Walking
Delegate', part political fable against socialism, part experiment with
the varieties of American vernacular, and in neither respect very successful, though it earned him $135 per thousand words from *The
Century*. He lamented to Sarah Orne Jewett that 'the mass of material . . .
to work at in this land' must be 'done by an inhabitant' (*Letters*, II.165),
but in truth he had seen all he wanted of America during his first visit
in 1889, and once settled in 'Naulakha' he made no effort to explore
further. He made some local friends, including Molly Cabot, who had
been a friend of Wolcott's, and James Conland, the doctor who attended Carrie after the birth of Josephine, and when he was not writing or
looking after his property he read up on the flora and fauna of

Vermont, learned to walk in snow shoes, and organised Christmas parties for the local children, but otherwise he showed little interest in his neighbours. The Brattleboro press was left to wonder why he and Carrie dressed for dinner, and over the number and duties of the servants, including maids, a nanny and a liveried coachman; requests for interviews were firmly declined.

Where Kipling did make new American friends, they tended to be rich, well-connected and cultivated. Perhaps the closest was Charles Eliot Norton, Professor of the History of Art at Harvard, whose daughter Sally he had met during his childhood visits to The Grange, the home of the Burne-Jones family. Norton was one of the old stock of New England Brahmin gentry, now losing ground as symbolic and material power shifted towards the more entrepreneurial New York. He had not only visited India but knew or had known everybody in both England and America, and the two men and their families soon became friends, with Norton assuming his habitual role of mentor. Later, Kipling's enthusiasm for the Anglo-Boer War made him uneasy, but the two shared an aversion to literary biography – Norton had attacked Froude's biography of Carlyle for what he took to be its indiscretion, and as Ruskin's executor would soon begin another of those bonfires of private papers that mark the age – and, more positively, an affection for Edward Burne-Jones. It was to Norton that Kipling wrote a long and touching letter after Burne-Jones's death in June 1898 (*Letters*, II.338–42).

Henry Adams, whom the Kiplings had met on their voyage out to New York, provided another point of entry into American life. Adams was part of a Washington circle that included the diplomat John Hay, soon to become Ambassador to England, the lawyer William Hallett Phillips, whose influence was decisive when Kipling wanted to establish a new post office within easy reach of his home, and Theodore Roosevelt, the American statesman he came most to admire. In *Something of Myself*, Kipling recalled telling Roosevelt of his wonder at a people who had 'extirpated the aboriginals of their continent more completely than any modern race had done', and now 'honestly believed that they were a godly little New England community, setting examples to brutal mankind' (*SM* 73). If he had remembered that within his own lifetime the British had eliminated the native people of Tasmania he might have been less free with his irony.[7] Roosevelt's Democrat opponents, led by President Grover Cleveland, were much less to Kipling's liking; a note in Carrie's diary dismisses them as a 'colossal agglomeration of reeking bounders'.

There were occasional visitors to 'Naulakha', including Kay Robinson from the Lahore days, and Conan Doyle, who stayed long enough to give Kipling a golf lesson, while urging him to tone down his attacks on the country. Frank Doubleday arrived on behalf of his company, Scribner's, to open negotiations for an edition of Kipling's complete works, and soon became a close family friend.[8] But with Carrie to guard his privacy, Kipling enjoyed his relative isolation. His letters from 1894 and 1895 suggest a man in full command of his powers, and confident of their worth. From time to time he threw out *obiter dicta* on the art of writing: reproving one writer for an over-elaborate attempt to represent dialect ('All you have to do is to give the reader a notion'), another for explaining too much ('I loathe an explanation'), and himself for writing with too evident a purpose ('Purposes are good things but they are apt to make writing stodgy – same as this last page and a quarter').[9] He remained shrewdly practical in his comments on literary rights and property. In a letter to *The Critic* he defended the literary agent as a man whose 'special knowledge of a highly specialized trade' enabled him to save the author a 'mass of profitless temper-wearing detail' (*Letters*, II.190); he urged the Society of Authors to establish an agency in New York to look after the interests of English authors hoping to be published in America (*Letters*, II.196–7); and he reacted quickly and angrily when G. W. Dillingham in New York published an unauthorised book based on his Indian journalism (*Letters*, II.208–9). When the opportunity arose to buy back the copyright, outside India, of the six volumes published in the Railway Library series, he took it eagerly, meeting the costs from a royalty offer from Macmillan: 'It means a good deal to me – even at long prices – to control my early books' (*Letters*, II.169–70).[10]

The summers of 1894 and 1895 were spent in England. Lockwood and Alice had settled at Tisbury in Wiltshire, where they had been taken up by the landed gentry in the area, in particular by the Wyndhams at 'Clouds' and the Arundells at Wardour Castle, and Rudyard and Carrie rented a house nearby. The trip in 1894 allowed Alice to see her granddaughter for the first time, but a letter from Kipling to Stanley Baldwin hints that she and Carrie were at odds over Josephine's upbringing; on the second and shorter visit the following year Josephine was left with Carrie's mother and sister, and a tentative plan to build a holiday cottage in neighbouring Dorset was abandoned.[11]

During these summer visits Kipling was able to re-enter the world he had left, but in his new role as a married man and a writer of established reputation. He had lunch at the Savile Club, attended a dinner where he sat next to his military hero Field Marshal Lord Roberts, and made a visit to his old school to mark the retirement of Cormell Price. If it was a pleasure to be lionised, it was also unsettling, and back in Tisbury, where the miserable weather kept him indoors, he pondered the differences between England and America. It was here that he wrote his carping poem 'An American', as well as the farcical 'My Sunday at Home', in which an American visitor to Wiltshire becomes entangled in what proves to be 'an alien life', and 'The Puzzler', in which three Englishmen set an organ-grinder's monkey to climb a monkey-puzzle tree. He described these tales as 'full of the purely male horse-play and schoolboy rot that womenfolk bless 'em find it so hard to understand' (*Letters*, II. 143), but the male world they belonged to was also definitively 'English'. Appropriately, one of their guests in Tisbury was Henry James, who had made the international theme his own. Two years later, however, as James was settling into his home in Rye, Kipling was ready to end his experiment with America.

The Jungle Books

The first of *The Jungle Books* was published in May 1894, during the Kiplings' visit to England; during the 1895 visit, Kipling enjoyed watching his father at work on the illustrations for the second, which came out in November of that year. The stories had been appearing in magazine form since the end of 1892, but now they were published together they were an overwhelming success. One of the few dissenting voices was that of Henry James: '*how* it closes his doors & sets his limit! The rise to "higher types" that one had hoped for – I mean the care for life in a finer way – is the rise to the mongoose & the care for the wolf.'[12] No doubt it is unfair to note that 'The Death of a Lion', James's story warning against the dangers of the kind of popular acclaim he was himself never to receive, had just appeared in *The Yellow Book*.

The sources for *The Jungle Books* were many and varied. During his time in America Kipling's imagination had returned continually to India, and it had been spurred on by his father's visit in 1893. In the autobiography, he suggested that the stories had emerged along three different routes: his own tale 'In the Rukh', which deals with Mowgli after he has emerged from the woods and is working as a forest ranger; a story remembered from the *Boy's Own Magazine*, in which a hunter falls among a group of lions who recognise him as a fellow Freemason; and Rider Haggard's novel *Nada the Lily* (1892), in which Umslopogaas is rescued from a lioness by Gehazi the wolf. Behind these are other textual sources, in particular a pamphlet by Sir William Sleeman, *An Account*

of Wolves Nurturing Children in their Dens (1852), Robert Sterndale's
Natural History of the Mammalia of India and Ceylon (1884), and
Lockwood Kipling's *Beast and Man in India*, published in 1891.

But there is also an unmissable undercurrent of personal investment
in the story of Mowgli's triumphs. Left by his parents at Southsea,
Kipling had felt neglected and starved of affection; Mowgli finds himself adopted by a family of wolves who are ready to fight to the death
for him, and then by the whole jungle, which comes to recognise his
'true' qualities. If there are times when he knows himself to be a
stranger and alone, the difference in his nature allows him to take on a
heroic role, as in the battle against the dholes in 'Red Dog'. At one level
the story is a thrilling medley of childish daydreams: the wolf pack battling for its very survival, the enemy aliens who attract no sympathy
and deserve no mercy, the wise counsellor who accompanies the hero,
the lone wolf fighting to avenge his murdered family, and the lament
over the leader fallen in the final battle. This kind of fantasy is hardly
peculiar to Kipling, but he develops it without talking down to his
young audience. On the contrary: he instinctively felt the world was a
cruel and dangerous place, and that exposure to cruelty might in itself
be a kind of education. Mowgli laughs 'a little short ugly laugh' on the
day he kills Shere Khan, and he is 'shaking all over with rage and hate'
as he prepares to destroy the village by letting in the jungle. *The Jungle
Books* are written for children, and they deal for the most part in emotions children can recognise, but Kipling knew from his own experience
that these emotions can be bitter and passionate.

The Mowgli stories are clearly designed to appeal to children in other
ways too – hence the running, swimming and climbing, the passwords
and the secret fellowships. But they also belong to the tradition of alle-
gories or beast fables; Kipling himself cited the ancient *Jataka* tales of
India, in which the Buddha appears in different animal forms. This is a
level which the reader can pick up or set aside according to mood,
where Shere Khan represents an unreasoning and finally self-destroying
hatred, the Bandar-log a foolish instability of purpose, and so on. Yet
the moral lessons are rarely insistent, unless the stories are read in the
depressingly wooden versions Baden-Powell made of them for *The Wolf
Cub's Handbook*. So, for example, in 'Kaa's Hunting' Mowgli is torn
between the lawlessness of the Bandar-log and the wise counsel of
Baloo, but the moral outcome is never in doubt, and the real power of
the story comes from the account of the Cold Lairs, derived from
Kipling's memory of the ruined cities at Amber and Chitor. Both here
and in 'The King's Ankus' the 'rows and rows of roofless houses . . . like

empty honeycombs filled with darkness' are a reminder of the ultimate futility of human effort. Kaa too is a disturbing presence in the story. His slow dance before the Bandar-log, his body making 'soft, oozy triangles that melted into squares . . . and coiled mounds', is more terrible than an allegorical battle between wisdom and lawlessness, and more memorable. Another writer might have seen the Bandar-log, with their delight in mimicry and in irresponsible play, as avatars of the artist, but not Kipling. In this story Kaa is an artist in killing, who compels admiration by the perfect adjustment of means to ends.

The underlying concern at the allegorical level is the importance of the Law, with upper-case L. The lower-case laws communities have made for themselves may be open to question; the Law is not. It is significant that the Law is born from Fear, in the story Hathi the elephant tells in 'How Fear Came'. Tha, the first of the elephants, institutes Law and Fear together, since 'only when there is one great Fear over all . . . can we of the Jungle lay aside our little fears, and meet together'. Law, like Fear, imposes a discipline. It stands between the individual and the anarchy that threatens from without, such as the attack by the Red Dogs, and the still more dangerous threat of madness or despair to which the animals in the jungle give the name *dewanee*. Only unquestioning obedience to the Law can shield us from the 'horror of desolation, abandonment, and realised worthlessness' which Kipling had known in his own life.[13]

This defensive mood explains Kipling's hostility to those who evade or ignore the Law; the actions of such people lead to anarchy, and that way madness lies. The Bandar-log are to be taught if possible and punished if not, but there is no point in trying to understand them. Kipling's Law has little in common with the Christian idea of a Law which reconciles Justice and Mercy. In the *Jungle Books*, Justice is a matter of debts to be settled, and Mercy is irrelevant. Mowgli's error in going off with the Bandar-log causes harm to Bagheera, who has therefore to punish him: it is the Law. Mowgli tells Messua that he does not understand what she means by Justice, but he sets about destroying the village in which he and she have been mistreated: it is the Law. Bagheera buys the life of young Mowgli with the bull that he has killed, and he frees him from the Jungle by killing another. This is closer to the world of taboo and the evil eye than it is to the moral schemes of Victorian England. Critics like Shamsul Islam have shown how Kipling's 'philosophy' of Law conjoins three interrelated elements, 'namely moral values, the Imperial Idea, and the Doctrine of Action'.[14] But for Kipling it was less an idea to be thought through than an instinct to be obeyed. If the Law is disturbed, it can only be restored if the due price is paid in full.

There is affection as well as cruelty in *The Jungle Books*, for the Jungle, for Baloo and Bagheera, and for Mowgli himself. Like the imaginary Bombay of Kipling's childhood, the jungle is an Edenic space in which divisions of race, caste and creed can be set aside, but without prejudice to the final superiority of the young Sahib/hero.[15] In this respect, the stories prepare the ground for *Kim*, though there are notable differences: Mowgli becomes the Master of the Jungle, but Kim is the Friend of all the World; Mowgli insists on his authority, whereas Kim is impelled by curiosity. Closer to *Kim* than the Mowgli stories is 'The Miracle of Purun Bhagat', which follows 'How Fear Came', and in many ways runs counter to it. Purun Bhagat embodies within himself the two opposing worlds of *Kim*, the Western code of decisive action, and the Eastern (in this case Hindu) way of passivity, which in *Kim* is given to the Lama. Retiring from years of political service, Purun Bhagat enters a life of meditation and the road to spiritual peace. In the end, however, love for his fellow-man forces him back to the world of action when the nearby village is threatened by an avalanche – though since he dies in the position in which the holy man or Sunnyasi is supposed to be buried Kipling perhaps wanted to suggest that there is no final incompatibility between the two ways. The Law desired by Purun Bhagat has nothing to do with Fear, and the balance he seeks belongs to the inner life, not to an outer world where debts must be paid. His Law finds its expression in love and contemplation, not in codes and rules, and it is all-encompassing, not reserved for the members of the Pack. If it is not quite the rise to 'higher types' that James was looking for in Kipling's work, 'The Miracle of Purun Bhagat' provides an important counterweight to the stories of violence and competition that otherwise dominate *The Jungle Books*.

Quarrels and departure

Kipling enjoyed writing *The Jungle Books*; in *Something of Myself* he recalled that once he had begun, 'the pen took charge', and he could surrender himself to the pleasure of the work (*SM* 67–8). But there are moments of disquiet in the stories too, not just in the presence of the Cold Lairs, or the Red Dogs, but in the precariousness of Mowgli's own position. Delightful as it often is, he belongs finally to neither animal nor human worlds; each demands from him as much as it offers. As Alan Sandison has argued, Kipling valued social life as a necessary defence against the horror of isolation, but he also feared it as an erosion of individual selfhood.[16]

And America was coming to seem a threat. In the autobiography, this is attributed to an inherent incapacity for 'law-abidingness' (*SM* 71), running in tandem with a racial declension as the old stock was invaded by immigrants recruited as cheap labour. One aspect of this was an anti-English sentiment, ready to be whipped up whenever it suited the press and the politicians. In 1895 a long-running dispute over the boundary between British Guiana and Venezuela intensified when gold was found in the region. The Venezuelan government thoughtfully offered a concession in the disputed area to an American syndicate; President Cleveland appointed a commission to define the boundary, and invoked the Monroe Doctrine to caution against British intervention. In the closing weeks of the year there was the prospect, loudly welcomed in the American press, of a trans-Atlantic war.

The dispute was eventually settled peaceably, but it highlighted the problems Britain would face in defending itself if the dangers posed by Germany in Europe were compounded by threats elsewhere. Tensions were rising in the Transvaal in South Africa, where the government of Paul Kruger had imposed uncompromising conditions on the immigrants, or 'Uitlanders', who had come to work the goldfields. The majority of these were British, and they were increasingly restive. Cecil Rhodes in South Africa and Joseph Chamberlain in London looked for ways to exploit the situation. In response, Kruger began to make friendly overtures towards Berlin. Then, on 29 December, with the Venezuelan dispute at its height, Leander Starr Jameson launched his Raid into the Transvaal, ostensibly to protect British nationals during a popular uprising against Boer rule. The plan was as bungled in execution as it was dishonest in conception; the anticipated rebellion failed to take place, and on 2 January the raiders were forced to surrender.[17] The following day the Kaiser sent a telegram in support of the Boers, to show that Germany no longer considered itself bound not to interfere in the affairs of the Transvaal.

Watching these developments from Vermont, Kipling became convinced that he and his family were in personal danger:

I seem to be between two barrels like a pheasant. If the American mine is sprung it means dirt and slush and ultimately death either across the Canada border or in some disembowelled gunboat off Cape Hatteras. If the German dynamite is exploded equally it means slaughter and most probably on the high seas. . . . it is borne upon me by the inner eye that *if* trouble comes I shan't live to see it out. . . .[18]

He had already contributed to the increasingly anxious debate about Britain's military position. The nation's security was assumed to depend on the supremacy of its fleet, but measured by what was known as the 'two-power standard', that the strength of the Navy should exceed that of any two other powers combined, this supremacy could no longer be counted on. The British government had embarked on a programme of naval building, and it had been proposed that the colonies should help meet the costs. In October 1895 *The Times* published Kipling's poem 'The Native-Born', which insisted on the common destiny and heritage of those who called England 'home', even though they lived scattered across the world.[19] Kipling told the editor, Moberley Bell, that he had kept the verses back until the time came to intervene: 'I may be a verse-writer by accident but I am a journalist by education' (*Letters*, II.207). Because this was a poem written in the national interest, he refused a fee, accepting instead the offer of a free subscription.

Early the following year he sent Bell another poem, the 'Hymn Before Action', in which his personal fears were projected in terms of a national emergency:

> The earth is full of anger,
> The seas are dire with wrath.
> The Nations in their harness
> Go up against our path . . .

Wisely, Bell declined; the threat of an Anglo-American war receded almost as quickly as it had sprung up, and Kipling calmed down. In February 1896 his second daughter, Elsie, was born, and his attention turned back to domestic matters, and to work on a novel, *Captains Courageous*.

The impetus for the story came from conversations with James Conland, the Kiplings' family doctor in Vermont, who had once been a fisherman working on the Grand Banks. The plot, such as it is, is simple. Harvey Cheyne, the brattish fifteen-year-old son of a railway millionaire, falls from an ocean-going liner, but is rescued by the *We're Here*, a fishing vessel operating out of Gloucester, Massachusetts. Over the next few months he is compelled to play his part as a responsible member of the crew, a process of chastening and education which transforms him from a spoiled mother's boy into a man, ready to become his father's 'companion, partner, and ally'. There are elements of fable here. Harvey's fall overboard is a parabolic drowning, from which he emerges into a new life; the life of the fishermen is treated realistically, but it also functions as a pastoral, contrasting with the empty life of the wealthy young men Harvey once seemed set to join; and there is a suggestion that the world of the *We're Here* will eventually yield to a new era of technology, in which men work indirectly, via machines, rather than with their hands.

But this is a story without conflict. There are times when it seems that Cheyne Senior will be seen as a typical example of the greed and lawlessness Kipling had stigmatised in *From Sea to Sea*, as when he contemplates 'a pleasant but unscrupulous campaign' against his business rivals, and laments that his lack of formal education means that he 'can't . . . hurt 'em where they live', but in the end there are only a few gestures in this direction.[20] Like Disko Troop, the captain of the *We're Here*, he has 'the faith that comes of knowing men and things', and his record-breaking railway trip across the continent when he hears that his son is safe makes him as much a force of nature as the skipper. The opposition between past and present, sea and land, fades from the story, as both the new-made Harvey, and Dan, Disko's son, transfer easily from the fishing fleet to work on Cheyne's liners. Cheyne is a man of the future, but he embodies the native energy of his country; in his time he has been 'deck-hand, train-hand, contractor, boarding-house keeper, journalist, engineer, drummer, real-estate agent, politician, dead-beat, rum-seller, mine-owner, speculator, cattleman [and] tramp'. Like Whitman, he contains multitudes.

The absence of conflict marks the tale in another respect. The crew of the *We're Here* includes a Portuguese, a negro cook who speaks in Gaelic, a former preacher traumatised by an accident, and a former farmer, but despite this diversity there are no real disputes. The obvious contrast is Conrad's 'The Nigger of the "Narcissus" ', published a year later. In both texts the ship stands as a model of society, but Kipling's crew is rather a team, or a tribe, united in pursuit of a single, agreed goal. Harvey is socialised into a world of shared tasks, memories and customs, right down to the need to spit over the side before announcing the schooner's position after reading the quadrant: 'There is an etiquette in all these things.' These codes are normative, and final; men either accept them, or face death at sea. There is no room and no need for question or speculation. Life is simple; as Harvey tells his mother: 'I worked like a horse and I ate like a hog and I slept like a dead man.' He has learned what is already known, in order to meet the needs of the day. Such knowledge can be deepened, but not challenged.

Kipling himself enjoyed acquiring this knowledge, not least because it allowed him to turn his attention away from a family crisis. The relationship with Beatty had become increasingly sour. There were disputes about money, about his right to mow a meadow, and about his drinking. A startlingly tactless proposal that the Kiplings should support Beatty's wife and daughter for a year, while he went away to find regular work, did little to reconcile the two families, and by the summer of 1895 they had ceased to be on speaking terms. In March 1896, a month after Elsie's birth, Beatty filed for bankruptcy. Two months later, on 6 May, the two men met, Beatty on his buckboard, Kipling picking himself up after a fall from his bicycle. Beatty challenged Kipling about remarks he was reported to have made, to the effect that he had been supporting Beatty and his family. Kipling replied that if he had a complaint, he should make it through his lawyer. Beatty then made some kind of threat. By his account, he meant nothing more than a beating; according to Kipling, he threatened to blow out his brains. There the matter might have been left, but the next morning Kipling went to his lawyer, and Beatty was arrested on a charge of 'assault and opprobrious and indecent epithets and threatening to kill'. For a man who wanted to protect his privacy, Kipling's decision to involve the courts was bad enough, but worse was to follow. When it seemed that Beatty might be kept in jail over the weekend, Kipling offered to stand bail; Beatty raised the money himself, and used the weekend to contact the newspapers. By the time the case came to court, on 12 May, it had already attracted wide attention. Kipling was the only witness, and during cross-examination he was obliged to admit both that he had claimed to be supporting Beatty, and that he had been repaid all the money he was owed. Asked whether he would retract his words, Kipling replied: 'I would not retract a word under threat of death from any living man.' This sounded well, but everyone knew that he had been the one to call in the lawyers. Beatty, relaxed and confident, was bound over to keep the peace, and required to attend at the County Court in the following September. Kipling returned home, as Carrie recorded in her diary, 'a total wreck. Sleeps all the time. Dull, listless and weary.'

The idyll in Vermont was at an end, though it is unclear when the decision to go was finally made. Kipling wrote to Howells to say that he did not intend to leave permanently; it would be hard 'to go from where one has raised one's kids and builded a wall and digged a well and planted a tree' (*Letters*, II.244). Nonetheless, over the summer he settled with *McClure's Magazine* to publish *Captains Courageous* for $10,000, to be paid in gold dollars, sent off the last pages of *The Seven Seas*, and wrote to Frank Doubleday to discuss the first instalment of the proposed Outward Bound Edition. On 1 September he, Carrie and the children left quietly for England on the SS *Lahn*.

5
The Song of the English

On their return to England, the Kiplings rented a house in the village of St Marychurch, near Torquay, where forty years earlier the young Edmund Gosse and his father had studied the rock pools along the shore, and pondered the relation between Genesis and geology. Carrie enjoyed the view of the sea, but it hardly compensated for the breach with her own family, and the unwelcome prospect of ever greater contact with her parents-in-law. Both she and Rudyard found Torquay stuffy, and disliked their house. Its only real advantage was its nearness to the navy base at Dartmouth, and Kipling happily accepted an invitation to visit the Royal Navy's training school, the three-decker HMS *Britannia*. Here he found new material to explore, though his status as a celebrity guest meant that he had less rapport with the ordinary seamen than he had enjoyed with the soldiers in India.

Kipling's first task was to correct the proofs of *The Seven Seas*, due to appear in October, and of *Captains Courageous*, which began publication in *McClure's Magazine* in November.[1] He was also rearranging his stories for the Outward Bound Edition, for which Lockwood was to provide the illustrations, in the form of clay plaques moulded in relief and then photographed for reproduction. But he was busy too with new ideas, including his first stab at what was to become *Stalky & Co.* In this two-part story, 'The Slaves of the Lamp', the boys outwit a master in the first part, and the same stratagems are then applied by Stalky while on campaign in India in the second. Kipling was revisiting his schooldays – Cormell Price of the USC was one of their guests at St Marychurch – and finding a new means to explore how England should fit its young men for an ideal of service. The stories are both a way of holding to his own personal past, and of exploring his relation to England's present. If nothing else, his four years in America had given him a new perspective. It has often been said that Kipling liked to write as an insider, but his position was more often that of the incomer, consciously learning the rules of membership.

He continued to follow affairs in America, and rejoiced in the Republican victory in the Presidential election. But Torquay offered little other than fly-fishing to interest him, he was suffering from problems with his teeth (not helped by the use of arsenic dressings to control the pain), and the weather was damp, so it was with a sense of relief that he and Carrie moved up to London in May to continue the task of re-entering English society. His celebrity made it easy to him. He was made a member of the Athenaeum without the trouble of a formal election, attended a banquet at the Royal Academy, where his uncle Edward Poynter was now President (and newly knighted), went out on the steam trials of the destroyer *Foam*, and joined Sir William Hunter, whom he had known in India, as an honoured guest at Balliol College in Oxford. He also found time to write a poem, 'The Vampire', to help publicise a painting by Philip Burne-Jones, who had become infatuated with the actress Mrs Pat Campbell:

> A fool there was and he made his prayer
> (Even as you and I!)
> To a rag and a bone and a hank of hair . . .[2]

It was not the first time he had come to his cousin's aid. In 1889 he had helped him to recover an autobiographical article he had sold, and at once regretted. Such acts allowed him to repay part of the debt he owed to Edward and Georgie Burne-Jones for their kindnesses to him in the Southsea years.

In the summer of 1897, as a Parliamentary Select Committee carried out a half-hearted inquiry into the Jameson Raid, the nation was preparing to celebrate Victoria's Diamond Jubilee. This had been conceived as a statement about Empire, with a main part in the ceremonies to be played by the prime ministers of the colonies, along with delegates from India and the dependencies. Rudyard had matters to discuss with many of them – he had just published 'Our Lady of the Snows', welcoming Canada's support for a system of preferential tariffs – but London was unpleasantly crowded, and he and Carrie gratefully accepted Burne-Jones's invitation to use his home, North End House, at Rottingdean, near Brighton. From there Rudyard and his father went to see the naval review at Spithead, where 165 ships of the Royal Navy lined up over thirty miles of the English Channel. Here he renewed his acquaintance with Captain Edward Bayly, whom he had met in South Africa in 1891, and at his suggestion spent two weeks in July on manoeuvres with the Channel Fleet.

Kipling was thrilled by the scale of naval operations. In *Something of Myself* he remembered that the national mood of optimism 'scared' him (*SM* 86), but his most recent collection of poems, *The Seven Seas*, published in October 1896, had already contributed to it. This was his first volume of verse for three years, and the public was eager to hear from him; more than 20,000 copies were sold prior to publication. Most of the poems had been written in Vermont, but their argument was of a piece with what became known as the 'New Imperialism'. The British, Sir John Seeley had suggested in 1883, seemed to have 'conquered and peopled half the world in a fit of absence of mind',[3] but the new imperialists had their minds fixed firmly on the extension and consolidation of Empire, preferably in some form of federation or customs union. Underpinning their ambition was the conviction that the British – though they typically spoke of the English, and of the virtues of the Anglo-Saxons – were ideally suited to govern the world, and the world ideally available to British rule. 'We happen to be', said Cecil Rhodes, 'the best people in the world, with the highest ideals of decency and justice and liberty and peace, and the more of the world we inhabit, the better for humanity.'[4] The claim was repeated by politicians, headmasters and speech-makers up and down the land, and any number of journalists, both in the periodical press and in Alfred Harmsworth's new halfpenny evening paper, the *Daily Mail*.

The reviewers recognised a similar conviction in *The Seven Seas*. Charles Eliot Norton drew attention to the 'passionate, moral, imperial patriotism' running through its pages; William Dean Howells described Kipling as 'the laureate of that larger England' of the English-speaking peoples.[5] A year later, *Blackwood's Magazine* hailed the Jubilee celebrations as 'an outward and visible sign of the reawakening of the national spirit', and Kipling as the writer who had 'seized upon the national thought and enshrined it in imperishable verse'.[6] In the past, Kipling had been identified by his subject matter, as the poet of India and of Tommy Atkins. Now he was being identified with a political position and, increasingly, as the spokesman for a political group.

Not all the poems were overtly political. One of those singled out for praise was 'McAndrew's Hymn', a celebration by a 'dour Scots engineer' of machines, the men who tend them, and the world in which they work. Some readers took exception to a further set of 'Barrack-Room Ballads', finding the language used unpleasantly coarse, but the soldiers who spoke in these poems could still be imagined as playing their part, like McAndrew's rods and pistons, in a larger and grander whole:[7]

> Now, a'together, hear them lift their lesson – theirs an' mine:
> 'Law, Orrder, Duty an' Restraint, Obedience, Discipline!'

As the reviewers noticed, McAndrew's prayer, 'Lord, send a man like Rabbie Burns to sing the Song o' Steam', was answered in the poem.

The first poem in the volume, 'A Song of the English' (1893), set the tone of the whole. Here was a voice with which the middle-class reader could feel at ease: formal, masculine, rich with biblical echoes and cadences. The dedicatory stanzas insist on the need for humility ('Humble ye, my people'), but the tone is confident and assertive. Kipling's subject is the 'goodly . . . heritage' given to the English by 'the Lord our God', who had opened up for their use 'a pathway to the ends of all the Earth'. In the past the English had been led astray by 'evil counsellors'; the task Kipling sets himself in the poem is to recall 'us', the English, to the Faith that those who doubted England's imperial mission had betrayed.

Kipling admits a commercial logic to the Empire, acknowledged in the image of the nation's clippers, cargo vessels and whaling ships as the 'shuttles of an Empire's loom', but insists that there is more at stake than the success of a trading enterprise. In the section called 'The Song of the Dead' the vision of an imperial destiny comes like the Holy Spirit:

> Came the Whisper, came the Vision, came the Power with the Need,
> Till the Soul that is not man's soul was sent us to lead.

Elsewhere in the volume, in 'The Lost Legion', he paints a different picture of the forerunners of English imperialism, seeing them as a 'wholly unauthorised horde' of 'Gentlemen Rovers', driven to 'go and get shot and be damned' because they were too restless to stay at home. But whether summoned by God or lured by the desire of adventure, those who had laid down their lives for the Empire were now calling to their sons to 'follow after'.[8] They, the forerunners, had paid the 'price' in blood, and it was the duty of their descendants to accept the 'pride and doom' of 'admiralty' over the seas and the nations. The call runs figuratively through the generations, but literally through the undersea cables, out to the colonies and dominions where, in 'The Song of the Cities', it is heard and answered. In a series of quatrains, the Cities offer to bind themselves together in a 'well-forged link', provided only that

England will match their loyalty with her own. In the last part of the poem, 'England's Answer', England promises to do so, and to accept the Cities as 'Sons of The Blood': independent and autonomous, but bound to each other and to the motherland by a shared destiny and a common speech, the 'straight-flung words and few' of the English. Like Carlyle before him, Kipling was prone to write at length in praise of taciturnity.

'A Song of the English' spoke to the national mood, but it is not an easy poem to admire. It goes some way to justify James's view that the volume was 'all *violent*, without a dream of *nuance* or a hint of "distinction"; all prose trumpets and castanets and such – with never a touch of the fiddle-string or a note of the nightingale'.[9] The violence is only partly concealed. The conviction of England's God-given task to '[c]lear the land of evil, drive the road and bridge the ford', is at odds with the reference to possessions 'Snatched and bartered', cunningly got 'between greed of gold and fear of drouth'. In the resounding line,

> By the peace among Our peoples let men know we serve the Lord!

the phrase 'Our peoples' suggests those whom 'we' have colonised, and over whom we now claim rights of possession. Kipling uses the poem to speak of peace, and the need for obedience to the Divine Will, at the same time as he urges the constituent parts of the Empire to band together in preparation for 'the last great fight of all', in keeping with an increasingly predatory view of international affairs.[10] The overarching problem is the arrogance masquerading as humility, evident in the biblical diction and the willingness to make free with religious ideas, as in the notion of a priest-like succession of responsibilities, but only on the assumption that the divine purpose and the will of the English are one and the same.

The same problem attends 'Recessional', Kipling's poem on the Jubilee. He had at first intended not to write one, but in the end did so as 'a *muzzur-wattu* (an averter of the Evil Eye)' (*SM* 86). The title is appropriate; a recessional is a hymn sung during the withdrawal of the clergy at the close of a service, and the poem, shaped to the tune of the hymn 'Eternal Father, strong to save', invites the reader to pause in the midst of the national celebrations. Kipling insists that there is a distinction between mere Jingoism and a responsible imperialism:

> If, drunk with sight of power, we loose
> > Wild tongues that have not Thee in awe,

Such boastings as the Gentiles use,
    Or lesser breeds without the Law –
Lord God of Hosts, be with us yet,
Lest we forget – lest we forget!

The humility is superficial. Kipling is not warning against the claim to supremacy, but reminding his readers that the supremacy must be continually justified before those 'lesser breeds' unlucky enough not to have been born English. This phrase has troubled many readers, and not only, as Orwell has it, those in 'pansy-left circles'.[11] In Kipling's defence, one might read it as suggesting not that there are some lesser races who are eternally incapable of recognising the Law, but rather that those who deny the Law are for that reason less than they might be. This would be easier to accept if he had not accused so many races of lawlessness: not just the Indian peoples, in need of constant reminders of British authority to keep them in order, but the Americans, Germans and Irish, as well as the Jews.[12] However we read it, the line is rebarbative, inviting the question asked by Martin Seymour-Smith: 'Are there, humanly, *any* "lesser breeds"?'[13]

'Recessional' was published in *The Times* on 17 July, beneath a letter from the Queen thanking her subjects for their expressions of loyalty. If the conjunction of the two voices, of the Empress and her unofficial laureate, seemed appropriate, so too did the note of caution. While some Britons boasted of their 'splendid isolation', others were growing concerned that as the scramble for the world grew more intense, the British position looked more dangerous than splendid. When J. W. Mackail, the pacifist husband of Kipling's cousin Margaret Burne-Jones, applauded 'Recessional' because it seemed to urge a check on Britain's imperialist aspirations, Kipling was quick to correct him. It was the other nations that needed to be checked: 'seeing what manner of barbarians we are surrounded with, we're about the only power with a glimmer of civilization in us'. When the 'big smash' came, however, the British would pull through: 'It will be the common people – the 3rd class carriages – that'll save us' (*Letters*, II.306). For all their suspicion of democracy, the leaders of late Victorian imperialism agreed that strength overseas depended on what Alfred Milner termed 'soundness at the core'. The health of the nation required that social reform and imperialism should be regarded as 'inseparable ideals, absolutely interdependent and complementary to one another'.[14] The composite nature of *The Seven Seas*, the first part dominated by solemn statements of national duty, the second given over to the rougher voices of the common soldier, reflects Kipling's sense of the need to bind all classes to a common cause.

Behind the Jubilee rejoicings, the Kiplings had another reason to ward off the evil eye. On 17 August, a month after 'Recessional' was published in *The Times*, Carrie gave birth to John, 'a black haired boy who howls like a month-old baby' (*Letters*, II.311). The new arrival made it all the more necessary to find a place to live, and at the end of September they took out a three-year lease on The Elms, a red-tiled house with a fine garden on the edge of the village green at Rottingdean. There followed a series of visitors, among them Cormell Price, to whom Kipling read stories for *Stalky & Co.*, Beerbohm Tree, who wanted Kipling to write a play for him, and Arthur Sullivan, who wanted to set 'Recessional' to music. Despite these interruptions, Kipling found time to lobby for a pension for William Henley, who had fallen on hard times.[15] But he was unsettled, still prey to the bouts of depression he had suffered since the retreat from Vermont, and in no mood to face another damp English winter. Earlier in the year he had met Milner, the new High Commissioner for South Africa, and may well have met Cecil Rhodes about the same time, during the inquiry in the Jameson affair. Now he decided that he, Carrie and the children, together with Lockwood, would visit South Africa in the New Year.[16]

Their arrival, on 25 January, was heralded by the publication in the *Cape Times* of a poem by Edgar Wallace, welcoming Kipling in the voice of Tommy Atkins as '*our* partic'lar author':

> You're the poet of the cuss-word an' the swear,
> You're the poet of the people, where the red-mapped lands
>   extend . . .

It was a shrewd move; Kipling invited Wallace to dinner, and offered his assistance for the future – though in acting as godfather to nearly 150 stories about 'Sanders of the River', an uglier version of his own accounts of the role of the district commissioner, Kipling did his own reputation little good. Over the next ten weeks, while Carrie stayed in the suburbs of Cape Town, Kipling met Rhodes and Milner, travelled to the diamond mines at Kimberley, and made a speech to the Rand Club in Johannesburg, where he was lionised by the Uitlanders, and assured that they wished the Transvaal to be brought under British control. He also renewed his acquaintance with Olive Schreiner, whom he had met on his visit in 1891. They disagreed about politics – Schreiner was committed to a multi-racial, independent South Africa – but got on well.

The change of scene and weather, and the political excitement, did much for Kipling's mood; as he wrote to Conland in America, 'You never dreamed of such a country' (*Letters*, II.336). In India he had been occasionally near the centres of power, but as an onlooker, only a half-step ahead of the crowd who gathered around Mrs Hauksbee: a gadfly, not a player. The visit to South Africa left him impatient to influence events, rather than merely report on them. When Rhodes asked him, 'What's your dream?', he answered that Rhodes was part of it (*SM* 87); increasingly, he would find his friends not among writers, but among financiers, newspaper magnates and politicians. After Vermont, it was good to have a dream again. With the American invasion of Cuba, and the annexation of the Philippines, America too seemed to be coming on board, taking up its share of 'The White Man's Burden'. The Dutch and the Spanish could be swept aside – 'There is no place in the world today for worn-out nations' (*Letters*, II.335) – and the English-speaking peoples could take their place as the acknowledged leaders of a new era.

The Kiplings returned from South Africa in good spirits, but only six weeks later Burne-Jones died suddenly of a heart-attack. The body was cremated, and the ashes taken to Rottingdean, where Kipling took his turn to watch them. Next to his father, Burne-Jones was the man he most loved and looked up to, and he was too distraught even to weep: 'It's all a sort of clot in my head because one has to realize that the man won't come back. . . . It's all in the day's work of course and one must hold on to the end of the day but, sometimes one gets a wee bit tired' (*Letters*, II.342). Despite their political differences – 'Ruddy (beloved of my heart) is in South Africa', Burne-Jones lamented; 'he would go – and he will always be going away – any place where mankind is flighty' – they had loved each other since the Southsea days, and it was a hard loss to bear.[17]

The Day's Work was to be the title of Kipling's collection of stories from the American years, published in September 1898. Not all have worn well. 'William the Conqueror', the story of 'a wooing in the thick of a Madras famine – man and girl together working hard among the starving and feeding the abandoned black babies and generally going through deep waters' (*Letters*, II.176), was nicely suited to Christmas publication in the *Ladies' Home Journal*, but its idea of the 'new woman' resolves itself into a female version of the heroic administrator he had already described to the world; she cheerfully answers to the name William, dislikes poetry, rolls cigarettes for her brother, and until the last few pages of the story is almost comically lacking in sexual identity.[18] 'The Brushwood Boy' is a fantasy about an ideal subaltern – strong, inarticulate, and oblivious to the women who seek to attract him – who is troubled by recurring dreams which feature a pile of brushwood on a beach, and a girl who grows older at the same time as he does. The climax of the story comes when he meets a girl who closely resembles the one in his dream-world, and has dreams similar to his own; they at once fall in love, and become engaged. 'The Brushwood Boy' prefigures Kipling's later interest in the supernatural, but the dream-life has little or no connection with the outer action, and George Cottar, the Boy, is a mere cipher for the values he is meant to embody. The story is overlong, and frankly tedious in its admiration for the Boy. Kipling is rarely silly, but here he is.

Much more successful is 'The Bridge-Builders', the story of Findlayson, an engineer, on the night his all but completed bridge over the Ganges is threatened by a flood. Together with his Indian foreman, Peroo, Findlayson is driven on to a small island. There, in a trance brought on by the opium they have taken as a precaution against fever, they witness a *punchayet* or assembly of the gods, convened to debate their response to Findlayson's bridge.

Despite its supernatural elements, this is a story deeply concerned with the day's work, in almost Carlylean terms.[19] Drawing on his journalism, including his account of the Kaiserin-i-Hind bridge across the Sutlej River in March 1887, Kipling follows Findlayson's reverie as he looks out at his bridge, and reflects on the obstacles he has had to overcome: red tape, last-minute changes to the specifications, and even corruption on the official side; cholera, smallpox and 'the riots of twenty warring castes' on the Indian side. Here in microcosm are key themes in Kipling's stories of Anglo-Indians: the need for a rite of passage by which the young can be tested and proved ('Cub thou wast; assistant thou art,' reflects Findlayson about his sole British co-worker), and the belief that a sense of individual identity can only be conferred by others – and, therefore, that without their approval it can also be lost ('his own kind would judge him by his bridge, as that stood or fell').

The sense of an identity founded – or foundering – in the material world, is challenged by the opium trance in the central section of the story. The debate among the gods reflects not just the complex hierarchies of the Hindu pantheon, but also the social reality of conflicting responses to the impact of the West on the life and traditions of India. Some of the gods want the bridge destroyed, and payment made in blood for the insult to the sacred river; others are untroubled, confident that the ancient beliefs will absorb and outlast the ideas represented by the bridge-builders, as they had absorbed others before them: 'Let the dirt dig in the dirt if it pleases the dirt.' The gods represent the forces against which Kipling's Anglo-Indians conceived themselves to be fighting: the resistance of climate, fever and famine, and of traditions and customs, to Western ideas of change and progress.

Against these voices are set those of Indra and Krishna. Indra re-states the Riddle of the Gods: 'When Brahm ceases to dream, the Heavens and the Hells and the Earth disappear. . . . The dreams come and go, and the nature of the dream changes, but still Brahm dreams.' In Hindu teaching, Brahm or Brahman is the Absolute, from which proceed the manifold, individuated forms of Nature. While Brahm dreams, what we know as the universe exists; when Brahm ceases to dream, the universe ceases to exist. The true significance of men and bridges, and even of the gods, is to be measured against these vast cycles. Only Brahm is immutable: 'The Gods change, . . . – all save One!'

Indra's statement is in reply to Krishna, the only one of the gods to appear in human form. In Hindu art he is variously depicted as a child or a warrior, but often, as here, as a pastoral figure, coming up from the water with 'a snatch of a love-song'. He appeals to Mother Gunga, the god of the river; life is brief, and there is no need for destruction: 'Have pity, mother, for a little – and it is only for a little.' He warns the gods that the changes introduced by the bridge-builders cannot be resisted: 'my people see their work, and they go away thinking.' To Indra's concession, that even the gods must change, 'all save One!', Krishna responds: 'ay, all save one that makes love in the hearts of men.' It is possible to take Indra's words as final, and make the centre of the story a vision of transcendence which reduces the world, and Findlayson's bridge, to an illusion, but Krishna's reply sets against that view another, centred on human love. Their differing emphases foreshadow the double vision at the end of *Kim*: the Lama's, of his soul 'passed beyond the illusion of Time and Space and of things', and Kim's, of roads, fields, cattle, men and women, 'all real and true'. Rather than the final meaninglessness of the bridge, Krishna's words suggest the pathos, and perhaps the foolishness, of Findlayson's self-exclusion from the world of 'love in the hearts of men'.

Kipling does not attempt to nail down the story. As the dawn comes and the gods depart, the vision is dismissed: 'in that clear light there was no room for a man to think dreams of the dark.' The last section brings two other instances of East meeting West. Peroo, the foreman, hearing from the gods themselves that they cannot outlast the material world and will eventually die with it, returns to work with Findlayson, meditating on the beating he intends to give his priest. Skilled, energetic, loyal to the bridge and to Findlayson, he clearly has Kipling's sympathy. All too clearly, the Rajah whose boat picks up the two men does not. In 'tweed shooting-suit and seven-hued turban', complaining in Babu-English of 'dam bore' religious ceremonies, but unable to back his launch out into the river, he is exactly the kind of Indian that Kipling despised.

But this routine judgement is at odds with the shifting perspectives and narrative modes – British and Indian, realism and fantasy – of the story. Just as the *punchayet* is both an illusion brought on by the opium and a 'real' event, so elsewhere in the story Kipling is content to lay one kind of understanding against another. Findlayson's belief that his identity is bound up with the strength of his bridge is played against the Hindu teaching that the goal of existence is to recognise the identity of the individual soul (Atman) with the Absolute (Brahm), and each of these against Krishna's affirmation of the enduring value of life in those villages which have figured to Findlayson only as possible aids or hindrances to his work. No one view is consistently maintained or privileged; each modifies the other. Findlayson's bridge has a military as well as a civil purpose, flanked as it is by guard towers 'loopholed for musketry and pierced for big guns', but the story remains the most sympathetic of Kipling's accounts of the work of Empire.[20]

America: the final visit

The summer saw Kipling engaged in a variety of activities. He was at work on the stories for *Stalky & Co.*, published in magazine form between August 1898 and April 1899, as well as on the *Just So Stories*, and he continued to write poems addressed to the political needs of the nation. He was annoyed when one of these, 'The Truce of the Bear', appeared in *Literature*, the new supplement to *The Times*, where he felt its political meaning – a warning that Russia was not to be trusted – might be 'smothered'; the poem was addressed to the world of affairs, not to 'literature' (*Letters*, II.349).

The high point of his summer came in September, when he joined HMS *Pelorus* on manoeuvres in the Channel. The turn of the century saw a series of technological developments in the design and engineering of warships and naval gunnery, which required corresponding shifts in political and military strategy. The chief threat came from Germany, which under the direction of Admiral von Tirpitz had begun to invest massively in the development of an Imperial German Navy. In six articles in the *Morning Post*, under the title *A Fleet in Being*, Kipling pleaded the Navy's cause for expansion, constantly asking his readers to consider how it might be when rather than on exercise the Navy was confronted with 'the Real Thing'. Behind this immediate purpose, and alongside his fascination with the technology of ships and warfare, there was a further sense that the Navy naturally stood for morality and order:

> under the shell of the new Navy beats the heart of the old. All Marryat's immortals are there, better fed, better tended, better educated, but at heart unchanged.[21]

To celebrate the Navy was to describe an essential Englishness: 'the whole thing was my very own (that is to say yours); mine to me by right of birth. . . . The wind, and the smell of it off the coasts, was mine, and it was telling me things it would never dream of confiding to a foreigner.'[22] *A Fleet in Being* is a celebration of the 'admiralty' of which he had written in 'A Song of the English', paid for in blood by generations of English seamen from Drake to Nelson, and still embodied in the officers and ratings, cooks and signalmen, on board the *Pelorus*.

The closing months of 1898 brought a family grief, when Trix, who had returned to England a year earlier, suffered a mental breakdown. The nature of her condition is unclear, but the symptoms were disturbing: hypermanic phases, periods of mutism, outbursts of rage at her husband's presence. Neither he nor her parents could afford the cost of a private hospital; Rudyard, who could have done, seems not to have made the offer. Alice Kipling was convinced that she was the only one who could look after her daughter, but the effort took its toll, to the point that the rest of the family were almost as concerned for her as for Trix. On the political front however the news was good: Kitchener had defeated the Dervishes at Omdurman, the French had backed down before the British at Fashoda, and in New York Teddy Roosevelt had returned from the war in Cuba as a national hero. Encouraged by these events, Rudyard and Carrie decided it was time to revisit America. He had a copyright problem to resolve, and Carrie wanted to see her mother; perhaps they hoped that the birth of their son might help to heal the family breach.

They set sail on 25 January. The weather was rough, and the children were sick. By the time they arrived at their hotel, Josephine was feverish, and Carrie too was ill. News arrived that Beatty was threatening to sue Rudyard for malicious prosecution, and their hotel was besieged by reporters. For a time, with the help of their old friend Dr Conland, up from Brattleboro, Josephine's condition seemed to stabilise, and Carrie recovered. Kipling set about his copyright problem, trying to prevent Putnam from bringing out an unauthorised edition of his work to rival the authorised Outward Bound edition from Scribner's.[23] Then, on 20 February, he too fell ill, with inflammation of the lung. As his condition worsened, so did that of Josephine. For reasons it is now impossible to understand, she was moved to the Long Island home of a friend, the sister of Lockwood de Forest, leaving Carrie to tend her husband while agonising over the condition of her daughter. Over the next two weeks Kipling's life hung in the balance, and the news of his illness travelled across the world, with daily bulletins published in *The Times*.[24] By 4 March he was pronounced out of danger, but even as the telegrams of congratulation flowed in, the six-year old Josephine was slipping away, and on the morning of 6 March she died. For a time Kipling was thought too ill to be told the news, and for his sake Carrie had to pretend to be cheerful. When at last, against the advice of the doctors, she asked Frank Doubleday to tell him, 'at first . . . he was too ill to realise it quite, but now every day he feels it more'.[25]

It is a simple and terrible story. Angus Wilson writes that Carrie's conduct in the crisis was 'beyond praise'; returning from the funeral, with Kipling still unaware of Josephine's death, she was about to enter his room wearing her black shawl, but remembered just in time to catch up a red one instead.[26] Those who knew Kipling thought that he was a sadder and a harder man after Josephine's death, and it is as well to notice that some of the less charitable accounts of Carrie's nature also come from these later years.[27] Neither of them spoke much about their grief; Kipling was too ill, and Carrie coped by attending to an assortment of business matters. They were helped through the crisis by a number of friends. Lockwood Kipling and Watt came over to offer what comfort they could. Charles Norton's daughter, Sally, acted as Carrie's confidante, while Doubleday – 'Effendi', after his initials FND – assisted with the correspondence, prepared Kipling's meals, and sat by his bedside while Carrie rested. As soon as Kipling was able to stand the journey, Doubleday took him off to convalesce at a private hotel at Lakewood. Kipling made a slow return to health, and in June, accompanied by Doubleday and his wife, he, Carrie and the two children returned to England.

The first few weeks at Rottingdean were intensely painful. Kipling seemed to see his daughter round every corner. There was no thought of consolation from religious belief; nothing more hopeful than Lockwood's letter: 'I can't help fancying all this weight of love may count for some thing.'[28] Trix remained ill. There was tension between Alice Kipling, grieving over her daughter, and Carrie, grieving over the loss of hers; one of Carrie's stranger actions had been to ask Doubleday to write to Watt, who in turn was to write to Lockwood and Alice, to say that she would never be able to talk to them about what she and Rudyard had gone through. But it was necessary to pick up the threads. The Kiplings engaged a secretary, Sara Anderson, who had worked for Ruskin during the years of his severest breakdowns, and could be relied upon for her total discretion. Philip Burne-Jones came to paint the portrait of Kipling at his desk that now hangs in the National Portrait Gallery. They spent a month at Creich in Scotland, staying in a house lent them by the steel magnate Andrew Carnegie, where Burne-Jones started work on a companion portrait of Carrie. And so, over the summer, they began the process of recovery. They never returned to America. Their former coachman, Matthew Howard, stayed on to look after 'Naulakha', until it was sold in 1903.

Stalky & Co.

In October, seven months after his illness had drawn the attention of readers around the world, Kipling presented another side of himself to the public, with the publication of *Stalky & Co.*, his stories of life at the United Services College. By the 1890s the boys' school story was a well-established genre, traceable to two books in particular: *Tom Brown's Schooldays* (1857), Thomas Hughes's story of life at Rugby School under Dr Arnold, and Dean Farrar's *Eric, or Little by Little* (1858). Both were remarkably successful; by the end of the century there had been more than fifty editions of *Tom Brown's Schooldays*, and more than thirty of *Eric*. Over the same period there had also been an increasing market in 'penny dreadfuls', sensational and often brutal stories aimed at the audience created by the Education Act of 1870, with little or no didactic element. To counter what it considered the dangerous influence of these stories, the Religious Tract Society began in 1879 to publish its own penny magazine, the weekly *Boy's Own Paper*, known as BOP, and the BOP style of healthy adventure story, in particular the stories contributed by Talbot Baines Reed, effectively institutionalised the genre. P. W. Musgrave notes four defining features: 'the plot is seen from the boys' point of view; the school is seen as an organisation; the character of the hero or heroes develops during the story; and, last, there is a morally didactic element in the story.'[29] In *Stalky & Co.* Kipling both employs and subverts this genre.

The first paragraph of the first story suggests that *Eric* is to be his main target: 'In summer all right-minded boys built huts in the furze-hill behind the College . . . a place of retreat and meditation, where they smoked.' The phrases 'right-minded', 'high-minded', 'pure-minded', echo through the stories, and are taken directly from Dean Farrar's novel, which tells how Eric slides 'little by little' into error – laughing in chapel, drinking, not owning up when challenged – until he is suspected of theft, runs away from school in disgrace, and dies in the knowledge that his backsliding has hurried on his mother's death. Kipling's trio, Stalky, M'Turk and Beetle, are familiar with *Eric*, and turn to it from time to time, but only to laugh at it:

> 'Here we are!' said M'Turk. ' "Corporal punishment produced on Eric the worst effects. He burned not with remorse or regret" – make a note o' that, Beetle – "but with shame and violent indignation. He glared" – oh, naughty Eric! Let's get to where he goes in for drink.'

But Kipling has Hughes in mind as well. The reading from *Eric* is interrupted by their housemaster, Prout, complaining that the three take no interest in house-matches and 'the honour of the house'. Prout's notion, 'that by games, and games alone, was salvation wrought', derives if not directly from Hughes then at least from books inspired by *Tom Brown's Schooldays*. But the three boys in *Stalky & Co.* care nothing for the honour of the house, or for games. Beetle's views on the former are said to be 'incendiary', and in their eyes one house-match is much like any other.

The phrase 'right-minded boys' invokes several aspects of the traditions of nineteenth-century education. These may be said to begin with the appointment in 1828 of Dr Arnold as Headmaster of Rugby School. It was Arnold's ambition to turn 'boys' into 'Christian gentlemen', and to persuade them to see manhood as the goal of Christian training, the time when one put away childish things and accepted one's duties in the world. He defended corporal punishment as appropriate for those who had not yet reached this goal, but were still in the 'semi-barbarous' condition of boyhood.[30] But Kipling's trio accept their beatings as part of the natural order of things, and show no ambition to become 'men' in Arnold's sense. Though the stories take place over several years, there is no development in their characters, no progression towards the Sixth form, still less the role of prefect. They simplify the school hierarchy into three levels, which remain constant throughout the book: house-masters and prefects, who must be warred on with care; the lower forms, who can be treated more or less with impunity; and the Head, 'that amazing man', who alone commands their admiration. The *Bildungsroman* element identified by Musgrave as a central feature of the school story, bound up with its didacticism, is notably absent in *Stalky & Co.*

Kipling's relation to the Hughes/Farrar tradition is apparent in the most unpalatable story in the collection, ironically titled 'The Moral Reformers'. Both Hughes and Farrar depict their heroes at a moment of moral crisis. In Hughes's novel Tom's form-master recognises that his pupil is beginning to run wild, and recommends that he is given 'some little boy to take care of'. Accordingly Tom is asked to share a study with young George Arthur, whose health is delicate and who has never been away from home before. The critical test comes in a chapter entitled 'How the Tide Turned', when Arthur kneels to say his prayers and is jeered at by a bigger boy. Tom leaps to Arthur's rescue, and soon after he himself begins to say his prayers in public. Despite occasional faltering, he has made the choice for good rather than evil. Under Arthur's influence, he begins to accept that he has a responsibility towards the school as a community, summed up by his recognition that team games like cricket represent a higher moral good than 'fives or hare-and-hounds, or any others where the object is to come in first or to win for oneself and not that one's side may win'. The distinction, made explicit in the novel, is parallel to that between 'working to get your living', and 'doing some real good in the world'.

Eric's crisis is a mirror image of Tom's. One night in the dormitory one of the older pupils uses foul language in the presence of a new boy at the school. Like Tom, Eric knows he should protest, and Farrar underlines the importance of the moment: 'Now, Eric, now or never! . . . Speak out, boy!' But Eric fails to do so, and soon 'the poison of evil communication' is flowing into his veins. He makes periodic attempts to reform, encouraged by one of the masters, but fails more than he succeeds. In the Preface to an edition of 1889 Farrar remarked on the 'inherent nobleness' of Eric's disposition, but in fact the book testifies more strongly to its author's sense of human sinfulness, and each chapter sees Eric slip a little further down the slope leading to his eventual disgrace.

The parallel story in *Stalky & Co.* occurs when Stalky, M'Turk and Beetle are invited by the Chaplain to protect a younger boy, Clewer, who is being bullied by two of the senior boys in the school. Beetle (based on Kipling) has known what it is to be bullied, and suggests that Clewer should become their study-fag, which would provide him with a retreat. M'Turk flatly refuses, because Clewer is 'a dirty little brute, and he'd mess up everything'. Evidently Clewer has little in common with the saintly George Arthur. But M'Turk's main objection is that 'we ain't goin' to have any beastly Erickin''. The complex of moral values ascribed by Hughes and Farrar to the protection of the weak by the strong has been reduced to a verbal form, 'Ericking', with an added element of homophobia ('beastliness' is a code word for homosexuality). Far from exercising a moral influence on his protectors, Clewer is never seen in the story, while the Chaplain turns a blind eye as Stalky, M'Turk and Beetle trick his tormentors into a situation where they can be subjected to physical torture and emotional humiliation. With heavy irony, this is referred to as a process of 'moral suasion': precisely the means which Kipling is dismissing. An episode which in *Eric* or *Tom Brown's Schooldays* would have been a turning point in the lives of those involved has become simply another schoolboy battle, no more significant, morally, than any other of the disputes which make up the daily lives of 'right-minded boys'.

The topos of the crisis or turning-point was not specific to the boys' school story; conversion episodes are to be found everywhere in Victorian fiction, as well as in the autobiographical writing of the period. Their effect, in the fiction, is to import quasi-religious motifs into a predominantly secular genre: in particular, the distinction between the sinful and the elect, and the idea that moral life is to be construed teleologically, in terms of development. But in *Stalky & Co.* Kipling sets himself against this narrative shape. He even introduces a brief parody of the conversion topos, when one of the younger masters is persuaded that Stalky and Beetle have been stealing. The boys delight in leading him on: 'Stalky went to his study and pretended to blub, and told Mason he'd lead a new life if Mason would let him off, but Mason wouldn't.' They attribute Mason's gullibility, predictably, to his reading of *Eric, or Little by Little*, and give him another of Farrar's school stories, *St Winifred's, or the World of School*. The world of *Stalky & Co.*, unlike that of St Winifred's, is resolutely secular, and its moral scheme unrelentingly pragmatic.

This is not to deny that Kipling's stories were, as he claimed, written as 'tracts or parables on the education of the young' (SM 79). When the boys see through what in their terms is the cant and humbug displayed by the less respected masters – though not by the Head – they do so in the name of the values they reject in their debased form. This becomes obvious when the school is visited by the 'Jelly-bellied Flag-flapper' in 'The Flag of their Country'. His lecture on patriotism, and particularly the flourishing of the Union Jack with which it concludes, coarsens what the boys believe at a level too deep for speech, and they are outraged, as their choice of nicknames suggests. They bait masters like Prout and Mason not because they are unable to admit any authority, but rather to test authority. In the form of their housemasters it fails them because it can offer only platitudes; in the form of the Head, it answers to their deepest needs. When he beats them it is, as he says, 'a howling injustice', because technically they are innocent; but he is also paying them 'a tremendous compliment' by acknowledging that they (unlike the housemasters) can understand that it is sometimes necessary to set aside the formality of rules. In spirit they are guilty, and accordingly to be punished; to defer to the rules would be morally feeble, dangerous to the institution, and unhelpful to the boys themselves. Real authority, Kipling suggests, lies not with those who recite tired phrases about fair play and the honour of the house, or cling to the outworn creeds of Arnold, Hughes and Farrar, but with those who have the courage to flout the rules. Authority is wise, is the message of the book; it can be trusted. The function of the stories is to make it express itself.

In reality, Cormell Price, headmaster at the USC, had little in common with the cane-wielding Head of the stories. But the interest of *Stalky & Co.* has less to do with its representation of Kipling's schooldays, than with the way it conducts a serious and complex argument with the traditions represented by Dean Farrar and Thomas Hughes. When Farrar wrote to protest, Kipling replied courteously, acknowledging Farrar's books as classics, but pointing out that 'there are boys – ignorant and vulgar minded it may be – who take less interest in the moral teaching of the two books than in their divergencies from the facts of school-life as boys know these today' (*Letters*, II.381). Other readers reacted more sharply than Farrar. Robert Buchanan claimed that 'only the spoiled child of an utterly brutalized public could possibly have written *Stalky & Co.*'.[31] H. G. Wells, initially an enthusiast, attacked 'The Moral Reformers' for promoting 'the ugliest, most retrogressive, and finally fatal idea of modern imperialism; the idea of a *tacit conspiracy between the law and illegal violence*'.[32] More than any other, *Stalky & Co.* was the book which turned away Kipling's admirers. Clever, sure-footed, unappealing, it remains as a challenge to new readers.

South Africa

The virulence of Buchanan's attack can be explained partly by the fact that *Stalky & Co.* appeared in the month which saw the outbreak of the

Anglo-Boer War, fuelled, it seemed to him, by the 'spirit of mercenary militarism' he suspected in Kipling. But while Kipling may have helped to stir the pot in readiness for war, the ingredients were already in place. South Africa comprised four states: the Cape Colony and Natal, and the two Boer-dominated interior states, the Orange Free State and the South African Republic in the Transvaal. To those who admired them, and there were many in Britain who did, the Boers were a god-fearing, rural people; to men like Rhodes and Chamberlain, they were a backward and undeveloped race, in need of a push into the modern world. The British had attempted one such push in 1877, when they annexed the Transvaal, but the Boers fought to regain their independence, and in February 1881 the British were defeated at Majuba Hill. To the dismay of the Queen, Gladstone decided to enter into negotiations. Under the Pretoria Convention, the Transvaal reverted to full independence, with the British retaining a nominal suzerainty in respect of its relations with foreign powers. In the mid-1880s, however, the discovery of gold desta-bilised the situation. The Transvaal became the economic hub of South Africa, drawing in capital and manpower from overseas, and shifting the balance of power away from the Cape. Its political structure, how-ever, remained conservative and agrarian, to the frustration of the immigrants (Uitlanders), faced with laws which made it difficult for them to acquire citizenship and political rights, and of the capitalists, burdened by levies and tariffs which hindered the development of the mining industry.

The botched Jameson Raid of 1895 added to the atmosphere of uncer-tainty, not least, in British eyes, when it persuaded President Kruger of the need to strengthen his military defences. Now the Boers had money, men and Mauser rifles. Into this inflammatory mix – the increasing power of the Transvaal, the claims of the Uitlanders, the demands of the mining industry, the British claim to supremacy as an imperial nation – came Alfred Milner, appointed High Commissioner in 1897. No less determined than Chamberlain to secure an integrated imperial order, Milner had no interest in compromise or the waiting game. In his view British interests could best be served by clearing the decks for war, and resolving the conflicts once and for all. By October 1899 Milner had manoeuvred Kruger into issuing an ultimatum requir-ing the withdrawal of British troops from the borders of the Republic and the removal from South Africa of reinforcements sent out in the previous months. The ultimatum was rejected, and on October 11 Kruger invaded the territory of Natal, while troops from the Orange Free State invaded Cape Colony. This supposed proof of Boer intransigence helped to create popular support for a war which would provide an opportunity to avenge the defeat at Majuba Hill. But from the first the war had its opponents, some of them openly pro-Boer, others arguing that the British had become the pawns of Johannesburg miners and cosmopolitan financiers who stood to gain from the crisis. There had been voices raised against earlier Victorian conflicts, but no other divided public opinion so deeply.

Kipling's immediate response was his poem 'The Old Issue', published in *The Times* on 29 September.[33] The introductory stanzas suggest that the British had the same duty to resist Kruger's claim to authority as their forebears had to oppose the claims of King John and of Charles 1, making Kipling perhaps the only writer to cast Rhodes, Milner and Chamberlain in the role of the Barons at Runnymede. But his first real contribution to the poetry of the war in South Africa was 'The Absent-Minded Beggar', an unblushing exercise in fund-raising, on the principle that we 'must help the girl that Tommy's left behind him':

> Cook's son – Duke's son – son of a belted Earl –
>   Son of a Lambeth politician – it's all the same today!
> Each of 'em doing his country's work
>   (and who's to look after the girl?)
> Pass the hat for your credit's sake,
>   and pay – pay – pay!

First published in the *Daily Mail*, then in pamphlet form with an illustration by Caton Woodville, set to music by Arthur Sullivan and sung or recited at theatres and music-halls, the poem raised more than £250,000 to provide clothes, tobacco and other comforts for the troops. It also led to the offer of a knighthood, which Kipling refused, as he was to refuse all other offers of political honours.

The success of the poem was not matched by the forces in South Africa. The war fell into three stages, beginning with a series of British defeats. Within a month Kimberley, Ladysmith and Mafeking were under siege; in 'Black Week', between 10 and 15 December, British forces suffered major reverses at Stormberg, Magersfontein and Colenso. This was not like the many 'little wars' the British had fought over the past half-century, essentially short, fierce assaults against non-white forces, and they were badly prepared. Their maps were inaccurate, they had too few horses, their intelligence about Boer numbers and dispositions was poor, and they were unimaginatively led. Faced with modern rifles and quick-firing guns, troops needed to be deployed in open order, taking advantage of available cover; the British infantry had been trained to march in straight lines, to fire in volleys under direct orders from an officer, and to concentrate their efforts on getting close enough to engage the enemy with bayonets. Sir Redvers Buller, in command, was out of his depth, and knew it; the losses he suffered at Colenso shattered his confidence, and that of the War Office. Lord Roberts of Kandahar, whose son had been fatally wounded at Colenso – like his father, he was awarded the Victoria Cross – was finally given the position he had been angling for, and took over as Commander-in-Chief, with Kitchener as his Chief of Staff.

By February 1900 Roberts had 180,000 troops at his disposal, more than the white population of the two Boer republics combined. The war was now on a huge scale; in all, it would involve some 500,000 men from across the Empire, as the colonies and dominions acted out the promises Kipling had written for them in 'The Song of the English'. With massive superiority in numbers, Roberts and Kitchener turned the war around. The sieges at Ladysmith and Mafeking were relieved, to national rejoicing at home; Bloemfontein fell on 13 March, and on 5 June Roberts entered Pretoria. It seemed that the war was virtually over, but it now entered a third phase, a prolonged guerrilla war which continued until the Treaty of Vereeniging was signed in May 1902.

Like most guerrilla campaigns, this third phase was bitterly fought. The British employed a scorched-earth policy, intending to persuade the Boers that it was not worth fighting on, and gathered around 136,000 people into concentration camps, ostensibly to protect the women and children from attack by black Africans – 'We are looking after their wives and kids so they have nothing to worry about,' wrote Kipling (*Letters*, III.41–2) – but effectively as hostages. When Emily Hobhouse drew public attention to the desperate conditions in the camps, in which some 28,000 died, mostly women and children, Kipling declared her 'unspeakable' (*Letters*, III.68); the official view was that the unsanitary habits of the Boers were to blame for the high death rate (Kitchener thought the women should be tried for the manslaughter of their children). Both sides in the conflict carried out summary executions; both deplored the other as uncivilised, the Boers condemning the British use of the lance, which they regarded as little better than the 'Kaffir' assegai, the British objecting that the Boers abused the white flag and fired on ambulances.

Kipling had anticipated the war, and despite the early setbacks he welcomed its arrival. 'The war is having a splendid effect,' he wrote to

Norton, 'and all fires will burn more clearly for the fierce draft that has been blown through them' (*Letters*, III.10). Eager to see events at first hand, he arrived in the Cape with his family in February, four months into the action, and was soon in the thick of things. On 22 February he joined an ambulance train to the Modder River, where he distributed some of the funds earned by 'The Absent-Minded Beggar', and found himself a hero among the rank and file (*SM* 88). In March he had lunch with Rhodes, who had just returned to the Cape from the siege at Kimberley. The great majority of the 1500 who died during the siege were black Africans, which did little to support the British claim that they, unlike the Boers, acknowledged a duty of care towards the black population, but Kipling's admiration for Rhodes was undiminished. Then, at the end of the month, he was summoned to Bloemfontein, where Lord Roberts had revived the local paper, the *Friend of the Free State*, and wanted Kipling as one of the editors.[34] He and his fellow-editors once came under fire during a minor skirmish, though there were no casualties; the experience was still vividly in his mind when he came to describe it in *Something of Myself*.

These were joyous times for Kipling, though hardly for Carrie, left to her own devices at the Cape. One of their regular visitors was the explorer Mary Kingsley, now working as a nurse with Boer prisoners in Simonstown.[35] She was contemptuous of Rhodes, and sympathetic to the case for African nationalism, but nothing that she said or he saw could shake Kipling's belief that the British were not only right, but absurdly scrupulous in their conduct of the war. Returning to England at the end of April, he pushed this conviction at every opportunity. He spent time and money setting up a Rifle Club in Rottingdean, organised celebrations following the relief of Mafeking, and spoke on behalf of the Conservative candidate for Tisbury (his father's constituency) in the 'Khaki Election'. He also wrote four war stories for the *Daily Express*, though since three of these remained uncollected until the Sussex Edition he presumably did not think highly of them. With an eye to the longer term, he advocated 'planting clean white men of colonial experience' in South Africa (*Letters*, III.15). This was to be the theme of a post-war poem, 'The Settler', in which he envisaged the peaceful coexistence of Boers and British, with trees growing and wells dug where once 'the senseless bullet fell, / And the barren shrapnel burst'. Andrew Rutherford applauds the 'combination of humane wisdom and poetic power' in the poem, but this has to be balanced against Kipling's unhesitating support for Milner, 'this silent capable man', who had done more than most to bring about the war, and was ready to prolong it if by doing so he could ensure a dictated rather than a negotiated peace.[36] 'Humane' and 'wise' are not words that could be applied to most of Kipling's statements about the war.

The following Christmas saw the Kiplings back at the Cape, staying this time at The Woolsack, a house in the grounds of Rhodes's Groote Schuur estate which he had put at their disposal. The war was entering its guerrilla phase, and the British had begun burning farms. Kipling was entirely in favour, believing that until 'the horrors of war [are] thoroughly realized through every part of the colony the people won't be quiet . . . Sherman would have wound it up in six months but we seem to delight in stopping to caress the enemy' (*Letters*, III.42).[37] In a story written during this visit, 'A Sahibs' War', he suggested that the British way of war was not horrible enough. The Indian narrator, Umr Singh, recounts the death of Kurban Sahib, the English officer he has served and loved from his childhood, following an act of treachery by a family of Boer farmers. In Umr Singh's eyes, at least, the family is entirely hideous – an old man with a wart on his neck, a fat woman with the eyes and jowl of a swine, and an idiot son: 'His head was hairless, no larger than an orange, and the pits of his nostrils were eaten away by a disease.' Umr Singh intends to hang the child in front of his parents, in exchange for the life of his 'child', Kurban Sahib. But at the critical moment the spirit of Kurban Sahib speaks to him: 'No. It is a Sahibs' war.' As an English Sahib, Kurban cannot allow an ethic of personal revenge, nor can he sanction a policy of reprisals. Umr Singh is compelled to defer to a code which, like Kipling, he knows but does not share.[38] Nonetheless, at the end of the story, the farmhouse has been destroyed, the cattle are gone, and except for two trees withered by fire the land around the farm is desolate. There is no place here for the compassion of 'The Settler'.

But while Kipling's opinions on the war had hardened, this was a more relaxed visit, some of it spent nursing a lion cub from Rhodes's private zoo, in between conversations with Rhodes and Baden-Powell, the hero of Mafeking in the popular estimate if not that of later historians. The war, he told Norton on his return to England, had been a 'wholesome' experience, which had taught a people 'bung-full of beastly unjustified spiritual pride' that what they called 'civilization' was only 'another name for shirking' (*Letters*, III.53). It is hard to imagine a person less likely than Norton to sympathise with this view of 'civilization'; that Kipling could write to him in such terms suggests the depth of his alienation from what he regarded as the decadence of English society. It was in this spirit that he wrote 'The Lesson':

Let us admit it freely, as a business people should,
We have had no end of a lesson: it will do us good.

His argument was the double one that the nation as a whole was morally unprepared for war and that those who were charged with its defence
were incompetent. The second part of this argument was undoubtedly
correct, but it was, ironically, under a Liberal administration, with
Richard Haldane's appointment as Secretary of State for War in 1906,
that the process of reform began to take place. Over the next few years
Haldane created an Imperial General Staff, built up an Expeditionary
Force and consolidated the existing auxiliary forces into a new
Territorial Army. The changes were far-reaching and effective, but noth-
ing short of compulsory military service could satisfy Kipling, and
Haldane became another on his list of despised Liberal politicians.

There were other reasons for Kipling to feel tense during the summer
of 1901. His suits against the publishers, G. H. Putnam and R. F. Fenno,
had been costly and unsuccessful; the death in June 1901 of Walter
Besant, founder of the Society of Authors, added salt to the wounds.
Trivially, his first motor-car, an American steam car, broke down as
often as it ran. More seriously, Carrie, approaching her forties, was
unwell. She was ordered rest and massage rather than the operation she
had feared, but towards the end of July, while Kipling was visiting his
parents before going out again with the fleet, she became severely
depressed. Martin Seymour-Smith offers the bizarre speculation that she
was afraid for his moral welfare in the company of sailors, but it is more
likely that she feared his parents as the rivals for his affection.[39] In a letter to Carrie's mother, Kipling wrote that his wife was 'a sweet and win-
ning woman', but she took life 'too blame seriously' (*Letters*, III.63).
Given that this was a family letter, the tone suggests complaint rather
than sympathy. No doubt it was a trying position for them both. Carrie
was aware of the increasing demands on her husband's time, now a
political figure as well as a man of letters, and she must have known
that she no longer had the first or even the second claim on him. We
are, wrote William Butler Yeats, 'forced to choose / Perfection of the life,
or of the work'; but the reality is more often an untidy balance between
the two, with a consequent mix of pleasures and pains. Like other cou-
ples, Rudyard and Carrie sometimes found it hard to achieve the compromise.

Kipling continued to intervene in political debates. His poem 'The
Reformers', published in *The Times* in October, argued that those who
had fought in South Africa would return as the engineers of change. He

was persuaded that the 'common ordinary gordam average white man', if not the upper classes, recognized the need for action, and for 'compulsory service for home defence' (*Letters*, III.80–1). He returned to this theme in 'The Islanders', a scathing attack on the inadequacies of the ruling class. His claim is that those who should have led the nation had instead been preoccupied with 'witless learning', or amusing themselves with 'the flannelled fools at the wicket or the muddied oafs at the goals'. They had failed in their duty, and it had been left to the working man, and the men of the 'Younger Nations' (the six Australian colonies had federated in 1900), to save the day. Like Carlyle berating a 'Do-Nothing Aristocracy', Kipling accused the nation's rulers of having forgotten that they had to earn the advantages they had inherited; they enjoyed 'the lordliest life on earth', but

> It was not made with the mountains, it is not one with the deep.
> Men, not gods, devised it. Men, not gods, must keep.

The poem prompted a furious debate in *The Times*, but by the time it appeared Kipling was already on his way to South Africa, where the war was moving into its final stages. Rhodes would not live to see its conclusion. He died on 26 March 1902, and Kipling composed a poem, 'The Burial', to be read at a service at Groote Schuur, celebrating him as an 'immense and brooding Spirit': 'Living he was the land, and dead / His soul shall be her soul!' Rhodes's death made him feel 'as though half the horizon of my life had dropped away', but the pull of South Africa remained strong (*Letters*, III.87), even as his hopes that the war would leave England invigorated and united were fading. In a letter to Leander Jameson, signed 'Yours disgustedly', he wrote that 'England had better be put into a dry larder till some one scrapes the mould off her' (*Letters*, III.92).

Returning for what he intended to be a short visit, to attend the coronation of Edward VII, he met one example of a disunited people in Georgiana Burne-Jones, indomitable as ever, and increasingly radical in her politics. In the Methodist tradition of bearing witness to the truth, she responded to the news of the Boers' surrender by hanging out a banner protesting 'We have killed and also taken possession', and Kipling had to intervene to defuse a demonstration outside her home.[40]

He had planned a speedy return to South Africa, but the King's sudden illness caused the coronation to be delayed, and in the interim he and Carrie discovered that a house they had admired two years earlier had come on to the market. This was Bateman's, a Jacobean mansion near the village of Burwash, without electricity and with no bathroom. Undeterred, they negotiated to buy it, together with a water-mill and some surrounding farmland, for £9300. Kipling's cousin, Ambrose Poynter, now with his own practice as an architect, was hired to supervise the necessary improvements. In August they attended the coronation, the arrangements made for them by another cousin, Stanley Baldwin, and in September they moved into their new home. The work was incomplete, and they had to share the space with plumbers and decorators, but they were in. This, at last, was 'The Very-Own House'.

6
Kim

In 1902, as the war in South Africa was coming to an end, Kipling was arranging the *Just So Stories*: in its volume form, twelve tales and twelve poems, with 23 full-page drawings and numerous smaller illustrations.[1] He had begun them in very different circumstances. The first story, 'How the Whale got his Throat', had appeared in the 1897 Christmas issue of *St Nicholas Magazine*, in time for Josephine's fifth birthday, followed in the next two months by 'How the Camel got his Hump' and 'How the Rhinoceros got his Skin', but all three must have been told to her many times before then, perhaps to reassure her in the months leading up to John's birth in August 1897. The magazine version of 'How the Whale got his Throat' includes a preamble which admits her right over the stories, as the child who insisted that they must be told 'just so', and who discovered that some were morning stories, others stories for bedtime.[2] This was removed for the 1902 edition, but the completed volume confesses her absence, most openly in the poem attached to 'How the Alphabet was Made', the only one of the stories not to have been published separately:

> For far – oh, very far behind,
> > So far she cannot call to him,
> Comes Tegumai alone to find
> > The daughter that was all to him.

In this story, and in 'How the First Letter was Written', Effie, as the family called her, becomes 'Taffy', lodged safely in the prehistoric past; the 'five whole years' she and her father Tegumai spend in creating between them the 'magic Alphabet-necklace' match both the five years of Effie's life, and the five years it took her father to integrate the stories he had

116

written for her into a volume including stories written after her death. Even so, and although the necklace was made of 'the finest and strongest reindeer-sinew', the narrator reports that some of the letters were lost, 'a long time ago, in a great war', and the necklace mended 'with the dried rattles of a rattlesnake'. Taffy and Tegumai share their alphabet with their tribe, but its origin, like that of the stories, is a 'secret' shared by a father and his daughter.

Angela Mackail recalled the fun of hearing the stories told at Rottingdean, 'in Cousin Ruddy's deep unhesitating voice. There was a ritual about them, each phrase having its special intonation which had to be exactly the same each time and without which the stories are dried husks.'[3] This is unjust to the printed texts, but the courtly addresses ('Before the High and Far-Off Times, O my Best Beloved'), the repetition of phrases, and a running joke involving the mispronunciation of long words ('seruciating', 'curtiosity'), all invite oral delivery. Angus Wilson writes of the implied 'interplay' between adult and child when the stories are read aloud; the illustrations, many of them packed with detail, invite an accompanying commentary from the adult reader, and provide the child listener with an opportunity to delay the linear progress of the narrative.[4] The ritual element in the telling recalls Kipling's own childhood, at play in the basement at Southsea, within the magic ring of his own imagination (SM 8). Fenced around by the stories, telling them 'just so', perhaps the daughter who was all to him did not seem quite so far away.

The *Just So Stories* helped to reassure those of Kipling's admirers dismayed by the brutality of *Stalky & Co*. Far more important in this respect was *Kim*, which began serialisation in *McClure's Magazine* in December 1900, and appeared in book form in October 1901. If it seems appropriate that this, the most generous of his books, should have appeared almost exactly half-way through his life,[5] it remains difficult to reconcile his delighted account of life on the Grand Trunk Road with the support he was giving, even as the novel came out, to Kitchener's scorched-earth policy in South Africa; one is left to wonder if the intensity of his anger at the war exorcised his imagination when he turned to India. To contemporary readers, however, it seemed that he had recovered his true voice. Henry James, who had disliked *Stalky* as much as anyone, rejoiced at *Kim*, and wrote urging Kipling to 'chuck public affairs, which are an ignoble scene, and stick to your canvas and your paint-box'.[6] Kipling could never have made so determined a separation between literature and politics, but he did concede that his 'long leisurely Asiatic yarn' was 'a bit more temperate and wise than much of my stuff' (*Letters*, III.11), and most readers have been as much captivated by the novel as James. Kim himself is one of the most lovingly imagined child characters in fiction, and the Lama one of the most sympathetic figures in the long tradition of the holy fool. Their love for each other is entirely convincing, and untroubled by the racial difference – though even here the relationship is not one between Englishman and Indian, since Kim is Irish, and the Lama Tibetan. This was to be Kipling's last significant story about India, and it captures his nostalgia for a country more imagined than remembered, in which the opposition between the coloniser and colonised has melted away: an India of plenitude, of innumerable differences of caste, creed and custom, but without internal conflict. Even the external threat posed by the Russians, although it has to be resisted, is never felt to be serious.

The novel is not quite as 'nakedly picaresque and plotless' as Kipling said it was (*SM* 132), but the pleasures of life on the road count for more than the excitements of the spy plot. This is partly in homage to Cervantes and to Chaucer, who stand as remote godfathers to the novel, but more importantly because the picaresque is concerned with movement rather than with the goal. In picaresque fiction the central characters are in the society, but not of it; neither is seen teleologically, in the processes of change and development. The purposes of history are lost sight of in the rewards of the present moment:

> One thing after another drew Kim's idle eye across the plain. There was no purpose in his wanderings, except that the build of the huts near by seemed new, and he wished to investigate.

This has a negative side, in that the novel is drawn to generalisations ('an Oriental's views of the value of time', 'the Oriental's happy indifference to mere noise'), and to the presentation of types, like those Kim meets on the train to Umballa – the Jat cultivator, the Amritsar courtesan, the Hindu money-lender, and so on. Such figures, the novel suggests, cannot be the agents of history. Because they are offered as types, they are denied the possibility of change.

The positive side is the delight in spectacle for its own sake. India is felt in the novel to be endlessly there, submitting patiently to the idly 'approving eye'. Nothing that Kipling had written before exceeds the visual brilliance of *Kim*, though it is hardly less rich in accounts of noise and smell:

The diamond-bright dawn woke men and crows and bullocks together. Kim sat up and yawned, shook himself and thrilled with delight. This was seeing the world in real truth; this was life as he would have it – bustling and shouting, the buckling of belts, and beating of bullocks and creaking of wheels, lighting of fires and cooking of food, and new sights at every turn of the approving eye. The morning mist swept off in a whorl of silver, the parrots shot away to some distant river in shrieking green hosts: all the well-wheels within earshot went to work. India was awake, and Kim was in the middle of it . . .

There is no gap here between Kim and the narrative voice: each is thrilled with pleasure. It is in the same spirit of delight that Kim, narrator and reader take up the Lama: 'This man was entirely new to his experience. . . . The Lama was his trove, and he purposed to take possession.'[7]

Kim's desire to participate in this world, and the chameleon qualities which allow him to play so many parts in it, are as useful to the novelist as they are to Colonel Creighton, who wants to recruit him into the Great Game. As Edward Said has argued, Kim's easy identification with different castes and creeds allows Kipling to '*have* and enjoy India in a way that even imperialism never dreamed of.'[8] But this India, as Said goes on to show, is awkwardly removed from the India of 1900. Most obviously, it includes nobody who resists English rule. The Ressaldar is the only person who remembers the Great Rebellion of 1857,[9] and his account of it endorses the British view, that it was an outbreak of 'madness' and cruelty on the Indian side, justly met by the British with a calling to 'strict account'. For the Ressaldar, as for Kipling, the British presence in India provides the security which makes the Lama's quest possible: 'if evil men were not now and then slain it would not be a good world for weaponless dreamers'. Kipling was not to know that in 1903–4 Lord Curzon would send a British force into the Lama's native Tibet, still less that the London newspapers would carry photographs of troops with Maxim guns mowing down monks armed with hoes, sabres and flintlocks: not quite weaponless dreamers, but hardly a threat to the Empire. But he must have known that Indian nationalists of 1900 saw the Rebellion as a step towards independence, not as an act of madness. In *Kim*, Kipling allows himself to forget the warnings he had issued in 'Recessional', that even the British Empire was not eternal.

Its picaresque elements distinguish *Kim* from the realist fiction of the nineteenth century. Rastignac and Emma Bovary in France, like Pip and Jude Fawley in England, are confronted by barriers. Paris, London and

Christminster are the names for a world of desire which they cannot reach, and where, if they do win entry, the glittering prizes turn to dust and ashes. Not so for Kim, who is welcomed everywhere as the Little Friend of all the World. The gates of St Xavier's school clang shut on him for a time, but when he emerges he is enlarged, not diminished. Here again there is some sleight of hand. In the early chapters, before Kim's admission to the school as a Sahib, he plays 'the game for its own sake'. He executes commissions by night in Lahore, or follows the Lama, as a free agent, for the delight of doing so. After he has left the school, however, he is acting under orders. Kipling contrives to make this a change without a difference. Initially, as Kim enters on his new role, the Grand Trunk Road appears to him as simply one part of 'great gray, formless India', an India drained of life and colour, seen through a Sahib's eyes, but this is only for a time, and his old eagerness is quickly restored.

Yet the change from child to spy, from Friend of all the World to a member of the governing race, is not seamless. As a participant in the Great Game, Kim has an altered relation to India. This casts a new light on the opening chapters. What it reveals is that the leisurely India of the first pages, 'the only democratic land in the world', where the policeman and the water-carrier smile at Kim, Chota Lal and Abdullah at their game of king-of-the-castle, was an illusion. The India of Kim's childhood was already the site of the Great Game. If it seemed 'free' of politics – as Kipling puts it, 'plotless' – that was because its political life was being carried on behind the scenes, by men like Creighton and Mahbub Ali. The historical plot is invisible not because it is not there, but because Kipling represents it as inevitable, as much part of the fabric of Indian life as the climate or the geography. Politics, when practised by the British, is 'natural'.

The novel is shaped by the double quest of Kim and the Lama. In narrative terms, the two quests run along parallel lines; morally, however, they are antithetical. Kim's is an attempt to make sense of the complex and ambiguous pedigree he is given in the opening pages, where we are told first that he is English, and therefore in his rightful place astride the gun, Zam-Zammah (those who 'hold Zam-Zammah . . . hold the Punjab'); next that he is 'burned black as any native', thinks in the vernacular and is at home in the bazaar; and finally that he is Irish, and carries in an amulet around his neck the documents that will prove him to be Kimball O'Hara, and a Sahib. He is, after all, as Father Victor observes, 'not very black'. The education these papers earn him will also transform him into a spy like 'R 17' or 'E 23', but this, it transpires, is a role which he can play properly only when he has again been 'de-Englishized' under the guidance of Hurree Babu. As part of his training, Kim learns to make maps for the Indian Survey Department. Like the Wonder-House in Lahore, or Colonel Creighton's papers for the Ethnological Society, the Indian Survey was part of the British attempt to control the country by knowing it, even where, as in its North-Eastern corner, it could not be occupied. As a 'de-Englishized' Sahib, Kim is uneasily situated as both an agent of the work of imperial surveillance, and as one of the objects of study. The transformation of his father's regimental badge into 'a sort of fetish' is, Creighton remarks, 'very interesting': the kind of topic on which one might write a paper. But it also earns Kim his admission into St Xavier's school, and the world of the Sahibs.

There is, then, no easy answer to the question, 'Who is Kim?' But if his place is uncertain, that of the Lama is entirely unmappable. Even the Curator of the Wonder-House, with his photographs, his documents, and his 'mighty map, spotted and traced with yellow', cannot help him find the River which marks where the Arrow of the Bodhisat alighted. At the end of the novel, his search accomplished, the Lama has a vision of 'all Hind, from Ceylon in the sea to the Hills, and my own Painted Rocks at Such-Zen [and] every camp and village, to the least, where we have ever rested'. This is a vision which simultaneously exceeds any map the Indian Survey could produce, and denies the meaning of such maps, since they necessarily defer to those illusions of Time and Space which the Lama has rejected. The conclusion of Kim's quest asserts, if only ambiguously, his identity among those who seek to map the world; the Lama fulfils his quest by denying the reality of the world, and surrendering his identity.

The relation between the two quests moves towards a crisis at the end of the novel. Edmund Wilson argues that the reader expects that 'Kim will come eventually to realise that he is delivering into bondage to the British invaders those whom he has always considered his own people, and that a struggle between allegiances will result.' But then there is no struggle; Kim and the Lama achieve their goals, but 'the parallel lines never meet'.[10] There is neither opposition, nor synthesis. Kipling, according to Wilson, refuses to face conflict.

There is some justice in the response that in Kipling's view there is no conflict, because he would not admit words like 'bondage' or 'invaders', but it applies to the novel only at the political level, not at the personal one. On their journey back from the hills, Kim feels the burden of having betrayed the Lama's trust, and the reader feels it with him. Here, certainly, there is a conflict. But rather than a resolution, Kipling contrives a conclusion that is both inevitable and impossible. The novel ends with the Lama following the way of the Boddhisattvas, who on the threshold of Nirvana chose to remain in this world out of compassion for others. In the last sentence, the Lama smiles, 'as a man may who has won salvation for himself and his beloved'. It is a measure of the novel's achievement that this allusion, to Christ and the beloved disciple, seems so remarkably unforced. To imagine Kim as rejecting the salvation offered to him by the Lama would be to imagine his rejection of the love that has existed so beautifully between them throughout the novel. Most readers will find this hardly possible. Equally, however, it is impossible to imagine this salvation wholly accepted, as the Lama innocently does when he suggests that Mahbub Ali might become Kim's disciple. *Kim* is, as in other ways are stories like *Great Expectations* and *Tess of the d'Urbervilles*, a novel which teases the reader with the unwritten page, the page after the last full stop. Whether Estella will stay with Pip, or Angel with 'Liza-Lu, or Kim will remain in the Great Game, is beyond the boundaries of the text: a question we ask knowing it has no answer, which we can consider only by returning to the first page to read the story again.

7
In a Hidden Kingdom

Kipling's position in England was an ambiguous one. The move into his new home filled him with excitement: 'England is a wonderful land. It is the most marvellous of all foreign countries that I have ever been in. It is made up of trees and green fields and mud and the Gentry: and at last I'm one of the Gentry!' (*Letters*, III.113). As he improved and extended his property over the next few years, his enthusiasm for the land, and his sense of the history underlying it, deepened and intensified. Yet he was unsure about 'the Gentry'. His estate included an old water-mill, dating back, he liked to believe, to the thirteenth century, which he decided to put to use, buying a turbine and generator and laying 250 yards of underground cable to supply electricity for the house. These improvements provided the basis for his story 'Below the Mill Dam', in which a Grey Cat and a Black Rat, living complacently together in an old mill, are disturbed by the introduction of new turbines. If the Cat and the Rat represent the old guard, clinging on to unearned privileges but forced to change their ways when 'the unvisited darkness of the old mill [is] scattered by intolerable white light', the light itself stands for the war, which had, Kipling wrote to Norton, challenged every part of the national life 'to show cause why it should continue on the old unthinking hide-bound lines' (*Letters*, III.53).[1] England might be 'a wonderful land', but its people had not yet faced the truth of their moral and military weakness. Kipling was still an angry man.

The South African war had undermined the nation's faith in imperialism. It had been fought between two Christian peoples, unlike most of Britain's imperial wars; it had been expensive and inglorious, costing over £200 million, and 22,000 British lives.[2] The crowds gathered to cheer British victories, but in the 'Khaki Election' of 1900, fought on the claim that a vote for the Liberals was a vote for the Boers, the

Unionists increased their majority by only four seats. The new leader of the Liberal party, Campbell-Bannerman, meant to cause a stir when he spoke of the 'methods of barbarism' used in the war, but his views reflected public concern at the number of deaths in the concentration camps. Meanwhile the economic case for imperialism was being challenged, notably in J. A. Hobson's *Imperialism. A Study* (1902). Hobson argued that the nation's economic difficulties were the result of under-consumption at home. His remedy, the redistribution of wealth in order to stimulate home consumption, seemed to offer a peaceful alternative to the expansionist policies followed in South Africa. The Imperialists had won the war, but not the battle for hearts and minds, and they found themselves on the defensive. Kipling had, as he told Milner, tied himself personally and poetically to Chamberlain's chariot wheels (*Letters*, III.127). With any fall in his reputation, or in that of the Imperialist cause, Kipling's too was likely to suffer; and so it did.

Early in January 1903 the Kiplings were back at the Cape. Chamberlain too was in South Africa, urging conciliation. Kipling took a harsher line, arguing that it would be dangerous to restore constitutional government until the Boers had been outnumbered by 'loyal' British immigrants. Milner, now ruling the Transvaal and the Orange Free State, shared Kipling's mistrust of the Boers. Over the next two years he worked hard to repatriate the 300,000 people displaced by the war, and to reconstruct the economy. To do so he spent far more than the three million pounds promised in the peace agreement, as Kipling grumbled in 'Piet':

> Ah there, Piet! with your brand-new English plough,
> Your gratis tents and cattle, an' your most ungracious frow,
> You've made the British tax-payer rebuild your country seat . . .

But Milner was not intending to be magnanimous. His ambition was to transform Boer culture – he founded schools, but the education was to be in English; he re-stocked farms, but urged British farmers to develop them – and Kipling continued to give him his support, noting every move made by his opponents, and working to strengthen the Progressive Party under Jameson. In the event, Milner pleased no one. The Boers refused to serve on his legislative council, the Uitlanders resented being taxed to help resettle their recent enemies, and the Indian and Bantu populations were dismayed that white South Africans, whether British or Boer, were to maintain their superior position. Matters drew to a head in 1904, when Milner agreed to the importation of Chinese coolies to work in the mines. By 1905 there were more than 50,000 indentured Chinese labourers, living in compounds, with no legal or political rights, and subject to punishment by flogging. Opinion in England was outraged; Milner resigned his position, and 'Chinese slavery' became a key issue in the election of January 1906.[3] The election result was a landslide victory for the Liberals.

Kipling's position was consistently illiberal. He visited the Chinese camps, and could see no hardship in their conditions – no bars or padlocks, and 'rather better grub than in barracks' (*Letters*, III.206); he even wrote to congratulate Milner on an outbreak of bubonic plague among the Indians in Johannesburg (*Letters*, III.149). The Tories' defeat at the election only proved 'how close and intimate were the relations between the reb[el]s and the Liberals' (*Letters*, III.200). The problem as he saw it was what it had been in India twenty years before, where 'picked men at their definite work' (*SM* 27) – in this case picked by Milner, and familiarly known as 'Milner's kindergarten' – were hindered at every turn by a home government in thrall to liberal sentiment. Campbell-Bannerman's concession of self-government first to the Transvaal, and six months later to the Orange Free State, was to Kipling an immense betrayal, both of England and the Empire, and of the 'loyal Dutch'. He continued his visits until 1908, but by then the country seemed to him 'a land without hope: under the rule of a semi-civilized people of primitive tastes' (*Letters*, III.299).

The clearest expression of his response to the war and its results came in *The Five Nations*,[4] published in October 1903, and composed largely of poems written during the war years. Whereas *The Seven Seas* had celebrated duty, *The Five Nations* attacks default and betrayal, especially by the ruling caste. This is the theme of poem after poem. 'The Islanders' and 'The Lesson' have become anthology pieces, but the argument is the same elsewhere: in 'The Wage-Slaves', for example, which contrasts the 'guardian souls' living serenely but ineffectively on their 'guarded heights' with those who 'simply do the work / For which they draw the wage'; or in 'The Old Men', an attack on men no longer fit to lead, who 'assume that we are alive, whereas we are really dead'.

The keynote of the volume is sounded in 'The Dykes'. Instead of ruling the seas, the speakers in 'The Dykes' merely watch as the waves nibble away at the English shoreline. Unlike their forebears, the men who made the dykes, they 'have no heart for the fishing', and 'no hand for the oar'; they have stood too far from the beach 'to know how the outbreaks stand', and now it is too late. In an echo of Matthew Arnold's 'Dover Beach', they are left 'uneasily pacing the shore', 'surrendered to night and sea – the gale and the tide behind!', conscious that they have no one but themselves to blame for their unprotected position:

> Time and again were we warned of the dykes, time and again we
>   delayed:
> Now, it may fall, we have slain our sons as our fathers we have
>   betrayed.

The mood varies from anxious premonition to self-pity, but neither of these lead to action. Where, in some of the other poems, the speakers do have the nerve to act, they are men from outside the ruling caste. 'The Explorer', called by God, makes his way through a difficult and dangerous terrain till he comes to 'White man's country':

> It's God's present to our nation.
> Anybody might have found it, but – His Whisper came to me!

All is not lost, since where the Explorer leads, others will one day follow – men like the Wage-Slaves, or 'Sergeant Whatisname', who can drill 'a Black man white' ('Pharaoh and the Sergeant'). But in the *Service Songs* which make up the second part of the collection, Kipling hints that men like the Explorer, the Sergeant and the Wage-Slaves have become unsettled, even disaffected. In 'Chant-Pagan', an 'Irregular' speaks of his fear that back home 'there's somethin' gone small with the lot'; in the same vein, the speaker in 'The Return' recognises that the war has changed him – 'I started as an average kid, / I finished as a thinkin' man' – and wonders if he can endure to 'do with little things again'. In both poems the implication is clear, that England has declined from what it must again become, 'the England of our dreams'.

But while the *Service Songs* speak up for the ordinary man, Kipling is not writing as a democrat. His concern is with the ruling class, who must learn that what they worship as 'civilization' is only 'shirking' under another name (*Letters*, III.53). This is the argument of 'The Islanders', with its demand for universal conscription, 'each man born in the island broke to the matter of war':

> Soberly and by custom taken and trained for the same;
> Each man born in the island entered at youth to the game . . .

The true 'England of our dreams', in *The Five Nations*, is one which gives a central place to military preparedness. What this might mean is the subject of the two-part story, 'The Army of a Dream', published initially in the right-wing *Morning Post*: school-children drilled in classes from the age of six, followed by periods of training in camp to the age of eighteen, then part-time service in a volunteer corps (with voting rights refused to those who failed to volunteer), in support of a regular professional army of 100,000 men. That Kipling knew the chances of his vision being fulfilled were remote is evident in the form of the story, in which the narrator is constantly baffled by the dream being enacted before him, and underlined by the poem which prefaces it, 'Song of the Old Guard', in which an unreformed ruling class sings of its refusal to change. In 'Recessional', or in 'The Absent-Minded Beggar', Kipling could claim to be speaking to the national mood, but now he was clearly writing against it. Even so, when 'The Army of a Dream' was included in *Traffics and Discoveries* (1904), he wrote to Edmonia Hill that it was the central story in the volume (*Letters*, III.181).

Life at Bateman's

Kipling's life at Bateman's provided a partial antidote to his disquiet about South Africa. If metropolitan, political England had disappointed him, the England of the Sussex countryside was another matter. Within months of moving in, he was reading Rider Haggard's survey of *Rural England*, and looking forward to washing his apple trees with oil and limewash. He and Haggard had much in common. Haggard was as closely associated with Africa as Kipling was with India, and no less committed an imperialist; he had been in Pretoria when Britain annexed the Transvaal in 1877, and had helped to run up the Union Jack. Like Kipling he had known what it is to lose a child, when his son Jock died at the age of nine, and, like Kipling, he had found that working on the land gave him some sort of comfort. Over the past ten years he had been writing about the depressed state of English agriculture, beginning with *A Farmer's Year*, which Kipling had admired for its treatment of 'the sane, common (which is uncommon) quiet humorous real country life of England'.[5] The two continued to exchange opinions on books, farming and politics until Haggard's death in 1925.

Kipling and Carrie steadily increased their property, eventually acquiring 300 acres, some of it let to tenant farmers, some farmed by themselves. Kipling had become a wealthy man. Andrew Lycett estimates his earnings at the start of the century as around £15,000 a year, at a time when £1000 was enough to set up a middle-class household.[6] The sale of 'Naulakha' in 1903, to Molly Cabot's family, brought £1000 to Carrie, as the nominal owner. She too invested in land, not just because it was profitable, but as part of a protective buffer around their home. One disagreeable consequence was that the District Council proposed to double the rateable value of their property. Concerned that they were being taken advantage of, they dug in, and eventually agreed a compromise. It was one thing to 'pay – pay – pay' for the sake of Tommy Atkins in time of war, quite another to pay into the local community.

Kipling enjoyed his dealings with the local workforce. Learning to get along with men of varied skills, 'most of them . . . artists and craftsmen' (*SM* 106), with their own lore and traditions, was a domestic version of the challenges faced in his Indian stories by men like Deputy Commissioner Yardely-Orde in his dealings with the Khusru Kheyl. He was pleased too with his neighbours. The nearest of these was Colonel Feilden, effectively the local squire, who had served with the British army in India and China before attaching himself to the Confederate army in the American Civil war, and had later travelled as a naturalist to the Arctic expedition of 1875–76. Others included Sir Abe Bailey, a mining millionaire from the Cape, who had risked imprisonment for his support for the Jameson Raid, and Moreton Frewen, whom Kipling had known in Allahabad. Conan Doyle became a neighbour in 1907; he shared Kipling's views on the war in South Africa, during which he had served in a field hospital, and on the need for tariff reform. Not much further afield was another South Africa connection, Lady Cecil, who had lived at Rhodes's home Groote Schuur while her husband was besieged in Mafeking. Milner, whom she would later marry, had his home at Sturry Court, near Canterbury. Henry James was along the coast at Rye. As the political climate grew more turbulent, Kipling's life in the Sussex countryside provided a compensating image of order and continuity.

He soon began to turn his experiences into fictional form. In his poem 'The Recall', the land (England) speaks of her children:

> I am the land of their fathers.
> In me the virtue stays.
> I will bring back my children,
> After certain days.
>
> Under their feet in the grasses
> My clinging magic runs.
> They shall return as strangers.
> They shall remain as sons.

There is an ambiguity here about whether what constitutes 'English-ness' is a matter of blood or race, figured as a 'virtue' passed down the family line, or the result of the magical power of certain places, something like that 'touch of English soil' which, according to Ford Madox Ford, is enough to transform even those born outside the race into 'Englishmen'.[7] Having lived half his life in India and America, Kipling could hardly escape a conflict between the stranger and the son, the discoverer and the inheritor. His Englishness was inevitably equivocal, less a matter of celebrating his roots than an attempt to will them down into the English soil, and there are hints of strain in the way his Sussex is so often defined by negatives, in opposition to the decadence of London intellectuals in the rather snappish story ' "My Son's Wife" ', or to the stresses brought on by work in the more relaxed 'An Habitation Enforced'.

This is the story of George Chapin, a wealthy American who breaks down from overwork, and after wandering across Europe arrives with his wife Sophie in Sussex, where they decide to buy an old manor house and its accompanying farms. They, like Kipling, are set on becoming 'gentry', but know better than to push themselves. The secret of their success is partly Sophie's belated discovery that she is in fact returning to her family home (Carrie too was to discover remote family connections in England). Their neighbours suppose that she had always known this, but had chosen not to mention it, it being held, in this story, that the English do not explain, but allow their customs to be discovered. 'This is like all England', Sophie comments: 'Wonderful, but no explanation. You're expected to know it beforehand.' The sign of their acceptance is the birth of a son and heir, who will resume the old family name.

The story is consciously charming. On the Chapins' first visit to what will be their new house, Friars Pardon, they are taken through a 'maze of back-kitchens, dairies, larders, and sculleries', in which one almost expects to find the National Trust Shop that will surely be built in time. The message that ownership brings duties is spelled out all too clearly: 'Your people', Sophie is told as she is saluted and curtsied to on leaving Church, and she soon learns that an outbreak of mumps imposes responsibilities on her. As George puts it: 'It's not our land. We've only paid for it. We belong to it, and it belongs to the people – our people they call 'em.' But for all the talk of work on the farms, the estate is a 'hidden kingdom', bounded externally by three main roads but within traversed only by footpaths, 'soft-footed ways by woodland, hedge-row, and shaw'. A 'kink' in the line of telegraph poles connecting Friars

Pardon to the outside world is explained in the story by the need to avoid felling a clump of elms, but invites an alternative explanation: that even as he surrendered to the charm of Old Rural England, Kipling was unable to draw the line which would connect the past to the present, and the secret places of Sussex to a new and invigorated England of turbines, the motor-car, and a reconstructed army.

The last paragraphs echo Kipling's own experience as a landowner, constrained by the customs of those who in theory worked for him. George has asked for a bridge to be built across a stream, and expects it to be put up swiftly, and made of larch. His workforce are intent on using oak, which will last. 'You've got no call to regard my words,' says one of them, 'but you can't get out of that.'

'No,' said George after a pause; 'I've been realising that for some time. Make it oak then; we can't get out of it.'

George and Sophie embrace Friars Pardon as their home and their destiny: an enforced habitation. Like Forster's *Howards End*, the story faces the future by looking to the past. Forster ends with a harvest ('such a crop of hay as never') and Kipling with an oak bridge. The images are determinedly robust, yet both writers are in retreat, dreaming of a return to lost origins, and the restoration of an almost forgotten and now subtly feminised Englishness.[8] Despite his place among the gentry, Kipling's imagination declared him still a stranger in the land.

In between writing and politics, and work around his estate, he found time to receive a steady stream of visitors to Bateman's. One of these was Joseph Conrad, who called in 1904. Kipling admired Conrad's sea tales, but 1904 was the year of *Nostromo*; it is hard to imagine Kipling having much sympathy with Conrad's critique of 'the buying and selling gang' which dominates a South American republic through its interest in its silver mines. Percy Grainger visited in 1905, while collecting material for the English Folk Song Society, a project which fitted well with Kipling's explorations of Sussex lore and dialect. Perceval Landon, a friend from the Bloemfontein days, was such a regular guest, between trips abroad as a war correspondent, that in 1912 a cottage on the Bateman's estate was refurbished for his use as a second home. Kipling was wary of interviews, but he did grant one to Jules Huret, a correspondent for *Le Figaro*, who came to Bateman's in August 1905; he evidently spoke more freely than he had intended, and had to ask Huret to delete a string of anti-German remarks before the interview was published (*Letters*, III.192–3).[9] The French had been hostile towards the

British during the South African war, but since then relations had improved with the *entente cordiale*. This had begun as a pragmatic agreement between the two nations that Egypt fell within the British sphere, and Morocco within the French, but the King's visit to Paris in May 1903 soon led to broader cultural exchanges. Kipling's reputation had been rising across the Channel, even as it declined in England, and Huret's visit helped to cement his love affair with France. As Thomas Pinney observes, it was to be the only country in which he was not disappointed.[10]

Kipling continued to intervene in domestic politics, especially where national defence was the issue. In 1903 Erskine Childers's *The Riddle of the Sands* helped to relaunch the genre of invasion stories begun by George Chesney's *The Battle of Dorking*, written in the aftermath of the Franco-Prussian war. For both writers, the external threat was from Germany, but the real enemy England's own laxity. Perhaps the most popular work in the genre was William Le Queux's *The Invasion of 1910* (1906); bound into every copy was a facsimile letter signed by Lord Roberts urging the reader to take up the cause of military preparedness. When, in 1905, Roberts became President of the National Service League and called on Kipling to back the conscription campaign, the support was gladly offered. Admiral 'Jackie' Fisher, who became First Sea Lord in 1904, also tried to enlist Kipling's help, but with less success. He shared Kipling's view that Germany was the potential enemy, and Kipling might have been expected to approve his plans to ensure that engineers and executive officers had more of their training in common – hitherto, senior commanders had often had little technical knowledge, and tended to look down on the 'greasers' – but Fisher's decision to concentrate the fleet in home waters ran up against Kipling's view of the Navy as the link between the far-flung parts of the empire, and he took every opportunity to snipe at the plan, and at Fisher.

His other priority was the need for preferential tariffs as a means to bind the empire into closer unity. Chamberlain had been urging this since the 1890s, but it ran counter to the policy of free trade which was thought to have secured national prosperity for 60 years, and the deep divisions it opened up among the Unionists contributed to the party's defeat in 1906. Later that year Chamberlain suffered a stroke and withdrew from politics, but the issue of tariff reform lingered on, with many of those who campaigned for it finding further common ground on still harder questions about Irish Home Rule and the power of the House of Lords.

It is a mark of Kipling's standing that men like Chamberlain, Roberts and Fisher hoped for his support, but power was moving towards the Liberals, and Kipling was moving further to the right. His role was to act as a gadfly, and an encourager of other gadflies, including Leo Maxse at the *National Review* and Howell Gwynne, one of Kipling's fellow-editors on the Bloemfontein *Friend*. In 1904 Gwynne became editor of the ailing Tory *Standard*, which had been bought by Arthur Pearson, founder of the *Daily Express*, to champion the cause of tariff reform. The *Dictionary of National Biography* unkindly describes Pearson's career as 'more alarming than edifying', but neither his understanding of mass-market journalism nor Gwynne's polemical skills could turn the *Standard* round, and in 1911 Gwynne moved to the *Morning Post*, a right-wing paper with a circulation of about 80,000. When Kipling had a more than usually vitriolic poem to publish, he could usually rely on the *Morning Post* to accept it; though even Gwynne declined 'Gehazi', Kipling's attack on Sir Rufus Isaacs, the Attorney-General implicated in the Marconi scandal of 1913.[11]

Kipling frequently wrote to Gwynne, as he did to other editors, to offer advice, support, or pieces of information he thought might be useful. His close relationship with *The Times*, however, was disrupted by the introduction in 1905 of *The Times* Book Club. In an effort to increase circulation, *The Times* offered to loan copies of new books to its subscribers, which could later be purchased at much reduced prices, thus undercutting other booksellers. Initially the publishers cooperated, but then came to feel that their trade was threatened, and retaliated by refusing to sell to the paper at the usual discount. *The Times* countered by accusing the publishers of excessive profits, and urging its readers to buy only those books included in *The Times Monthly Catalogue*. Kipling was among those who protested, on the grounds that the distribution of books would soon become a monopoly: the author would either have to 'write to please *The Times*', or cease writing, because he has no means of reaching his public except through *The Times*' (*Letters*, III.224). The 'Book War' ran on until 1908, when the paper agreed to the publishers' terms, in effect signing up to the Net Book Agreement which would last until the end of the century.[12] It was the paper's new owner, Lord Northcliffe, who took the decision to retreat – the editor, Moberley Bell, wanted to fight on – but Kipling mistrusted Northcliffe (*Letters*, III.351), and began to place his work with the *Morning Post* rather than *The Times*. The change, from a national newspaper to one frankly partisan, is a sign of how far he had moved from his position as the nation's unofficial laureate.

Traffics and Discoveries

Traffics and Discoveries, published in 1904, did little to win back those English readers who had begun to lose faith in Kipling, in tandem with his increasingly vigorous hints that he had lost faith in them. But while the volume exhibits the less sympathetic aspects of Kipling's 'insistence on the disciplines of the pack',[13] most obviously in 'A Sahib's War' and 'The Captive', other concerns emerge from within these insistent voices. Pyecroft, the least imaginative of Kipling's narrators, struggles to tell the story of 'Mrs Bathurst'; ' "Wireless" ' starts with the techniques of radio transmissions but evolves into an account of literary creation; ' "They" ' begins with Kipling's passion for the motor-car, but takes the narrator to a place which is not on any of his maps. All three stories foreshadow themes and techniques which were to dominate Kipling's later work.

In *Something of Myself* Kipling recalls that the face and voice of one woman in Auckland, and a comment he overheard about another in Cape Town, came together, 'and a tale called "Mrs Bathurst" slid into my mind, as smoothly and orderly as floating timber on a bank-high river' (*SM* 61). Most readers have found it anything but orderly. A year on from the Anglo-Boer war, four men exchange reminiscences in a railway-siding near Simon's Bay in the Cape. These turn on error and deception, and the loves of men and women, and draw gradually towards the story of 'Click' Vickery, a naval warrant officer who has deserted within eighteen months of his pension. It transpires that he was one of two men struck by lightning in the forests beyond Bulawayo; the bodies have been turned to charcoal, but one had the dentures which provided Vickery with his nickname. None of the men know much of him, except that he has been visiting the cinema obsessively to watch a piece of newsreel showing a woman alighting from the Plymouth–London train. This is Mrs Bathurst, the proprietress of a seaside hotel in New Zealand, who is also known to two of the men telling the tale. They agree that she was the kind of woman a man would go 'crazy' for, but neither can believe that she was in any way to blame for Vickery's eventual fate.

There are numerous mysteries in the story. Who was the person beside Vickery, also killed by lightning? (Hooper, who tells this part of the story, uses the nicely ambiguous word 'mate' to describe this figure, leading some readers to suppose it was Mrs Bathurst.) If Mrs Bathurst was looking for Vickery in London, as he states, did she find him, and if she did what happened? Did she know, before she arrived, that Vickery was already married? What is the relevance of the other stories the men tell, especially that of Boy Niven, who once 'lured' a group of seamen into walking around a barren island in the Vancouver archipelago?

None of these questions can be answered with certainty. In the autobiography, Kipling explains how he learned to revise his stories by shortening them as much as they could bear: 'a tale from which pieces have been raked out is like a fire that has been poked' (*SM* 121). A number of critics have concluded that in 'Mrs Bathurst' he took this process too far, and have gone on either to dismiss the story as a failure, or to view its indeterminacy as part of its meaning and a sign of its modernity.[14] Others, like Craig Raine, have argued that 'the story is as precise as a Swiss watch. Everything fits, but the reader has to wind it up.'[15] This would be consistent with what Kipling also says, that the stories had to be written long before they were cut down, but there is no consensus as to how the parts fit. Raine argues from Vickery's reference to 'my *lawful* wife' that he has married Mrs Bathurst bigamously. This is why he is afraid: Mrs Bathurst, we are told, 'never scrupled to . . . set 'er foot on a scorpion'. But the italics here are Raine's, and his reading remains suggestive rather than compelling.[16]

Elliptical as it is, 'Mrs Bathurst' can also be seen as a reworking of the earlier ' "Love-o'-Women" '. In both stories the narrators admit their inability to understand a man who has cut loose from the known world of the crew or regiment. Vickery, like Larry Tighe, is 'what you call a superior man'; both he and Tighe quote Shakespeare (Vickery's parting words are 'The rest . . . is silence');[17] both believe themselves doomed; both court death, Tighe in battle and Vickery by standing up to attract the lightning. Both have known love, betrayal, and isolation. But where ' "Love-o'-Women" ' evokes the heat and claustrophobia of an Indian barracks, 'Mrs Bathurst' ranges more widely. The tale jumps from New Zealand to Vancouver Island, from Paddington Station to a teak forest in Bulawayo, not to record and celebrate the reach of the British Empire, but to show how much world there is for a man to get lost in: not only Vickery, but those other men recalled by the narrators, who jumped ship, died of fever or went native, or joined the 'heaps of tramps' to be found in Rhodesia, forlornly keeping close to the railway line. Everywhere there are reminders of chance and disconnection, from the missed appointment with which the story begins to the broken and sabotaged machinery which litters its pages: a damaged brakevan, an ammunition hoist carried away, a platform submerged in sand at the appropriately named False Bay.

At the centre of the story is the piece of newsreel film, ironically titled 'Home and Friends', which shows Mrs Bathurst with her 'blindish look' arriving on the platform and walking 'on and on till she melted out of the picture': a human narrative held on a piece of celluloid, caught in an endless transit, seen but unseeing, while Vickery, his ill-fitting teeth clicking 'like a Marconi ticker', is compelled to gaze back, seeing but unseen. Like the newsreel, the narrative is composed of fragments in which the figures walk out of view, leaving the reader to search for a meaning which the known events will not disclose. Twice in the story Hooper, the railway man, touches something in his waistcoat pocket, which the reader expects to be Vickery's dentures, but on the last page of the story he brings his hand away '– empty'. 'Mrs Bathurst' teases us by withholding the evidence we expect, but which, even if we had it, would not resolve the narrative questions. We have both the illusion that there is a single determinate meaning to the story, and the fear that this *is* an illusion. 'I used to think seein' and hearin' was the only regulation aids to ascertainin' facts,' remarks one of the narrators, 'but as we get older we get more accommodatin'.' One of the things we have to accommodate in 'Mrs Bathurst' is that our wish to bring the facts into coherence may never be fulfilled.

The power of the mind to make things cohere is also an issue in ' "Wireless" '. In a chemist's shop on the south coast an electrician has rigged up a Marconi installation and is waiting to receive a radio message. In the shop itself, the chemist's assistant, a consumptive in love with a girl named Fanny Brand, takes some medication which causes him to fall into a trance, during which he composes verses which echo Keats's 'Eve of St Agnes' and 'Ode to a Nightingale', neither of which he has read. Meanwhile, a radio message does come through, but not the one expected: 'Signals unintelligible', and later, 'Disheartening – most disheartening.' The narrator struggles to draw an analogy between the radio message and the mangled attempts at poetry: in the radio installation a wire placed within the magnetic field of another can be charged with electricity; the chemist's assistant has somehow been caught in the field of Keats's influence – Fanny Brand (almost but not quite Fanny Brawne), the rich colours and smells of the shop, the drops of arterial blood on the handkerchief. . . . But there is no attempt to force the parallel. Instead, there is a series of recognitions: that exquisite poetry may take its origins in ordinary physical desire ('unwholesome, but human exceedingly'), that the power of the 'coherer' to receive incoming messages is linked to the quality of the 'home battery' (in this case Shaynor, the chemist, whose capacities are less finely tuned than those of Keats), and that the creative process which leads to poetry entails something very like inspiration. As many commentators have noticed, the story anticipates Kipling's observation to Rider Haggard in 1918, 'that any-thing which any of us did *well* was no credit to us: that it came from somewhere else: "We are only telephone wires." '[18] As one might expect, Kipling is delighted by the technical details of the radio experi-ment, but the heart of the story is his celebration of 'the pure Magic' of poetry, and the miracle of the gifted human coherer.

' "They" ' is one of the most moving of Kipling's stories, and one of the very few with a clear autobiographical impulse. The narrator of the story, whom the reader gradually realises is a bereaved father, makes three visits in a single summer to a mysterious but beautiful house, inhabited by a blind woman and filled with the laughter of children seen only momentarily, as a 'glint' of blue shirt, or a girl's form behind a window. The first visit suggests the entry into a fairy-tale, its highly wrought beauty owing something to Kipling's Pre-Raphaelite back-ground. This contrasts sharply with the second, in which a dishevelled woman, 'loose-haired, purple, almost lowing with agony', beseeches the blind woman's help for her sick grandchild, leading the narrator into a frantic search for doctor and nurse. On the third visit, the narra-tor for the first time enters the house, but despite all his stratagems is still unable to do more than glimpse the children. Only as he suspends his efforts, while watching the blind woman deal with a devious tenant, does he feel a child's kiss pressed into the palm of his hand: 'a gift on which the fingers were, once, expected to close . . . a fragment of a mute code devised long ago.' At once he realises what has already become clear to the reader, that 'They' are spirits, living in the house as chil-dren, even able to walk in the woods with their parents. Yet this discov-ery is for the narrator the sign that he can never return: 'For me it would be wrong. For me only . . .'. No explanation is offered as to why; it seems that for the narrator (and at this point it does not seem unrea-sonable to say, for Kipling) the pain of his loss has become an absolute, a part of his being that he cannot give up. Perhaps only the bereaved will admit the truth of this.[19]

From the outset there are clues that the story will be shaped by the emotional and psychological needs of the narrator. He is led to the house as if by the road itself ('one view called to another, one hill-top to its fellow'), through a landscape that already hints at the miraculous (the word is used in the first paragraph). He explains that he comes from 'the other side of the county'; the blind woman acknowl-edges that the house is 'so out of the world'. And from the first there are signs that he will be held back from what he seeks, such as the yew trees clipped into armed horsemen seeming to bar his way. His conversation with the blind woman is shot through with a similar ambivalence. She is unable to tell him how many children there are in the house, nor is she certain of her right to have them. Her literal blindness foreshadows his inability to see the children, while her hesitancy, and his lack of understanding, are both played off against the familiar clutter of children's toys – a rocking-horse, a wooden cannon – and the calm acceptance of Jenny, walking in the woods with her child, who 'placidly' tells the narrator: 'You'll find yours indoors, I reckon.' The effect is to poise the story on a boundary which seems always about to be crossed.

This sense of a boundary powerful yet somehow permeable is repeated on the second visit, which begins with the narrator's car seeming to take the road to the House Beautiful 'of her own volition', and ends with a desperate effort to get help for the dying child. This visit also helps to suggest what it is in the narrator which debars him from seeing his own lost child. He takes advantage of a mechanical fault to his car to set out his tools as if playing shop: 'It was a trap to catch all childhood.' Earlier he has prefaced a remark to the blind woman with 'if I know children . . .'. Evidently he does 'know' children, and loves them, but he expresses that knowledge in terms of rules and stratagems. Is it this cast of mind, this need for some mental purchase on and control of his deepest feelings of love, that binds him to his grief, and eventually exiles him from the house and its woods? Kipling was the most reticent of men. Perhaps for that reason, the three stories we can associate most closely with his own life – 'Baa Baa, Black Sheep', ' "They" ', and 'The Gardener', written after the death of his son at Loos in 1915 – are all laceratingly personal.

Evoking the poem in the first section of 'Burnt Norton', T. S. Eliot draws an appropriate conclusion:

> Go, said the bird, for the leaves were full of children,
> Hidden excitedly, containing laughter.
> Go, go, go, said the bird: human kind
> Cannot bear very much reality.

Kipling was always fascinated with non-physical modes of perception, but suspicious too. He viewed Trix's adventures in psychic research as one aspect of her mental breakdown, but at the same time he believed his own genius as a writer was 'given', and that it was his responsibility to follow the instructions of his 'Daemon'.[20] In this story, the child whose absence is so deeply felt becomes Kipling's Daemon. The writing of ' "They" ' both depends on and seeks to close the gap opened up by her loss. In the pain of this paradox lies the intensity of the story, and the narrator's recognition that he can never return.

Puck of Pook's Hill

Kipling liked to think of himself as a pioneer motorist; he even wrote a group of verses, *The Muse among the Motors*, for the *Daily Mail*. He could certainly claim to have suffered for his enthusiasm: his second car, a Lanchester bought in 1902, broke down so often he named it 'Jane Cakebread', after a prostitute notorious for a string of convictions. Its successor proved more reliable, and in it he set out to explore the southern counties of England. Each new place called up a different phase of English history, turning the car, as he wrote to Filson Young, into 'a time-machine on which one can slide from one century to another' (*Letters*, III.150). But he found at Bateman's that he could travel through time by exploring downwards instead, when the process of digging a well in the grounds unearthed a spoon dating from the time of Cromwell, a Jacobean tobacco-pipe and part of a Roman horse-bit. The discovery prompted a series of fictional excavations into the history of Sussex. The land seemed 'alive with ghosts and shadows' (*SM* 109), and when a performance by John and Elsie of *A Midsummer Night's Dream* suggested the figure of Puck as the bridge between past and present, a means to revivify the ghosts and bring them out of the past to tell their stories, the result was the two books for children, *Puck of Pook's Hill* (1906) and *Rewards and Fairies* (1910).

Kipling had considered such a scheme earlier, in 1897, the year of the Jubilee, and a time of national reflection on the past and future destiny of England. Historians like John Seeley and James Froude had moved the origins of 'Englishness' back from the settlement of 1688 to 1588, to the defeat of the Armada and the beginnings of an age of conquest and expansion. For these writers Englishness was not a matter of constitutional niceties, but of race, blood and instinct. Froude in particular valued the frontier spirit as a corrective to the decay of public life, military and moral decline and the degeneracy of modern towns. The colonist would redeem his own life, secure the defence of Greater Britain, and contribute to the national renewal which Kipling had called for in the poems of *The Five Nations*. It seemed to Froude that this spirit had all but disappeared from the British (he found it instead among the Boers); Kipling's aim was to recover and celebrate it. Rome fell, Parnesius is told by his father, because it forgot its own best traditions. With Puck's help, Dan and Una, as John and Elsie become in the stories, will remember.

Kipling described the Puck stories as 'a sort of balance to, as well as seal upon, some aspects of my "Imperialistic" output in the past' (*SM* 111).[21] The modern historian ascribes value to the empathetic understanding of forgotten modes of thought and feeling. Kipling belonged to an older tradition which mined the past to seek its authority for the present, and the Puck stories emphasise continuity rather than difference. The woods in which Dan and Una wander are as well known to the Norman knight, Sir Richard Dalyngridge, as to them. Hobden, who lives off and seems to emanate from the land, is the descendant of a former 'Hob of the Dene'; when the knight gives out his hunting call, Hobden answers instinctively from deep in the woods (as Puck comments, 'It's in his blood'). Dan finds a flint arrow-head in the grass; what was formerly a 'plague-stone' is now in use as a chicken's drinking-trough.[22] The old stories still matter, and the old songs live on: 'This I have heard sung!' exclaims Sir Richard, while Puck and Una join in reciting Richard Corbet's 'The Faeryes Farewell', written 300 years earlier.

Not only objects, but dialect words and local customs have survived down the generations: in one story, the ground is 'poached and stoached' rather than trodden into puddles; in another the Pharisees (fairies) are 'stenched up' rather than confined; 'Hal o' the Draft' includes 'ary', 'mell', 'seely', 'spaulty', 'swarved up', 'tod', 'vivers', 'willowtot' and 'wool-wain'. Kipling picked up some of this from conversations with the local artisans and craftsmen, and some from the dialect dictionaries that were one offshoot of the growing interest in local history around the turn of the century. Joseph Wright's *English Dialect Dictionary* appeared in six volumes between 1898 and 1905, and by the time Kipling joined the Folk Lore Society in 1911, 29 of 40 English counties had published fieldwork on their local customs. His interest was part of a widespread tendency of the age. In Dorset, both Thomas Hardy and William Barnes lamented the way dialect words were losing their hold; Barnes especially was an impassioned champion of what he called 'our own strong old Anglo-Saxon speech', who wanted to substitute 'English' words – words with a pre-Norman origin – for those derived from Latin: birdlore and folk-wain, for example, rather than ornithology and omnibus. Gerard Manley Hopkins struggled to build into his verse what seemed to him the purity of Anglo-Saxon. Edward Freeman, whose *History of the Norman Conquest* is echoed in the Puck stories, came to regard French and Latin words as dangerous intruders, and when revising his work took every opportunity 'to put a good English word' where he had earlier 'allowed a stranger to creep in'.[23]

The common theme here is the belief in an essential Englishness lying hidden in the language, waiting to be uncovered. The Oxford English Dictionary followed these movements in complex ways. The *OED* resisted the idea of a range of local dialects in favour of a single English language, not so much the creation of numerous interacting communities as the bearer of a 'national' literary heritage. It was accordingly unsympathetic to contemporary slang, but tolerant of older dialect words. It is not difficult to establish similar contexts for other aspects of the Puck stories. The concern for an Englishness stored in places and in artefacts, for example, is reflected in the founding of the National Trust in 1895, as well as a number of local or 'folk' museums (a recurrent theme in the stories is the persistence of genuine craftsmanship through the ages: what the carpenter Mr Springett calls 'workin' honest'). But there are other aspects of the stories which command attention. There is in particular an apparent conflict, especially in *Rewards and Fairies*, between a vision of Sussex as a kind of Neverland – 'a sort of thick, sleepy stillness smelling of meadow-sweet and dry grass' – and as an arena in which to examine the moral imperatives which engage the figures who come to meet the children. 'What else could I have done?' becomes the leitmotif of the tales.

This is the clue to Kipling's underlying purpose. In 'The Islanders' he had asked how the English were to be defended in the years ahead, 'when the restless lightnings wake / In the womb of the blotting war-cloud', and answered his own question: only the constant vigilance of each islander, and an ever-renewed readiness for sacrifice, would serve. The qualities that built the island's greatness are those needed to maintain it: 'Men, not gods, devised it. Men, not gods, must keep.' What Kipling does in the Puck stories is to read back through the sweetness of the landscape to the sometimes bitter and violent deeds by which it had been won. He was ready to endorse what has been called 'the Southern metaphor', the image of an essentially rural and apparently stable England, the home of the gentry rather than the industrialist or businessman, but he sought to incorporate into it a memory of the energies which had secured it for the English.[24]

The stories link the past world of action to the present state of possession. But the right to possess is won only by the willingness to sacrifice, to be dispossessed: many of the figures in the stories are dislocated – Romans born overseas who never see Rome, Norman incomers who will never return to Normandy, young men sent abroad to die. Behind the disruptions, however, England persists.[25] The Conquest of 1066 is a disturbance rather than a breach of continuity; in the final story in

Rewards and Fairies, the Saxon King Harold, supposed dead, reappears to die in the presence of the Norman Henry I, whose Charter was held by historians like Francis Palgrave and Edward Freeman to have restored the old laws of Edward the Confessor. England, in these stories, assimilates those who walk its soil: Parnesius the Roman, Sir Richard Dalyngridge the Norman, Kadmiel the Jew. As Kipling put it in a letter, 'the land itself compels the men it breeds to serve it' (*Letters*, III.424). In 'Weland's Sword', Puck cuts a piece of turf and gives it ceremonially to the children, explaining that they are now 'lawfully seized' of Old England. Their conscious knowledge of their various encounters is magicked out of them, but through Puck they possess the stories of the land at a deeper level, at the same time as they are, as Kipling's son and daughter, the legal heirs to its material possession.[26]

They are the land's, and it is theirs. Five years after *Rewards and Fairies*, John, like the brothers Elizabeth I sends out to fight the Spanish in 'Gloriana', would die for it.

8
Towards Armageddon

In *Puck of Pook's Hill* Parnesius and Una discuss families. Parnesius recalls how his father would tell his children to make less noise, and then join them in a wild romp: ' "Fathers can – if they like," said Una, her eyes dancing.' Kipling certainly could; he always enjoyed the company of children, and not only of his own. But more rapidly than Dan and Una, John and Elsie were growing up. In September 1907, at the age of ten, John began school at St Aubyn's in Rottingdean, where his great-aunt Georgie Burne-Jones still lived. Kipling had not forgotten his own unhappiness in his first months at school, and he felt the pain of separation keenly. His letters reveal a man desperate to express his love in a way acceptable to his son, and to himself, ever careful not to put an evil eye on their relationship by celebrating it too openly. They cajole, praise and caution a boy who was not especially gifted: slow to learn, but reasonably diligent; short-sighted, like his father, but gradually finding himself in games. Despite his own lack of sporting prowess, Kipling bowled to him in the nets, and even, when John was away, admitted to a plaintive wish that he had someone to drag him out for 'footer'. Each of John's successes, however trivial – moving up a place in form, bearing with a disappointment – is applauded, alongside warnings to avoid any boy suspected of 'beastliness', and cautions to keep warm and eat properly. The more than 200 letters which have survived are full of homely details designed to remind him of the family as a unit, and of his place in it:[1] Carrie's knitting, Elsie's tennis-playing, the hiving of bees, the damage caused by an autumn flood, or the tale, with illustrations, of how Gwynne fell from the canoe into the pond. There are very few references to Kipling's work, or his status as a public figure; lively as the letters are, they are also resolutely ordinary. It was in the mundane or the facetious that father and son could find common ground.

In letters to his friends Kipling brooded over the responsibilities of fatherhood. In November 1907, just after John had started school, he wrote to Edmund Gosse to congratulate him on the publication of *Father and Son*. Gosse had been brought up by his father, a member of the Plymouth Brethren, in the shadow of his mother's dying plea to them both to remember their faith. Reading Gosse's memories of the burden of Evangelical discipline and expectation, Kipling was inevitably reminded of his own experiences at the hands of Mrs Holloway. In the Epilogue, Gosse describes his struggle to resist his father's loving inquisitions, and to claim 'a human being's privilege to fashion his inner life for himself'.[2] Kipling's comment, that 'the last thing a parent learns is when not to love over-much' (*Letters*, 3.278), was an appropriate response to Gosse's words, but the fear of loving not wisely but too well was his own. Writing to Dunsterville, he pondered the need for parents to give their children 'enough of that judicious letting alone which makes and builds up a kid's character' (*Letters*, 3.325). If he reflected privately that his own parents seemed to have had no such problem, he did not say so. Yet from the moment of John's birth he had marked out for him a future in the Navy; when his eyesight proved too poor, his only thought was to make him a soldier. Letting alone was easier to write of than to achieve.

Immediately after delivering John to school, Rudyard and Carrie left for a six-week tour of Canada. At the Imperial Conference of Prime Ministers in May 1907, Canada had rejected proposals to establish a permanent secretariat to look after matters of common interest, primarily because its Québecois Prime Minister, Wilfred Laurier, was anxious not to offend French Canadian voters by conceding too much to British influence. Kipling's tour was intended to counter these concerns, and to shore up support among English-speaking Canadians. Because of his illness in New York in 1899 his honorary degree from McGill University in Montreal had been awarded in his absence. This visit gave him the opportunity to make amends.

It also made it possible for Carrie to see her mother, Anna Balestier, though they met in a hotel in Montreal; there was no question of crossing the border to call on her in Vermont. The Canadian Pacific Railway provided the Kiplings with a private coach, together with the services of a 'stately negro' who acted as Major Domo, in which they crossed the prairies to Vancouver and back. Rudyard's speeches were well received, but he found Canada 'a constipating land', albeit one redeemed by 'a certain crude material faith in the Empire' (*Letters*, III.330). When he wrote up his visit for the *Morning Post* under the title *Letters to the*

Family, he was more positive about the way Canada had learned to translate the moral virtues of 'insight, endurance, and self-restraint' into the material form of towns and railways. What the country needed now was a further 'influx of good men', demanding neither more nor less than 'the reward of their own labours', like those 'silent careful folk' he had celebrated in 'The Wage-Slaves' and 'The Explorer'. The presence of such people, driven from England by the dishonesty of a Liberal government, would create an Empire made of 'men and women of our own stock, habits, language and hopes'. Canada's future was assured; the 'only serious threat' to the Empire was in England itself, in 'that very Democracy which depends on the Empire for its proper comforts'.[3] As in India and South Africa, so now in Canada, the virtues of the colonist provided a standard by which those in government at home were found wanting.

There was another journey to make in 1907, an unexpected one. In November Kipling was awarded the Nobel Prize for Literature, and in December he and Carrie travelled to Stockholm to receive it. The ceremony was a muted affair, with the Swedish nation in mourning for the death of King Oscar II three days earlier. Kipling's account in his autobiography is properly sombre, but writing to his children he added a touch of comedy, saying that he felt 'like a bad boy up to be caned' (*Letters*, III.286), and adding a sketch of himself surrounded by hands reached out to congratulate him. He was an odd choice for the prize, which was intended for authors of 'an idealistic tendency' (as opposed to the naturalists, like Zola), but he appreciated the honour of being the first writer from the Empire to receive the award.[4] Earlier in the year he had received an honorary degree at Oxford, his first from a British university, alongside his hero Mark Twain. Like other writers before and since, he was finding official recognition even as his reputation, outside his own literary circle, was in decline.

He was about to receive further recognition, of a less intellectual kind. The first instalment of Robert Baden-Powell's *Scouting for Boys*, published in January 1908, included a summary of *Kim*, recast as a treatise on scouting, and a game, 'Kim's Game', based on the Lurgan episode in the novel. Kipling had evidently given Baden-Powell more or less a free hand, and while he declined to write a message for *The Scout*, he did agree, a year later, to write 'The Boy Scouts' Patrol Song'. Despite the efforts of the National Service League, it was clear that England was going to depend on a volunteer army – Baden-Powell had just taken command of the Northumbrian division of the Territorials – and while the Scout movement was not designed as a cadet corps, it was widely seen as a recruiting ground for the new Territorial Army. On these terms, Kipling, like Lord Roberts, was willing to give his support.

Since John attended only one Scout camp, it may be doubted whether he much enjoyed it. As Hugh Brogan points out, Baden-Powell and Kipling had less in common than might be supposed. Kipling's was much the darker vision. In 1915, after John's death at Loos, he wrote to Baden-Powell that 'there exists a residue of Ultimate Dirt – say 5% – which *must* be coerced by fear at the beginning. Later it learns honour and responsibility.'[5] This is far removed from Baden-Powell's individualism, reflected in his dislike of drill-based instruction, and from his commitment to social inclusiveness, exemplified in the ethos of the Scout camp. Nonetheless, Kipling gave his permission when Baden-Powell wanted to use *The Jungle Books* as the basis for a training programme for the Wolf Cubs, and the *Wolf Cub's Handbook* of 1916 includes an acknowledgement to Kipling as one 'who has done so much to put the right spirit into our rising manhood'.[6] By the time he published his *Land and Sea Tales for Scouts and Guides* in 1923 he had become a Boy Scout Commissioner, though his role was never more than an honorary one.

In January 1908 Kipling took his family to South Africa for one last visit, but they were merely going through the motions; he wrote to Milner that 'We do nothing: we see nobody. . . . We sit on the stoep and watch the hours go by' (*Letters*, III.303). He was glad to let his thoughts turn back to Sussex, and to ideas for *Rewards and Fairies*, but this was a year of low spirits, in which he published only one story, 'The Mother Hive', of any note. Not only was John away at school, but in the summer Elsie was in London, undergoing treatment to correct a mild curvature of the spine, while in November Carrie had to have three cysts removed from her head. He was worried too about his finances, as the Liberal government raised taxes to pursue its policies of social reform. He had already renegotiated terms with Alex Watt, so that any edition that had been on the market for ten years or more paid Watt five instead of ten per cent, and now he began writing to various well-placed friends for advice on how to invest his money, with a preference for investments overseas.[7]

For their winter holiday at the end of 1908 they chose Engelberg in Switzerland, more or less at random, but it proved to be a success, and they repeated the visit each year until the outbreak of the Great War. The holiday mood was broken, however, when they returned in April to the news of the 'People's Budget'. Lloyd George, the Chancellor, had faced a difficult task. In 1908 Germany had laid down four 'all big-gun' ships to Britain's two. The government's initial reaction was to lay down four at once, with contingency plans for another four, but it was soon forced to give in to a campaign to increase naval spending, under the slogan 'We want eight, and we won't wait'. Lloyd George was already struggling to fund the provision of old-age pensions; with the additional spending on the navy, he now had to raise £15 million by new taxation. Many of his measures might have been designed to offend Kipling personally: higher taxes on tobacco, taxes on petrol, motor licences, the creation of a new super-tax. The most controversial plan was to increase duties on unearned increment on the sale of land, necessitating a complete valuation of the land of Great Britain. The land-owning classes were predictably outraged, and against all precedent the House of Lords rejected the budget, triggering a new election in January 1910. This left the Liberals with a majority of two over the Unionists, with the balance of power in the hands of the 40 Labour members and the 82 Irish Nationalists. Since Nationalist support depended on a promise of Home Rule, which in turn would require an end to the Lords' power of veto, the country was now threatened by two constitutional crises, Irish Home Rule and the reform of the House of Lords. Kipling's fears about the dangers of 'Democracy' seemed to have been confirmed.

His private reaction was to seek further advice about investing overseas, to 'get every penny we can out of the country before the smash' (*Letters*, III.381). His public response was the poem 'The City of Brass', published in the *Morning Post* at the end of June. This was a furious attack on a government charged with abandoning the defence of the nation ('Swiftly these pulled down the walls that their fathers had made them'), and introducing a new and factitious ideology:

> They said: 'Who has hate in his soul? Who has envied his neighbour?
> Let him arise and control both that man and his labour.'
> They said: 'Who is eaten by sloth? Whose unthrift has destroyed him?
> He shall levy a tribute from all because none have employed him.'

The New Imperialists had argued for social reform as a means to strengthen the heart of the Empire; Kipling accused the Liberals of using taxation to wreck the Empire, flinging away 'imperial gains' to provide handouts to 'the shouters and marchers', in a cynical attempt to buy popular support. Liberal policies had put 'the heart of a beast in the place of a man's heart'; under their impotent leadership, it would be England's fate to pass 'from the roll of the nations in headlong surrender!'

He enjoyed writing the poem. He described its form, with the feminine end-rhymes supported by a complex pattern of internal masculine rhymes, as 'a "sport" from an Arabian one', and laughed off the denunciations it received in the press as 'great fun' (*Letters*, III.381). Yet 'fun' was not the issue. This was a time of crisis, and Kipling's poem added to the mood of uncertainty. He was not yet a rebel, though his opposition to Home Rule would soon make him one, but he was moving towards a position that could not easily be accommodated within the political process.

Actions and Reactions

Actions and Reactions was published in October 1909, in the run-up to the rejection of the budget in the House of Lords. Most of the stories had been written over the previous three or four years, but only one, 'The Mother Hive', bears directly on politics. It takes the form of a fable based on the social behaviour of bees, used here as in Shakespeare's *Henry V* to 'teach / The act of order to a peopled kingdom'. Liberal progressivism and individualism are the main targets. Because the hive is old and overcrowded, it fails to act when the Wax-moth insinuates her way past the guards. The younger bees are seduced by her arguments against the need to build defences, her refusal to work ('I don't like working. It's bad for the mind'), and her prophecy of a 'New Day' about to dawn. In a glance at contemporary fears of racial degeneration, the hive is soon filled with 'albinos, mixed-leggers, single-eyed composites, faceless drones, half-queens and laying-sisters'. The Wax-moth finds these misfits 'delightfully clever and unusual and interesting'; Kipling does not, and willingly hands them over to the Bee Master who comes to burn the hive, though not before a few uncorrupted bees, 'a handful, but prepared to go on', have left to establish a hive elsewhere. In 1897, in 'Recessional', Kipling had written:

> Judge of the nations, spare us yet,
> Lest we forget—lest we forget!

The cleansing flames at the end of 'The Mother Hive' suggest that he thought England had forgotten, and was due for judgement. His message is the one urged in *Letters to the Family*, that the nation was dying at the centre, and only the colonies could save it. But South Africa was lost and he had found Canada 'a constipating land', worthy but unexciting, and despite his conscientious admiration for 'the age-old instinct of loyalty and devotion to the Hive' which motivates the hero-bees, these are not the qualities which provoked his best work; substitute 'House' for 'Hive', and the story offers only a variant on the platitudes he had derided in *Stalky & Co.* It was the eccentric and the driven, not the dutiful and conformist, who engaged Kipling's imagination.

'The Mother Hive' is the most pessimistic of the stories in *Actions and Reactions* which begins and ends, as J. M. S. Tompkins has pointed out, with themes of healing.[8] There was to be no abatement in Kipling's political mood, or in his readiness to dismiss liberals and progressives as 'oddities' ripe for destruction; but increasingly, in the stories of the later years, the casualties in society, those who break down or lose their way, are treated with compassion. This is apparent in both the opening story, 'An Habitation Enforced', which develops from the Kiplings' life at Bateman's, and in the last, 'The House Surgeon', which recalls what they came to feel was the bad Feng-shui of the house they rented in Torquay after their flight from America (*SM* 79). The house in this story is new and brightly suburban, but afflicts everyone who enters it with the sense of 'a live grief beyond words', as if an unseen person were struggling to speak, until the narrator effects its exorcism by persuading the Evangelically minded Misses Moultrie, the former owners, that their younger sister died by accident, and not by suicide. The story succeeds because Kipling's sympathy extends to all the characters: nobody is condemned, all are forgiven. As Baxter, the Moultries' solicitor, puts it, 'The facts as God knows 'em – may *be* different – even after the most clinching evidence.' This is not a perspective allowed into 'The Mother Hive'. It is, however, in keeping with the poem which accompanies the story, 'The Rabbi's Song', which returns to the incalculable potentialities of human feeling. We carry, and we lay on others, unmerited burdens: 'The arrows of our anguish / Fly farther than we guess.'[9] Kipling and Carrie, both prone to depression, had reason to know how heavy the burdens could be.

Three of the stories reprise earlier themes and situations: 'Garm – a Hostage' was written in the 1890s, 'Little Foxes' and 'A Deal in Cotton' might have been so. 'With the Night Mail' is a new departure, an experiment in science fiction, though the term is misleading, since despite his fascination with technology Kipling had little interest in science. He was uncomfortable with Darwinian theories of evolution, and his response to the general theory of relativity was to suspect it as a Jewish contribution 'to assisting the world towards flux and disintegration'.[10] 'With the Night Mail' recounts an Atlantic crossing by airship in the year 2000, when nationalism has disappeared, war has been abolished, and everyone subscribes to a new motto: 'Transportation is Civilisation.' The story drew the attention of the air transport lobby, while Kipling himself became interested in the Aerial League of the British Empire: 'I don't think *yet* that air ships can paralyze a country or a fleet but it won't be many years before they do' (*Letters*, III.406). But the welter of cod-technical material in the story overwhelms what narrative energy it might have had, and the latent political meanings of the motto – reminiscent of Rhodes's conviction of the need for a railway running from the Cape to Cairo – were not to be teased out until Kipling published a sequel, 'As Easy as A.B.C.', in 1912.

The remaining story, 'The Puzzler', is a farce. This was a form Kipling enjoyed, though usually it is tied to a revenge plot. In this instance, three members of the English ruling class – a judge, an engineer and an artist – try whether a monkey can indeed climb a monkey-puzzle tree. Their efforts are observed by the narrator and a Colonial politician; when things go wrong, the latter improvises a solution, and is rewarded by being given access to the centres of political power. Helpless laughter, on this showing, is the English shibboleth. In a late poem, 'The Playmate', Kipling identifies a spirit of comedy in the universe, which presides over those moments when 'an earnest, baffled Earth / Blunders and trips to make us mirth'. The true Wisdom, at such moments, is to yield to the pattern of events.[11] In Shakespearean comedy, such a surrender typically leads on through love into a more complete integration into the community, signalled by the closing marriage. In Kipling, it leads to camaraderie rather than love – the actors in these stories are invariably male – and a shared collapse under the physical pressure of laughter. For the reader there is a sense of strain in all this, of the act of will by which Kipling sets aside the desire for self-possession that was habitual to him, in order to trust to chance and the initiatives of others; but there is no doubt that it was a relief for him to do so.

The reviews for *Actions and Reactions* were mixed. By and large the right-wing press approved, and the liberal press did not, with the *Standard* and the *Daily News* representing the extremes. But most of the reviewers had the same reservation: Kipling was no longer exciting. *The Times Literary Supplement* complained that 'the manner is stereotyped; it no longer surprises.' The *Athenaeum* worried that Kipling's 'genius has never matured', the *Academy* that he was 'blowing tunes on an old reed', and the sound had grown 'thinner and thinner'.[12] The reviewers were in one sense more right than they knew. The stirrings of literary modernism were about to make themselves felt. Joyce had already written *Dubliners*, though he had yet to find a publisher for it;

Pound had arrived in London in 1908 to publish *Personae* and *Exultations*; D. H. Lawrence had written and grown dissatisfied with a first version of *The White Peacock*; and in Harvard T. S. Eliot had discovered Laforgue and was about to write, in November 1909, his first poems in his own voice.[13] There is little in *Actions and Reactions* to suggest that Kipling belongs in this company. Nonetheless, the reviewers were mistaken if they thought Kipling had come to some kind of stop. In stories like ' "They" ' and 'Mrs Bathurst' he had experimented with imperfect narrators, elliptical methods of narration, characters opaque even to themselves, and open rather than closed endings, all of which have an affinity with modernist writing, and in his three final volumes of stories he would do so again. Kipling's work did change, but because he kept to his own trajectory, and remained largely indifferent to contemporary literature, the changes were easily missed.

Kipling read the reviews, but he had more pressing concerns. In October 1909 he learned that his mother was suffering from hyperthyroidism. A letter written at the time to his aunt Louisa is oddly defensive, and hints at a history of tensions.[14] He insisted he had done all he could for his parents – urged them to see medical specialists, volunteered to extend their property, even offered to build a home for them on his own land – but his efforts had been refused (*Letters*, III.397). He had told Edmonia Hill, in 1905, that 'they grow old – a disease for which there is no remedy' (*Letters*, III.196), but age had not mellowed Alice, and it is hard to imagine her consenting to live on the Bateman's estate as a virtual pensioner of her son and his wife. The mere thought of such an arrangement must have horrified Carrie, who was herself unwell again this autumn, with swollen glands and neuralgia. Their winter holiday in Engelberg went ahead as planned, but she took the opportunity to see a specialist in Zurich, who diagnosed arthritis. Kipling urged her to rest, but had to accept that with 'an executive temperament one *must* forge ahead on executive paths' (*Letters*, III.420). Carrie needed to be needed; being ill was one way to prove to her husband and her children how much she contributed, and at what cost to herself.

On their return Kipling sent *Rewards and Fairies* off to the publishers. Writing it had satisfied him as a craftsman, and he had enjoyed filling the stories with 'all manner of allusions and references and cross-references' and, so he said, 'anagrams and cryptograms', though if these are present they have remained undetected (*Letters*, III.467). Elsewhere, however, he wrote that he wanted his style to be as transparent as possible: 'the minute the reader begins to look at the glass instead of through it the game is up' (*Letters*, III.466). There is the same emphasis on linguistic efficiency in a letter to Gosse which stigmatises 'wordiness' as a mark of 'effeminacy' and urges him, only half-humorously, to discipline his style by writing telegrams (*Letters*, III.329). Fortunately for Gosse's self-esteem, *Father and Son* had recently been honoured by the French Academy, and he was busy manoeuvring to set up an English equivalent. Kipling acknowledged the need for 'a judicial body that can maintain and impose standards', but ducked the invitation to serve on an 'Academic Committee of English Letters'.[15] While they kept on amicable terms, Kipling was not fond of Gosse, and had no wish to work alongside him.

Political and literary debate alike came to a temporary halt in May 1910 with the death of the King, brought on, Kipling believed, by the pressures put on him by the Liberals, who wanted an assurance that he would back the Commons against the Lords if the constitutional crisis continued. Attending the funeral service with the Bateman's staff, the men wearing their medals, the maids lined up in their pews, Kipling was briefly reassured by the sense of a nation united in mourning. He wrote to John that the King was 'a great man', and his life and death 'a gentle hint to us all to play the game and do our work for the King did his and died in the doing of it' (*Letters*, III.432): a more restrained response than his proposal to Blumenfeld at the *Daily Express* that he should run a piece describing the Cabinet as 'The Regicides'. Blumenfeld wisely ignored the idea, and Kipling had to be content with a glance at it in his poem, 'The Dead King': 'When he was bowed by his burden his rest was refused him. / We troubled his age with our weakness – the blacker our shame to us!'[16]

The King's death overshadowed the news that Crom Price too had died, just two days before. In the same month Carrie's younger sister, Josephine, broke down after the death of twins at the end of a difficult pregnancy; Kipling's letters to her exhibit a tact and consideration notably absent from his political writing. There was however worse to come. Towards the end of November he was summoned by telegram to Tisbury, where his mother had been taken ill; she died a few days later. Carrie joined her husband for the funeral, but stayed in a local hotel, rather than at the house. Trix too was present, but in an excited and unstable mood. Her husband, or so it seemed to the rest of the family, was incapable of helping her, and Lockwood was left to find her a nurse, before fleeing to his friends the Wyndhams. Perhaps surprisingly, Rudyard and Carrie left with their children for their winter holiday as planned, on 29 December, believing, or hoping, that the need to care for Trix would blunt the edge of Lockwood's grief (*Letters*, IV.12). Three weeks later, however, came the news that he was ill, and before Kipling could get home, he too had died, less than three months after his partner for forty-five years.

Kipling felt this second blow hard. He wrote to Edmonia Hill that his father 'was more to me than most men are to their sons: and now that I find I have no one to talk or write to I find myself desolate' (*Letters*, IV.13). This seems ungenerous to Carrie, but while he could and did depend absolutely on her loyalty, her erratic nerves made it difficult to speak to her with complete freedom. Like Burne-Jones, his father drew him out of himself, whereas Carrie faced the world with a siege mentality. Nor, inevitably, could she help him as Trix's health went from bad to worse. After the funeral Kipling burned a number of family papers, not only his letters to his parents but also, Trix was persuaded, Lockwood's will. She was convinced that she had been cheated, and remained bitter towards her brother for many years, but his more immediate concern was that she be looked after. Like his mother, Rudyard was unwilling to have her confined in a mental institution, and she spent much of the next dozen years in a succession of nursing homes. She was not to be fully recovered until the 1930s.

Towards war

Between *Rewards and Fairies* in 1910 and *A Diversity of Creatures* in 1917, Kipling published a handful of stories in the magazines, but no new collections. In 1911 he and C. R. L. Fletcher, one of the founders of the history school at Oxford, brought out *A School History of England*, with a series of verses close in theme to many of those in the two Puck volumes: a centurion pleading to stay in Britain after his cohort is ordered back to Rome, a celebration of England being 'hammered into one' by the Normans after the Conquest, reminders that 'honour and dominion' are won by 'sword and shot', not by feasting and song.[17] Fletcher's fiercely anti-Liberal beliefs and his virulent hostility to Irish nationalism – the *DNB* splendidly understates in noting that he 'never concealed his strong views' – ensured the work received some attention, but this apart, it was Kipling's political activity, rather than his writing, that kept him before the public.

These were fraught years for the Tory interest. Throughout 1910 the reform of the House of Lords dominated political debate. The January election had the main parties level-pegging; a second election within the year, held in December, left the House of Commons almost unchanged, but the momentum had swung towards the anti-Unionist majority. When the Bill to limit the Lords' power of veto was brought back, the disclosure that King George V was ready to create enough new peers to ensure its passage ended the resistance of all but a minority of die-hards among the Tory peers, and the Parliament Act came into force in 1911. Recognising the scale of the defeat, Balfour resigned the Tory leadership, to be succeeded by the Canadian-born Ulsterman Andrew Bonar Law, a convinced tariff reformer and an eagerly confrontational politician. Kipling was encouraged by the change – he wrote that he loved Bonar Law 'because he hates' (*Letters*, IV.139) – as he was by his introduction to another energetic Canadian, Max Aitken, later Lord Beaverbrook, who entered the Commons in 1910. The two soon became friends, Kipling seeking Aitken's advice on how to get the best return on his money (he had some £3500 – about £300,000 in contemporary terms – which he wanted to invest in Canada and America), and in return offering his own ideas on how to revitalise the Tory party, in particular on the need to set up an effective press office; part of his frustration with Balfour was that he had not taken such matters seriously (*Letters*, IV.68–9).

In the long hot summer of 1911 the Kiplings and Aitkens travelled together into France. The journey home was complicated by the threat of a rail strike, one of a series of industrial disputes, some of them violent, between 1910 and 1914. Kipling was inclined to blame these on free trade, arguing that unrestricted competition led inevitably to depressed wages, the casualisation of labour and spells of unemployment for working men. These were the conditions, he warned, that bred socialism. In fact, Liberal politicians like Lloyd George and Churchill hoped to pre-empt socialism by introducing more effective welfare policies, in particular the right to sickness and unemployment benefits, but to Kipling, as to many Unionists, it seemed the government was offering to maintain the feckless and the work-shy at the expense of the honest and hard-working.

The political landscape was further challenged by the suffragette movement. The path to women's suffrage had constantly hit the same barrier: the Liberal party was philosophically willing to consider it, but feared that women would vote for the Conservatives; the Conservatives would have welcomed the votes, but were philosophically opposed to extending the franchise. In 1910 a Conciliation Bill, granting the vote to women with a householder or occupation qualification – about a million women – ran up against precisely this hurdle. Asquith's determination to halt its progress infuriated suffrage campaigners and prompted the 'Black Friday' demonstrations, when women and police fought a pitched battle in the streets outside Parliament. Suffragette action, including window-breaking and arson, led swiftly to imprisonment and hunger strikes, and these in turn to the hated 'Cat and Mouse Act' of 1913, which allowed for the release and subsequent re-arrest of hunger-strikers.

Kipling had no sympathy with the suffragettes, and wrote to Andrew Macphail, another Canadian friend, in terms that they might have thought wearisomely familiar: 'Women knock up, knock out, go into the rest-cures and under the surgeon's hand – disappear from their friends while the evasive husband says they are "not quite well" – and with them goes the promise of increase' (*Letters*, III.441). This echoes arguments which had long been used against women's education, and anticipates one of the more notorious statements on 'the Woman Question', Dr Almroth Wright's letter to *The Times* on the 'physiological emergencies' which lay behind the 'hysterical' behaviour of the suffragettes.[18] It may be, however, that Kipling was thinking more specifically of Carrie, all too often 'not quite well', and perhaps also of Trix – though not, presumably, of Georgie Burne-Jones, who had taken advantage of the 1894 Local Government Act to become elected to the Rottingdean parish council.

In 'The Female of the Species', published in the *Morning Post* shortly before the Black Friday demonstrations, Kipling adopts a different line. Here it is not women's supposed frailty that is held against them, but their capacity for violence and cruelty: 'The female of the species is more deadly than the male.' The claim made by some feminists, that women had already helped secure the peace and happiness of the Home, and might, given the opportunity, infuse the home spirit into the public arena, and take up their place as 'the mothers of the race', was precisely what alarmed Kipling; it was after all the women of the Ladies' National Association who had opposed licensed prostitution in India, so that 'nine thousand expensive white men a year' were laid up with venereal disease, and women like Emily Hobhouse who had crusaded against the concentration camps in South Africa (*SM* 34). In the poem, however, he resists the idea that women might bring a softening influence into public affairs, and chooses instead to see them bound into an aggressive-defensive role, 'white-hot, wild', and ready to go to war on their children's behalf, 'lest the generations fail'. Men are complex, moved to compromise by doubt or pity; women are simple, 'launched for one sole issue', and will attack even when 'Unprovoked'. The suffragists thought they had been more than enough provoked, and wrote in with their protests. Elsie, now fifteen years old, also took exception to the poem, and said so; Kipling wrote to Gwynne at the *Morning Post* that she wanted his 'editorial blood' (*Letters*, IV.67).

The Kiplings spent Christmas Day 1911 as guests of the Aitkens, before setting off on holiday to Engelberg, then to Venice and Florence, and then into France. Rudyard spent his time revising the proofs of *Songs from Books*, a compilation of the poems and verse headings which had accompanied his stories; one set, meant for Doubleday in America, went down with the *Titanic* in April, and the work had to be done again. His sequel to 'With the Night Mail', 'As Easy as A.B.C.', came out in the magazines at around the same time, though he had drafted it some years earlier. The 'A.B.C.' is the Aerial Board of Control, an international body responsible for the maintenance of traffic. Democracy has been outlawed, and the world runs as smoothly as a machine. When crowd behaviour breaks out in Chicago, the Board uses an immobilising ray to bring it under control, before depositing the troublemakers – the 'Serviles', who want to return to the old ways of speech-making and the popular vote – out of harm's way in London, where their worship of 'The People' can be used as a form of entertainment. Kipling shared the Board's suspicion of democracy; he cited the story when writing to Andrew Macphail that 'the people are fed up with "The People" – sick, and tired and most deadly of all, bored with the solemn pump . . . of Democracy' (*Letters*, IV.73). Even so, in this brave new world political stability, longevity, and technological advance go hand in hand with a declining birth rate, an absence of heroes, and the dreariness of having no 'spark of difference with a living soul'. The only art comes from Polly Milton, singing the old songs, and is provided by the impresario Leopold Vincent, whose task is to keep the world 'soft and united'. Whatever its political merits, a world run by the A.B.C. offers a poor home for a writer.

The Kiplings returned from their holiday at the end of March 1912, in the middle of another strike. Here was Demos in action, this time in pursuit of a minimum wage for miners. Kipling suspected foreign influences at work, and predicted that the strikes would be self-defeating, leading to a shift from coal to oil and a new range of fuels. The more urgent threat, however, came from the campaign for Irish Home Rule, demanded by the Nationalists in the south of Ireland and opposed by the Protestants in Ulster. As the Unionists saw it, this was a policy which entailed coercing a quarter of the people of Ireland into giving up their British allegiance. In April 1912, as a third Home Rule Bill was introduced in Parliament, all sides were prepared for a bitter and dangerous struggle.

Kipling was more than ready to play his part. He was close to some of the key players – George Wyndham, Chief Secretary in Ireland under Balfour, was a family friend, while Sir Edward Carson, the leader of the Ulster group in the Commons, had been a neighbour at Rottingdean – but his opinions on the Irish question had not changed since he had attacked the Parnell hearings in 1890. In October 1911 he spent a week visiting Dublin and Belfast: not long, but long enough to confirm his belief that the south was little more than a 'deboshed U.S.', and the north 'a new country of decent folk' (*Letters*, IV.59). On 9 April 1912, as Bonar Law and Carson stood together beneath the largest Union Jack ever made, ready to take the salute from 100,000 Ulster Volunteers, Kipling's poem, 'Ulster', was published in the *Morning Post*, with separate publication arranged for Belfast and New York. The poem was as inflammatory as the timing. It began with a warning that the 'dark eleventh hour' was drawing on, when the honour, laws, and even the lives of Englishmen, were to be sold to the 'traitor'. The result could only be war:

> We know the wars prepared
> For every peaceful home,
> We know the hell prepared
> For such as serve not Rome . . .

A Liberal MP, Joseph Martin, asked whether the poem provided grounds for Kipling to be prosecuted for sedition; the answer was 'No', but Kipling was in no mood to back down, and urged Aitken to get the verses recited in the House, preferably chanted in unison. He could see only two alternatives if the Liberals conceded Home Rule: either they would provoke an English nationalist uprising, comparable to the European revolutions of 1848, or a betrayed Ulster would call for military help from Germany, as the Jacobites in 1688 had summoned help from France. He took heart from the thought that the English were ready to revolt: 'when a decent folk learn at last to rebel against oppression, much may be expected' (*Letters*, IV.203). Nor was he alone in speaking of rebellion. In July 1912 Bonar Law told a Unionist demonstration that he could 'imagine no length of resistance to which Ulster will go' which he would not support. Asquith attacked the speech as furnishing 'a complete grammar of anarchy'; Kipling wholly approved of it.

But while tensions mounted, the ordinary business of family life had to be carried on. John had come to the end of his time at Rottingdean, and a new school had to be found. His poor eyesight denied him any chance of a naval cadetship, and he was entered instead for Wellington College, beginning in September 1911 in the next-to-bottom form and moving up slowly thereafter.[19] In May 1912 Kipling was invited to address the Literary Society there on 'The Possible Advantages of Reading', a task he was relieved to carry out to John's approval; he was ready to pull strings on John's behalf, but he did what he could to lighten his burden as the son of a famous father. Carrie meanwhile continued in poor health. In September 1912 she had to have several fatty tumours removed from her back by the family's surgeon friend, Sir John Bland-Sutton. It was a routine operation, but the experience left her worn out and depressed. Kipling too was feeling run down after a series of painful dental extractions, and with John away at school and Elsie with her governess in Paris, they decided to extend their annual holiday in Engelberg by going on into Egypt.

There were political reasons for wanting to visit the region. In October 1912 war had broken out between Turkey and the countries of the Balkan League, forcing the Turks to surrender most of their European territory. The Ottoman empire was crumbling in the face of nationalist revolts, and Kipling was anxious about the likely effects on India, especially if the instability should extend into the Middle East and threaten the Suez Canal. But the primary aim was to relax, and in February 1913 he and Carrie sailed from Marseilles to Port Said, then travelled down the Nile to Luxor and Aswan, before meeting up in Sudan with Frank Doubleday and his wife Nellie. In South Africa Kipling had written as if history began with the arrival of the white populations, but in Egypt he thrilled to both the landscape and the signs of an ancient culture, much as he had done on his visit to the native states of Rajputana in 1887. He wrote to John and Elsie from the temple of Abu Simbel, with its great statues of Rameses: 'You look up at them and feel a worm. That is all there is to it' (*Letters*, IV.159). Historical interest on a more human scale was provided by an invitation to take tea with the American artist Henry Newman, who had once painted flowers and cathedrals for Ruskin in Tuscany but now divided his time between Florence and Egypt. A less pleasant meeting was with Kitchener, the Consul-General, who had been in the Middle East on and off since 1874, and had little patience with anyone who questioned his proposals. Ever willing to intrigue, Kipling warned Gwynne that his 'butcherly arrogance' – he 'thinks himself a sort of second Rameses' – might harm British interests (*Letters*, IV.174–5).

When Kipling wrote up his visit in *Egypt of the Magicians*, he drew on his memories of India. The Sudanese, like the Indians, would demand self-government, forgetful of what the British had done to stabilise their country, according to the 'hard law' that 'if you give any man anything that he has not painfully earned for himself, you infallibly make him or his descendants your devoted enemies'. But Kipling's tone is mainly enthusiastic. Whether he is presenting himself as an experienced traveller, or as a tourist shuffling along under the direction of a guide, his sense of colour and light is as acute as ever:

> the glorious ritual of the Eastern dawn went forward. Some reed of the river bank revealed itself by reflection, black on silver; arched wings flapped and jarred the still water to splintered glass; the desert ridge turned to topaz, and the four figures [the statues of Rameses] stood clear, yet without shadowing, from their background. The stronger light flooded them red from head to toe, and they became alive . . .

For a time at least, his bitter mood had lightened. Even modern Cairo, dismissively introduced as 'an unkempt place', transforms itself into a 'Sorceress', dancing before him in the heart-breaking likeness of every city he had ever loved. There is however one dark, Hobbesian passage, in the letter on 'The Riddle of Empire'. Here Kipling reflects that fifteen years earlier the Sudan had been 'one crazy hell of murder, torture, and lust'; but 'at the battle of Omdurman the land was reduced to sanity by applied death on such a scale as the murderers and torturers at their most unbridled could scarcely have dreamed'. That battle, in September 1898, cost the lives of 11,000 Dervishes; few Englishmen had questioned the necessity for a decisive British victory, but fewer still could have written of a nation 'reduced to sanity by applied death'. The thought anticipates W. H. Auden's reference, in 'Spain' (1937), to the 'conscious acceptance of the necessary murder'. Auden later retracted his words; Kipling would have seen no reason to retract his.[20]

On their return to England, Kipling had business to attend to with Doubleday, who was to oversee the Seven Seas edition of his work, the American counterpart to Macmillan's Bombay edition. There were decisions to be made about the typeface, the use of the swastika imprint and the colour of the binding, as well as plans for *A Diversity of Creatures*, scheduled to appear in October 1914. He had also written a curtain-raiser, the one-act *The Harbour Watch*, first produced at the Royalty Theatre in April 1913, though he did not care for it enough to join Carrie and the children when they went to see it (he took them instead to a music-hall). In addition, he was determined to keep up the running battle with the publishers of pirate editions, with Watt threatening legal action, and Doubleday underselling the pirates. His efforts almost certainly cost him more money than he saved, but the only way to calm his anger was to follow up even the most trivial cases.

He and Carrie paid an occasional visit to Trix, who was making slow progress at a home in Scarborough. They were more worried about John's future. In May 1913 he failed the Army medical examination because of his poor eyesight, and the uncertainty affected both his health and his academic performance. Then in the summer he was laid up in the school sanatorium with glandular fever, prompting further parental warnings about the dangers of 'beastliness'. Bland-Sutton diagnosed a thickening of the thyroid gland, forbade running, and in November operated on John's tonsils. Kipling continued to shower his son with presents, including a motor-bike, while reminding him that he was 'a young man now, not a boy and must act accordingly'.[21] But he remained unsettled, and in March 1914 it was agreed that he should leave Wellington for a 'crammer' at Bournemouth, in preparation for his entrance examination to Sandhurst. At John's age, Kipling had just begun his stint in Lahore, and he could not help making comparisons: 'One sees oneself and yet *not* oneself looking and talking at one and its [sic] difficult to know how much is heredity and how much is the independent new soul' (*Letters*, IV.225). One display of independence came in July 1914 when John chose to be baptised into the Church of England. Perhaps his mind had been deepened by the threat of war; perhaps he wanted to impress his parents that he had indeed become a man, and put away childish things. There is no record of what Kipling thought of the decision. In retrospect, it must have seemed a timely rite of passage.

Through 1913 and into the summer of 1914, Kipling continued to watch political events with increasing fury. The news that Sir Rufus Isaacs was to be made Lord Chief Justice, only months after he had been implicated in the Marconi scandal, prompted his poem 'Gehazi', as well as a more general swipe at his enemies: 'As to the Liberals. My insular mind hasn't got further than saying: – "Thank God they ain't white." After all a Jew lawyer and a Welsh solicitor and Jack Johnson and rabbits are much of a muchness' (*Letters*, IV.181).[22] His disquiet at the situation in Europe was reflected in an invasion story, 'The Edge of the Evening', in December 1913. It includes as much farce as adventure, but the accompanying poem, 'Rebirth', is a grimmer piece, part Hardy, part Henley. It begins by imagining the world as it might be if a loving God chose to restore it, but ends by insisting that 'we are what we are' :

> So long subdued
> To sacrifice, that threadbare Death commands
> Hardly observance at our busier hands.

The Christmas holiday, in Engelberg and Paris, was quietly restorative, but Kipling's mind was turned towards Ireland, where volunteer forces in both the north and south were buying in arms from abroad. From Vernet-les-Bains, where he and Carrie were taking the waters, he added his signature to the British Covenant, published in *The Times* on 3 March 1914. This declared that if the Home Rule Bill were passed without a referendum or a general election, the signers would feel justified in taking 'any action that may be effective to prevent it being put into operation, and more particularly to prevent the armed forces of the Crown being used to deprive the people of Ulster of their rights as citizens of the United Kingdom'. A fortnight later, army officers at the Curragh demanded and were given the right to absent themselves from duty rather than move against the Ulstermen. Encouraged rather than deterred, Kipling addressed a rally in Tunbridge Wells, warning that Nationalist rule promised 'a despotism of secret societies, a government of denunciation by day and terrorism by night'. Published by the *Daily Express* as 'Rudyard Kipling's Indictment of the Government', the speech was widely sold at the news-stalls. On 21 May he brought out 'The Covenant', reminding Unionists of 'that last right which our forefathers claimed / When their Law failed them and its stewards were bought'. He did not use the words, but there could be no doubt that Kipling was urging the right to armed resistance.[23]

Attempts to work out a compromise, by which Ulster could opt out of Home Rule for a period of six years, foundered on protests from Unionists that this would be merely a stay of execution, and from Nationalists that such a measure would frustrate their demand for a united Ireland. Kipling himself had gone too far to draw back from the line separating protest from rebellion. If, as he predicted, events in Ulster were 'the first adumbration of the military power that invariably evolves itself out of a tyrannical democracy' (*Letters*, IV.240), he would have to stand with the new military power. Both he and Carrie anticipated a civil war; in June, Carrie joined a committee to look after the expected flood of women and children refugees. The following month British troops opened fire on a rioting crowd in Dublin, killing three and injuring many more. Then, only days later, affairs in Ireland were overshadowed by the outbreak of conflict across Europe. Kipling was not called upon to be a rebel. Rather than a civil war, England was to be engaged in a war of national defence.

9
The Great War and After

On 4 August 1914, as Britain declared itself at war with Germany, the Kiplings were at Kessingland Grange, on the Suffolk coast. Writing within earshot of the guns out at sea, Rudyard felt 'proud of the way in which England has bucked up at the pinch' (*Letters*, IV.250). He was proud too of John, who was eager to be among the first volunteers, but at the Army medical examination his eyesight again let him down. Kipling appealed to Lord Roberts, who was able to secure him a commission in the Irish Guards, a regiment which drew from both the Protestant and Catholic communities. John was promptly signed up as a Second Lieutenant, and on 14 September reported for duty at Warley Barracks in Essex.

The news was already worrying: reports of German atrocities in Belgium, the retreat of the British Expeditionary Force from Mons. The German army had since withdrawn to the River Aisne; barely six weeks into the war, the first trenches were being built. Over the next twelve months the family kept a proud but anxious watch as John undertook his training, seeing him whenever they could, and marvelling at his sudden maturity. 'We talked, and we talked, *and* we talked – this grown up man of the world and I', Kipling wrote to Elsie, assuring her that John got on well with his men: 'he talks to 'em when he can which is one of the great secrets of command' (*Letters*, IV.257–8). Evidently John had slipped easily into the paternalist manner adopted by most officers, even those who were still in their teens; his father had either forgotten the theory he had once given Mulvaney to express, that an inexperienced officer was the best to work with, 'on account of the surpassin' innocence av the choild', or was too proud of his son to mention it.

Meanwhile he was busy with his own tasks. On 2 September his poem 'For All We Have and Are' was published in *The Times*:

> For all we have and are,
> For all our children's fate,
> Stand up and take the war.
> The Hun is at the gate!

Bernard Bergonzi objects that the poem relishes the onset of war; Jon Silkin complains that Kipling failed to see how bloody it would be, or how long it would last.[1] Both criticisms are unfair. The poem describes the earth as 'sickened' by the cry for war, not as rejoicing in it. It is true that Kipling was stirred at the thought of 'mankind' united against a 'crazed and driven foe' (in his view the Germans stood outside mankind), but this is part of a wider recognition that the war would be a contest between nations rather than between armies. Nor did he underestimate the suffering it would involve; his guess, that it would last three years, was nearer than most, and he knew from the outset that John was likely to be among the casualties. Silkin also remarks that Kipling could never have written Wilfred Owen's line, 'I am the enemy you killed, my friend.' No doubt he could not; perhaps it was easier for a combatant to write than for the father of one. But such reflections could have no place in a poem intended to encourage the nation, at a time when it needed volunteers. There was 'one task for all', combatants and civilians alike, and that was to strengthen the war effort.

Kipling was once again speaking for the national mood. He had no doubt that the war was the outcome of plans laid over many years, but it was also the expression of an atavistic and ultimately self-destructive desire buried deep in the German national character:

> They paid the price to reach their goal
> Across a world in flame;
> But their own hate slew their own soul
> Before that victory came.[2]

Over the next few months he spoke in aid of the recruitment drive, visited Indian and Canadian troops in their barracks, and entered into an intense correspondence with his friends in America. He refused to plead for American intervention, except as a matter of self-interest – he warned Roosevelt that a German victory would mean German domination by land and sea across the Eastern hemisphere[3] – but he demanded that the Americans condemn the atrocities in Belgium: to remain silent in the face of such brutality was to commit 'moral suicide' (*Letters*, IV.372). This was the argument of his poem, 'The Neutral':

> If it be found, when the battle clears,
>   Their death has set me free,
> Then how shall I live with myself through the years
>   Which they have bought for me?

In the *Definitive Edition* the poem appears as 'The Question', but a note makes plain its meaning, and its target: 'Attitude of the United States of America during the first two years, seven months and four days of the Great War.'

Kipling was also involved more formally in the propaganda effort. His tour of army barracks was the basis for a series of articles on 'The New Army in Training' for the *Daily Telegraph*, where his theme was the coming together of men from different classes and regions, even different parts of the Empire, in a common cause, though he also noted the hostility of those who had enlisted to those who had not.[4] Back at Bateman's, Carrie and Elsie joined thousands of other women in knitting socks and gloves. Most of the young men they knew were at the front; some were already dead or wounded. Asked why John had joined the Army when there was no compulsion to do so, Carrie bravely replied: 'Precisely *because* there is no compulsion.'[5] But the strain was beginning to tell. Rudyard was ill with neuralgia, Carrie with neuritis, and on the recommendation of Bland-Sutton they went in March 1915 to Bath, where Carrie could try the waters. Rudyard spent his time visiting the hospitals, where he listened to the stories of Canadian and Australian soldiers, and relaxed when he could by reading Jane Austen.

On their return journey, they met up in London with John, by now impatient to get to France. In the event, Rudyard got there before him, leaving in August with Perceval Landon for a two-week tour of the French lines to gather material for a series of articles, *France at War*.[6] He was astonished at his reception; everyone seemed to know his work, and want to shake his hand. The visit excited him – at one point, he noted, he was within the length of a cricket pitch of the German trenches – but it also left him exhausted. The signs of war were everywhere: the fields bleached yellow by gas, the statuary at Rheims cathedral 'burned the colour of raw flesh' by incendiary shells, the trenchwork 'a white-hot gash . . . all across France'. Soon his son would be caught up in it. But the devastation was visible evidence of 'the all-embracing vileness of the Boche', and the reason the French would not be defeated: 'Their business is war, and they do their business.'[7]

Kipling was still in France when John went to Bateman's to take leave of his mother. Carrie wrote in her diary: 'He looks very straight and smart and brave and young as he turned at the top of the stairs to say "Send my love to Daddo".' Two days later, on his eighteenth birthday, he was in France. His letters home were reassuringly cheerful, mostly thanks for one parcel or pleas for another ('3 front studs & 3 back studs; also another pair of pyjamas'), interspersed with grumbles about the weather. Rudyard tried to match his son's mood, and to pass on advice, including the use of rabbit-wire to protect trenches against grenades – a suggestion John thought 'rather quaint', and in any case prohibited under standing-orders.[8] Then on 25 September, after a night march of 18 miles through the rain, he wrote that he had been ordered to the front-line trenches, as part of 'THE great effort to break through & end the war.'[9] On 27 September, with No. 2 Company of the Second Battalion of the Irish Guards, he advanced on Chalk Pit Woods, north of Loos, and was killed. The attack continued for three weeks, at the cost of 16,000 British soldiers killed, and 25,000 wounded, most of them shot down by machine-gun fire. All the British had achieved was a narrow salient some two miles deep. The battle in which John Kipling died was a German victory.

Precisely how he died is uncertain. One of Kipling's 'Epitaphs of the War' reflects what he wanted to believe:

> My son was killed while laughing at some jest. I would I knew
> What it was, and it might serve me in a time when jests are few.

The laughter is unlikely. Rider Haggard was told later by a Guardsman wounded in the same action that he had seen John with his face shattered by a piece of shell, but wisely kept this to himself.[10] The news that reached the Kiplings, on 2 October, was only that he was 'missing'. Since his body had not been found, they could cling to the possibility that he had survived and been taken prisoner, but as the months went by they had to give up hope.[11] Rudyard wrote to Dunsterville: 'It was a short life. I'm sorry that all the year's work ended in that one afternoon but – lots of people are in our position and it's something to have bred a man' (*Letters*, IV.345). He made no mention of John's death in his autobiography, but he did commemorate it in a poem, 'My Boy Jack':[12]

> 'Have you news of my boy Jack?'
> *Not this tide.*
> 'When d'you think that he'll come back?'
> *Not with this wind blowing, and this tide. . . .*

> 'Oh dear, what comfort can I find?'
>   *None this tide,*
>   *Nor any tide,*
> *Except he did not shame his kind –*
>   *Not even with that wind blowing, and that tide.*

In the *Definitive Edition* the note of personal loss is muted by the date attached to the title: 1914–18, not 27 September 1915. If John did not shame his kind, no more did those who died with him.

For the next few months the Kiplings kept to themselves. Rudyard avoided public engagements, but he continued to work on six articles for the *Daily Telegraph* on the North Sea and East Coast patrols. Like his account of the New Army, they were a celebration of unity and continuity, as men of different classes and professions, but all of them 'lineal descendants' of those who had fought with Nelson, willingly exchanged their civilian roles to fight a common enemy.[13] *Tales of 'The Trade'*, based on reports submitted to the Admiralty by submarine commanders, was similarly designed to publicise the results of naval operations. Faced with the difficulty of having his material at second-hand, Kipling took the brevity of the reports as a sign of British insouciance, and that in turn as a guarantee of their truth, since 'no pallid writer of fiction' would dare be so sparing of emotional detail.[14] One truth he insisted on was that the British never wittingly took the life of any non-combatant; unlike the Germans, they retained their moral codes even beneath the waves.[15] A third series of essays, *Destroyers at Jutland*, was intended to reassure the public that the Battle of Jutland, the only full-scale encounter between the British and German fleets, had been a success – something which the communications issued by the Admiralty had left in doubt. Though he spoke to some of those who had taken part, he was unable to penetrate the 'inevitable confusions and misreckonings of time, shape, and distance' over the 'illimitable grey waters'; all he could say was that the Service had achieved 'at the lowest, something of a victory'.[16] If British successes had been underestimated, as he allowed himself to hint, it was enough that the Germans knew the extent of their own losses.

Kipling's reputation, as well as his experience as a journalist, meant that he was inundated by requests for articles.[17] Some of these he declined, the more readily when he disliked the person who invited him, including one from Churchill to write about the munitions industry.[18] He was happier to write *The Eyes of Asia*, which evolved from letters sent home by Indian troops in France and made available to him through the censorship system and the India Office. It was a timely contribution, following as it did the failure of the campaign in Mesopotamia, where 13,000 British and Indian troops had been forced to surrender to the Turks at the end of April 1916. Predictably, however, Kipling was not among those who thought that India's massive contribution to the war effort – 62,000 Indian troops died in battle or of disease, more than from any other part of the empire – should be rewarded by moving closer to Indian self-rule.

Elsewhere too the war was going badly. In June he wrote to André Chevrillon that in choosing to offer themselves as 'a sacrifice for mankind' rather than 'perish in the spirit', the Allies had made 'the most tremendous affirmation of the immanent goodness of man's soul that Earth has ever known' (*Letters*, IV.378). Nine days later, however, on 1 July 1916, as the Allies began the 'Big Push' on the Somme, there was to be 'sacrifice' on a scale hitherto unthinkable, as 19,000 men marched to their deaths in a single day, over three times the number killed in action in South Africa; before the campaign petered out in the November mud, British losses had reached 420,000. By then Lloyd George had succeeded Kitchener as Secretary for War; in December he became Prime Minister. Max Aitken, who had campaigned against Asquith in the *Daily Express*, was duly rewarded with a peerage, and the Kiplings spent Christmas 1916 with the new Lord Beaverbrook. There was little else, a year on from John's death, for them to celebrate.

The propaganda work provided some relief, but there were other tasks at hand besides writing. An offer to allow Bateman's to be used as a hospital had been declined, but from May 1916 the Dudwell Farmhouse provided a temporary haven for wounded or shell-shocked soldiers, except when Trix stayed there for three months in 1917 – a visit which taxed to the limit Carrie's short supply of patience for her. Troops were occasionally billeted at the house, and after John's death there were regular visits from his friends, including Oliver Baldwin, Kipling's second cousin, who followed him into the Irish Guards in 1917. Invalids and friends alike found themselves asked to make up 'Kipling Scrapbooks', compiled from popular magazines and sent to the wounded in hospital. Meanwhile work continued on the farm, with the Rye Green Farmhouse used to accommodate an often difficult workforce of 'some twelve women and three small babies' (*Letters*, IV.384). Kipling drew on a quarrel among the women when he came to write 'The Wish House', but it was Carrie who had to dismiss one of those involved, and to deal with the task of running a farm of 200 acres. Even a calm and contented woman might have found it a heavy burden, and Carrie was neither.

In January 1917 Kipling agreed to write a history of John's regiment, the Irish Guards, an act of familial piety of a kind which in happier times might have fallen to the son, not the father. Until it was finished, five years later, he found it difficult to return to fiction. In April, however, he brought out the long-delayed *A Diversity of Creatures*.[19] The *Athenaeum* admired 'As Easy as A.B.C.', but thought the volume lacked 'the fundamental seriousness' of his earlier work; of the two stories written in the first year of the war, 'Swept and Garnished' and 'Mary Postgate', only the former is even mentioned.[20] Yet it is hard to imagine that Kipling ever wrote more seriously.

'Swept and Garnished' is the story of Frau Ebermann, a Berlin *haus-frau* who has never questioned the rightness of the war. While she is feverish with influenza, she is disturbed in her comfortable flat by the spectres of Belgian children killed during the German advance. She insists that their deaths must have come about by accident; she has her son's word that the German army has behaved impeccably. Kipling hints rather than states the horror that breaks her complacency. One of the rumoured atrocities was that German soldiers had cut off the Belgian boys' right arms, so that they would be unable to fight. When one of the boys cries as his sister plucks his sleeve, Frau Ebermann complains that it is inconsiderate of him to disturb her in her sick-room. 'Oh, but look, lady!' says the girl: 'Frau Ebermann looked and saw.' The story ends with her frantic attempt to clean the blood from the floor, and her instruction to her maid to find the children 'and give them cakes to stop the bleeding'.

'Mary Postgate' is a more elusive story. The companion of Miss Fowler, Mary is 'a treasure at domestic accounts', with a mind which does not allow itself to dwell on unpleasant things. The chief event of her life has been the arrival of Miss Fowler's nephew Wynn, 'an unlovely orphan of eleven'. She is content to be his 'butt and slave', meeting his endless demands on her, and acting as his intermediary with Miss Fowler. With the outbreak of war, he joins the Flying Corps; thereafter Mary's 'heart and interest' are 'high in the air with Wynn'. When the news arrives of his death in a trial flight, she reacts calmly: 'It's a great pity he didn't die in action after he had killed somebody.' After the funeral, she prepares to burn his things, 'deadly methodical' as usual. Going into the village for paraffin, she can 'almost' hear the beat of his propellers overhead, but it is misty and there is 'nothing to see'. She is with the village nurse when they hear 'a gun, they fancied', behind the Royal Oak; moments later they find the 'ripped and torn body' of the publican's daughter. It is Mary who concludes that a bomb has been dropped; the doctor speaks of an accident, due to the collapse of a stable. Kipling leaves the events ambiguous, allowing the reader either to take them at face value, or to suspect that at some point the external world drops away, and all that is left is Mary's fantasy.

As she burns Wynn's things (Kipling itemises them relentlessly), she sees a man sitting injured at the foot of a tree. Mary assumes that he is a German airman fallen from his plane, but again there are conflicting clues; he wears a uniform like Wynn's, and asks her for help in broken French, not German. But she knows that Wynn was a gentleman, who could never have caused a child's body to be torn into 'vividly coloured strips and strings. But this thing hunched under the oak-tree had done that thing.' Refusing to find a doctor, she fetches a revolver from the house, and waits for him to die, while working at the bonfire:

> Her long pleasure was broken by a sound that she had waited for in agony several times in her life. She leaned forward and listened, smiling. There could be no mistake. She closed her eyes and drank it in. . . . 'That's all right', said she contentedly, and went up to the house, where she scandalised the whole routine by taking a luxurious bath before tea, and came down looking, as Miss Fowler said when she saw her lying all relaxed on the other sofa, 'quite handsome!'

Oliver Baldwin called this the most wicked story ever written; others have argued that it shows not how the Germans should be treated, but how one woman feels about them – though the poem appended to the story, which explains how 'the English began to hate' makes this defence less persuasive. Yet its real centre is Mary herself, for whom the war has become wholly personal, an opportunity to let loose the mix of feelings she has towards Wynn – sexual frustration, anger at his taunting of her, even a parodic maternal attentiveness – on the airman who becomes his surrogate. Despite its reputation, 'Mary Postgate' is not without compassion; read alongside 'Swept and Garnished', it stands as another of Kipling's explorations of the nearness of love and hate, and of the inability of even the most orderly mind to keep them at bay. One can only guess with what feelings Rudyard and Carrie must have read it when it was first published, in September 1915, the month of John's death.

The stalemate on the Western Front continued throughout 1917, but the year brought one satisfaction. In February, Germany decided to resume unrestricted submarine warfare; a month later, the text of the Zimmermann telegram was made public; it included Germany's offer to

Mexico of financial support to recapture the territory ceded to the USA in 1848. The two events together pushed America to enter the war in April 1917, albeit in the semi-detached role of an 'associated power' rather than an 'ally'. Ignoring these subtleties, Kipling responded with a poem, 'The Choice', in which the American Spirit rejoices at the chance to 'recover the road we lost / In the drugged and doubting years'.[21]

With America now engaged in the war, the role of peacemaker devolved to the Vatican. Under Pope Benedict XV, Rome had maintained a policy of neutrality, and was consequently mistrusted by both sides. Kipling was invited to Italy by the English Ambassador, Sir Rennell Rodd, who wanted to counter British scepticism about the Italian commitment to the Entente. Kipling too had his doubts – Italy had entered the war late, and then only against Austria-Hungary, and on the promise of large chunks of Hapsburg territory – but he was eager to see the Italian war effort at first-hand, as well as to learn more about the Vatican's intentions. In May 1917, again with Landon, he left for a two-week tour.

Once in Rome he was then taken to meet an English cardinal, Francis Gasquet. Kipling had some liking for Roman Catholic priests – in 'The Record of Badalia Herodsfoot', as in *Kim*, it is the Catholic priest who understands human nature, not his Anglican counterpart – but his meetings with the Roman hierarchy left him uneasy; he wrote to Carrie that this was 'the d—dest queerest trap-doorest world I've ever got into' (*Letters*, IV.455). Nothing in Rome was what it seemed, and he was relieved to escape to the Dolomites and the campaign against the Austrians. The Italians were good hosts, and he admired their roads, and their soldiers – 'bigger men than you'd expect . . . with the swing of Roman legionaries'. General Cadorna, in command of the Italian forces, said what the generals always said, that sacrifice had united the country. Kipling was more impressed by his meeting with King Victor Emmanuel III, 'a man of affairs and knowledge *and* guts', who had chosen to spend the war at the front (*Letters*, IV.458–61).

He left on the eve of the tenth battle of Isonzo, persuaded that the Italians were a hard, fighting race, not the excitable Latins of popular fiction. Events did little to justify his confidence; the tenth battle proved little more than a prelude to the rout at Caporetto in October, when the Italians suffered 40,000 casualties, and lost 650,000 men through capture or desertion.[22] His suspicions about Vatican policy, however, seemed to be confirmed when in August 1917 the Pope again urged 'peace without victory'. Kipling responded with a poem, 'A Song at Cock-Crow', comparing the policy of neutrality to Peter's denial of Christ:

> The next time that Peter denièd his Lord
> 'Twas Earth in her agony waited his word.
> But he sat by his fire and naught would he do,
> Though the cock crew – . . .[23]

He wrote to Roosevelt that Rome's supposed neutrality was merely a cover for 'steady, unflinching and unscrupulous opposition' to the Entente, since the defeat of Austria would 'mean ruin for the Papacy materially and morally'. Catholic opposition to conscription in Ireland, even with the promise that it would be enforced only after the introduction of Home Rule, was merely a local instance of the way the Papacy had become 'civilization's great enemy' (*Letters*, IV.488).[24]

Kipling intended to stir up controversy with 'A Song at Cock-Crow'. He could afford to publish such work, he told Rider Haggard, because he had 'nothing to gain or lose from anyone'.[25] His determination to protect his independence had already led him to refuse a KCB in 1899 and a KCMG in 1903. On his return from Italy he found that he had been proposed, without his knowledge, for the new Order of the Companions of Honour, and this too he declined.[26] He could only write a poem like 'Mesopotamia', attacking those who had mismanaged the campaign, if he stayed outside the Establishment which gave them their posts. In the same spirit he resigned from the Society of Authors when it passed a resolution requiring its members to contribute to charity books only if they had been approved by the Society; his freedom was not to be compromised. He did agree to join the Rhodes Trust, but he was an awkward presence, opposing the award of scholarships to candidates who had not fought in the war, or who as married men would be unable to take a full part in Oxford college life. He was glad to resign in 1925, in protest at the appointment of Philip Kerr as Trust Secretary. Kerr had worked with Milner in South Africa, but Kipling thought him too liberal to be the vehicle for Rhodes's ideas.

He also became a member of the Imperial War Graves Commission. Once it was decided not to repatriate the bodies of servicemen but to bury them as near as possible to where they fell, commemorating them by name on a memorial or headstone, it was Kipling who chose from Ecclesiasticus the words for Lutyens's Stone of Remembrance, 'Their name liveth for evermore', and for those graves for which a name could not be found: 'A Soldier of the Great War Known unto God'. He strongly supported the most controversial of the Commission's principles, that the headstones should be uniform in size and shape, making no distinction for rank or social position. The need to recognise equality of sacrifice was the subject of the first of his 'Epitaphs of the War':

> A. 'I was a Have.' B. 'I was a "have-not".'
> (*Together.*) 'What hast thou given which I gave not?'

Kipling served the Commission unstintingly, attending numerous meetings, writing a pamphlet, *The Graves of the Fallen*, to explain the Commission's work, and playing a part in the decision to build the Indian war memorial at Brighton. After the war he made regular visits to the cemeteries as they were built; like those of many others, his holidays became acts of personal and national pilgrimage.

His attitudes had hardened as the war continued. In January 1918, as the Lords were debating the bill which would grant the vote to eight million women, he was at work on 'The Song of the Lathes', imagined as the words to a tune hummed by a war-widow at her work:

> Man's hate passes as his love will pass.
> God made Woman what she always was.
> Them that bear the burden they will never grant forgiveness
>   So long as they are here!

It was an old theme with him, but there was no sign that his own hate would pass, and no hint of forgiveness. His constant fear was that the politicians would stop short of an unequivocal victory, and he took every opportunity to attack those who argued for negotiation. He speculated to Almwroth Wright on the inherent masochism of those who sought peace, which made them respond to brutality with an interest amounting to sympathy; pacifism, he suggested, was a form of sickness, which should be dealt with 'scientifically', just as Wright would deal with his patients at a clinic (*Letters*, IV.420–2). He claimed that his view of the Germans was similarly informed by scientific detachment: 'Our concern with [the Hun] is precisely the same as our concern with the germs of any malignant disease . . . we clean out, sterilize, flush down, etc. etc. all places where they can get a foothold' (*Letters*, IV.405).[27] In reality his feeling was of hatred, passing into obsession. In 1918, on holiday in Cornwall, he was disappointed when a 'party of Huns – dog and three dry bitches' escaped a mob attacking their boarding house, and pleased when 'a Hun by the name of Waechter, with a bitch' was refused permission to stay at the hotel – this despite the fact that Waechter was eighty years old, and had been naturalised in 1865, the year of his own birth.[28] He and Carrie shared the instincts of those who wanted to revoke the citizenship of naturalised Germans: once a Hun, always a Hun.

Even the recognition that the war was in its final months did little to raise his spirits. He was persuaded that the nation was threatened by conspiracies, of Germans, Irishmen, Jews and Bolsheviks, in every combination, with the Catholic Church and the Germans working together in Ireland to undermine the Union, and in America to foment anti-British feeling. When it was declared that the goal of British policy in India was 'the gradual development of self-governing institutions with a view to the progressive realisation of responsible government' – in plain language, to allow a few steps towards self-rule – Kipling suspected the Jews as well as the Huns. Edwin Montagu, the Indian Secretary of State, he noted, was a 'Yid', and racially incapable of understanding the Empire (*Letters*, IV.509).[29] His earlier writing had been notably free from the casual anti-Semitism of so many of his contemporaries, but no longer. He blamed the publication in the *Daily Telegraph* of a letter arguing for a negotiated peace on the fact that 'the proprietor is a Hebrew . . . suffering from cold feet. It *is* a Semitic complaint' (*Letters*, IV.474). Labour unrest in the aftermath of the war was the work of 'the Hun, the Bolshevik and the Jew of Poland chiefly' (*Letters*, IV.572); he told Rider Haggard that 'we owe all our Russian troubles, and many others, to the machinations of the Jews'. On this occasion Haggard disagreed with his friend, preferring to blame the trade unions.[30]

The armistice signed on 11 November was technically a cessation of hostilities, much less than the victory Kipling wanted.[31] In his poem, 'Justice', syndicated in 200 papers across the country, he demanded that 'Evil Incarnate' be held to account 'till the end of time'. But a Germany crushed for all time could hardly make the reparations that were being demanded; more than that, there were fears that keeping Germany poor might increase the appeal of Bolshevism, and destabilise international trade. Whatever might be said at the hustings, the desire for retribution was in conflict with the demands of self-interest. Unsurprisingly, revenge proved a stronger motive than reason, with consequences which were to make themselves felt in the 1930s, but it was still not enough for Kipling. He and Carrie felt John's death all the more now that the war was over. One of the 'Epitaphs of the War', 'Common Form', suggests a deep underlying hopelessness:

> If any question why we died,
> Tell them, because our fathers lied.

With John dead, it was difficult to look forward, and hard not to look back with a sense of defeat, rather than victory.

A bitter peace

Two weeks after the armistice, Kipling wrote that 'One feels as if one were just coming out of an anaesthetic – before things had adjusted themselves to sight and hearing' (*Letters*, IV.522). There was much he did not want to adjust to. The politicians charged with the peace process were no better and no wiser than those who had made 'a barricade of the dead bodies of the nation's youth', and they had lost his confidence.[32] He thought Lloyd George corrupt and Woodrow Wilson an arid schoolmaster, too detached from reality to be an effective national leader. He was eager to see America play a larger role in world affairs, but under Wilson America was ready to claim the moral high ground but not to bear the costs of leadership. The problem with the League of Nations, Kipling wrote to Doubleday, was that it required 'an adequate force of police to watch the chief offender, and up to the present the U.S.A. don't seem inclined to help police the Hun border' (*Letters*, IV.548). In his pre-war invasion story, 'The Edge of the Evening', one of the characters suggests that the real America had died at Gettysburg, since when the country had been swamped with immigrants, and under 'a Government of the alien, by the alien, for the alien'. It had become his own opinion.

His deepest resentments were reserved for affairs in India and Ireland. Soldiers returning to India after 1918 found the country changed. Trade with the United States and Japan had increased, as had industrialisation; there were also food shortages, a 'flu pandemic and high inflation. All these added to the pressure for constitutional change. Ghandi had urged Indians to support the war as a means to prove their right to self-determination; they had done so, and expected to be heard. Discontent with the slow pace of reform led to sporadic rioting and some violence, and on 13 April 1919 a large crowd gathered in Amritsar in defiance of a curfew. Brigadier-General Rex Dyer ordered his troops to open fire; ten minutes later 379 Indians lay dead or dying, with more than a thousand wounded. The massacre was followed by a number of public floggings, and other humiliations.

In Dyer's view, as in that of his supporters on the political right, a strong man had taken strong action. His opponents criticised his conduct as illegal and excessive. They added, in the Parliamentary debate which followed, that India was to be governed by co-operation, not by the sword, and not as of right. The position announced by Fitzjames Stephen, and echoed by the Punjab Club, that British authority in India was non-negotiable, was being abandoned, and with it the basis of Kipling's views on the country of his birth. Despite a campaign in the *Morning Post*, to which Kipling contributed, Dyer was forced to resign his commission. There was to be one last imperial extravaganza, the inauguration of New Delhi as the British capital in India in 1931, but the tide had turned in favour of constitutional reform, and moves were already being made which would lead to the Government of India Act of 1935. Kipling became a Vice-President of the India Defence League, set up to oppose the Act, but he must have known it was a lost cause.

Political events in Ireland added to his bitterness. Legislation conceding Home Rule for all Ireland had finally been passed in September 1914. The operation of the Act had been suspended until the war was over, and it was planned to introduce an 'Amending Bill' to accommodate Ulster's fears, but the Easter Rising in Dublin in 1916 had shown that the demand now was for independence rather than Home Rule. In the General Election of 1918 Sinn Féin won 73 out of 79 seats in the south, set up an Irish legislature, and declared an independent Irish Republic. The Irish Volunteers, now the Irish Republican Army, began a campaign of terror against those they suspected of complicity with the British, prompting equally savage reprisals from the newly recruited Black and Tans. Yet another Home Rule bill, allowing for separate assemblies in Belfast and Dublin, failed to stop the violence, but in July 1921 a truce was arranged and negotiations begun towards an Anglo-Irish Treaty. With Ulster excluded, this gave to the 26 southern counties of Ireland the constitutional status of the Dominion of Canada: that is, its own army and navy, and control of its affairs at home and abroad, subject to an oath of allegiance to the Crown and membership of the Commonwealth. There was more violence to follow, but the Union for which in 1914 Kipling had been ready to rebel was effectively at an end.

Kipling regarded the Irish Free State as the forerunner of the 'Free States of Evil' which he predicted throughout the Empire. The treaty left him deeply depressed, and put an abrupt end to his friendship with Beaverbrook, who had supported it. Of his other friends, two had recently died, Jameson in 1917, and Roosevelt in 1919. There were other deaths to come to terms with. Carrie's mother, Anna Balestier, also died in 1919; despite the geographical distance, the two had stayed close over the years, and it was a hard loss for Carrie to bear, made no easier by the discovery that Beatty had spent most of their mother's money. A year later came the death of Georgiana Burne-Jones, still, despite her resistance to Kipling's political views, the Beloved Aunt. It was perhaps because they both felt the need to keep open a channel to the past that Kipling took Carrie to Southsea in February 1920, showing her for the first time the scenes of his childhood unhappiness.

There continued to be a steady stream of visitors to Bateman's, including men who had known John, or could advise Kipling on his history of the Irish Guards. One new acquaintance was T. E. Lawrence. They liked each other well enough for Kipling to read the typescript of *The Seven Pillars of Wisdom* in 1922, but there were matters on which they could not agree: Kipling was suspicious of Arab nationalism, Lawrence unhappy with the deal between Britain and France that would give Syria to the French and not, as he had promised, to the Emir Feisal. It was not easy to get past Kipling's reserve; Rider Haggard recalled him saying, 'grimly', that he could count those he cared for on his fingers, and found it difficult to make new friends.[33]

Elsie, meanwhile, was trying to do exactly that. Her 'coming out' season in 1914 had been disrupted by the war; aged 22 at its end, she had time to make up. Like her parents, she delighted in the occasional visits of Oliver Baldwin, who brought an unaccustomed gaiety into the house. Engaging but erratic, he was eventually to disappoint them in the role of surrogate son, not only becoming a socialist but living openly as a homosexual. It was through Oliver that Elsie met George Bambridge, who came with him to Bateman's in November 1919. An Old Etonian, ex-Irish Guards, and subsequently attaché at the British embassy in Madrid, he was an obviously suitable if unexciting partner. Her parents accepted rather than welcomed the relationship; the thought that Elsie would one day leave home filled Carrie especially with dread. The years ahead began to look increasingly lonely.

Preoccupied with his work for the War Graves Commission, and his research for the Irish Guards volume, Kipling found it hard to return to fiction. His sales had increased during the war to around 1500 volumes a week, but in 1919 they began to drop back to the pre-war level of about 1200 a week. When Macmillan suggested that some falling-off was to be expected, he wrote angrily to Watt, complaining that the publishers were failing to develop 'an extraordinarily valuable property', and demanding action (*Letters*, IV.588). For the time being, however, he could give them nothing new to work with, and they had to make do with another book postponed by the war, the *Letters of Travel (1892–1913)*, which appeared in 1920.

His prickliness is understandable. Earlier in the year, he had published his first volume of verse since 1903, *The Years Between*, to find himself described in the *Athenaeum* review as 'a neglected celebrity'.[34] The reviewer was T. S. Eliot, and in relation to the poetry it was a fair assessment. The 'Epitaphs' were being published for the first time, but most of the poems looked back to quarrels that had long since moved on to different ground: 'The Covenant' and 'Ulster' to the years when it still seemed possible to resist Irish Home Rule, 'Gehazi' to the Marconi scandal, 'The Rowers' to a dispute in 1902 about the collection of debts from Venezuela. The difficulty with such poems, Eliot argued, and the reason the 'conversational intelligentsia' would ignore them, was that they had palpable designs on the reader: 'their business is not to express, but . . . to impose on you an idea'.[35] Poetry with a purpose, in an openly rhetorical style, was out of favour. But the complaint was not merely that Kipling wanted to impose his ideas: the ideas themselves were felt to be outmoded, no less than the manner. His poetry enacted a kind of literary collectivism, which threatened to co-opt the individual into the general. The new poetry, whether Georgian or Modernist, found its basis in personal experience, even where it hoped to transform that experience into an image of wider significance.

The best of the poems in *The Years Between* are in fact the most personal, in subject matter if not in form, including 'My Boy Jack', 'A Nativity' and 'Gethsemane', but in the notes he made to help Doubleday advertise the volume Kipling insisted on his public, oracular role, describing 'My Boy Jack', for example, as 'Sung at concerts, etc. all over England', and 'A Nativity' as 'eminently singable' and much admired by Alfred Noyes (*Letters*, IV.542–3). Perhaps because he despaired of finding an audience ready to accept him as a prophet, Kipling wrote little political verse during the 1920s, and there were to be no new volumes of poetry after 1919.[36]

He remained busy, he told Dunsterville, 'at all sorts of jobs that don't seem to matter much. Nothing matters much really when one has lost one's son' (*Letters*, IV.560). The end of the war had not improved Carrie's health, or his own, and in February 1919 they were in Bath, where Carrie took the waters while he worked on his pamphlet for the War Graves Commission, *The Graves of the Fallen*. Their visits to Bath allowed Kipling to renew his friendship with George Saintsbury, who had moved there from Edinburgh in 1915. Saintsbury had little sympathy with modern literature, but he was hospitable, and Tory to the bone, and the two men enjoyed each other's company. Kipling continued to give most of his time and energy to his history of the Irish Guards, reading diaries and letters, and talking to survivors, some of whom came to visit at Bateman's. In September he relaxed long enough to enjoy a lazy fortnight with Carrie and Elsie in Perthshire, but politics were never far from his mind, and by the end of the year he was urging the *Morning Post* to explore a possible link between the locations of German prisoner-of-war camps and an outbreak of foot-and-mouth disease. The war, in his view, was not over, only hidden.

In March 1920, in need of the sun, and anxious to see the work being done by the War Graves Commission at first hand, he and Carrie spent six weeks in France, returning in time for his address to the Royal Society of St George, on 'England and the English'. Taking his cue from Defoe's lines on 'The True-Born Englishman', he argued that the complexity of their racial heritage gave the English an instinctive kinship with all men and races. He had suggested as much in the Puck stories, though even so his audience might have been surprised to hear Kipling of all people praising the 'imperturbable tolerance' of the Englishman. His conclusion, that 'the whole weight of the world' lay 'on the necks of two nations, England and France', was one he was to maintain till the end of his life.[37]

He had another and more demanding speech to make a few days later. The War Graves Commission had come under attack for its plans to use headstones rather than crosses, and to make no distinction of rank among the dead. With a Parliamentary debate scheduled for 4 May, Kipling went to the House to rally support from an audience of MPs. He also allowed William Burdett-Coutts to quote from a personal letter during the debate: 'You see we shall never have any grave to go to. Our boy was missing at Loos. The ground is of course battered and mined past all hope of any trace being recovered. I wish some of the people who are making this trouble realised how more than fortunate they are to have a name on a headstone in a known place.'[38] It was not a context in which to think of victory, and the arguments continued outside Parliament, but by the end of the debate, with the help of a closing speech by Churchill, the Commission had won overwhelming support for its work.

Rudyard and Carrie returned to France in July, visiting some thirty cemeteries, as well as the battlefield at Loos, where they made a fruitless attempt to find where John had fallen. The Commission had already begun designing, building and planting 800 cemeteries in France alone, and in many there was still little to show beyond wire fences, wooden crosses and the flowers of a single season. Even so, at Rouen, Kipling was struck by 'the extraordinary beauty of the cemetery and the great care that the attendants had taken of it, and the almost heartbroken thankfulness of the relatives of the dead who were there'.[39]

The following year the family decided to travel further afield, to Algeria, in part because Oliver Baldwin had spoken so highly of it. Their plans were threatened when Rudyard fell ill. Bland-Sutton announced that the problem was infected teeth, and that he should have them all removed. Still unwell, and with his new teeth not yet fitted, Rudyard was understandably miserable at the start of their journey, but he enjoyed Algiers, where the colour, light and heat reminded him of India, and he was pleased with what he saw of the way France looked after its colonies. On the journey home, however, when he was taken on a tour of the battlefields of Verdun, he was overcome by the scale of the suffering, and began to feel that 'if anyone gave me another idea my head would not stand it – it would burst'.[40] Back in France in November, where he was to receive honorary degrees from Strasbourg and the Sorbonne, he was still seized with horror at German 'barbarism'. He asked his audience at the Sorbonne to reflect that the 'folk-tales of a race never lie'. Those of England and France tell of young men rewarded for their courage and their kindness to others; those of Germany of the werewolf, which hides its bestiality beneath its adopted human form. The evil might be masked, but it would never go away; 'the cycle of suspense, treachery, and terror' would inevitably begin again. The only security for the future lay in making that truth the basis of common action between England and France.[41]

By the spring of 1922 Kipling was close enough to the end of the Irish Guards volume to take another holiday. March and April were spent visiting Gibraltar, where Elsie danced with Prince George on board the *Queen Elizabeth*, and Spain, where George Bambridge took Rudyard to a bullfight in Seville. In May they were in France again, at the coastal cemetery at Terlinchtun, to hear King George V deliver the speech Kipling had been asked to write for him. The poem he wrote at the same time, 'The King's Pilgrimage', warned sharply that those who had given their lives would feel betrayed if the survivors 'denied their blood / And mocked the gains it won'; his words for the King were more measured, and included the hope that he himself hardly shared, that the cemeteries, as visible memorials of the desolation of war, would encourage the nations to draw together 'in sanity and self-control'.[42] The speech was judged a success, and over the years the King and Kipling formed a quiet but genuine friendship.

In July *The Irish Guards in the Great War* was finally finished. Dorothy Ponton, his secretary between 1919 and 1924, remembered it as written 'with agony and bloody sweat', each chapter going through four or five drafts before the whole text was revised shortly before its publication.[43]

It is a determinedly reticent work, orderly, factual, and low-key, its tone typified by the sentence following the list of those killed and wounded at Loos on 27 September 1915, including John Kipling: 'It was a fair average for the day of a debut, and taught them somewhat for their future guidance.' Edmund Blunden complained that Kipling had failed to show 'the pandemonium and nerve-strain of war' or the 'enigma of war atmosphere', but he had made no effort to do so.[44] In his poem 'A Legend of Truth', Fiction asks Truth to keep 'the record of the War'. But when Truth is presented with dossiers of 'Facts beyond precedent and parallel', she summons back her sister:[45]

> 'Come at once.
> Facts out of hand. Unable overtake
> Without your aid. Come back for Truth's own sake!
> Co-equal rank and powers if you agree.
> *They need us both, but you far more than me!*'

The Irish Guards had been written as a report on a regiment, in the name of Truth; the nerve-strain and atmosphere of war, its impact on mind, body and spirit, were matters he could explore best in his fiction.

But the work had taken its toll, and after further medical examinations revealed an ulcerated colon he was put on a diet of milk and enemas. His mood was not helped by the publication in the New York *World* of what purported to be an interview he had given to Clare Sheridan, the daughter of his neighbour Moreton Frewen. The article contained a litany of his complaints about America: that it had entered the war late, forced the Allies into a damaging settlement at Versailles, and become overrun by immigrants of the wrong sort. Kipling was too ill to respond, and Carrie had to issue a statement denying that he had given Mrs Sheridan an interview. This was strictly true, in that he had thought of their meeting as a private conversation, but there was nothing in the article that he had not said or hinted before, and the denials were not convincing.

It was a hurtful episode, and may have contributed to his continuing ill-health, which in November required him to undergo an operation. Bland-Sutton declared himself satisfied with the outcome, and there was no trace of the cancer Kipling had feared, but in January he needed further surgery, this time on his eyes. Rider Haggard found him 'looking drawn and considerably aged', and pondering on mortality. He had come to think, he told Haggard, that the individual human being was 'not a mere flash in the pan . . . but an enduring entity that has lived elsewhere and will continue to live'. Both men were despondent about the future for the country, and rather proud to be 'out of touch with the times', since 'the times' were all wrong.[46] But with *The Irish Guards* off his hands, Kipling was at last returning to fiction, at work on 'The United Idolaters' and 'The Janeites', both published in 1924.

At the end of March 1923, the Kiplings sailed to Toulon, and then on to Monte Carlo and Aix. Rudyard began to recover his spirits, though he was distressed by a meeting with his friend Bonar Law, fatally ill with throat cancer. In May, Law resigned his office as Prime Minister, to be succeeded by Stanley Baldwin. Kipling was doubtful about Baldwin's politics, which were more conciliatory than his own, but the two liked each other personally, and they continued to exchange family visits. In October there was more good news, when Kipling was elected as Rector of the University of St Andrews, and was able to propose Baldwin, Bland-Sutton and Sir Henry Newbolt for honorary degrees. The Rector was chosen by the students – the first generation to have grown up with Mowgli, Stalky and Kim – and he was reassured to find that he had not, as he sometimes feared, lost his audience during the Great War.

The New Year brought less welcome news. Following Baldwin's defeat in the December elections, Ramsay MacDonald took office as Britain's first Labour Prime Minister. Kipling consoled himself with the improbable thought that the public would now come to see that the Labour party took its orders from Moscow. It was more difficult to face the fact that Elsie wanted to leave home. If, as seems likely, it was around this time that Kipling learned of Oliver Baldwin's homosexuality, he must have been concerned that George Bambridge, the man she wanted to marry, was Oliver's friend, and more than that had been at Eton, which in Kipling's view was riddled with 'beastliness'. But Elsie was determined; she would be 28 in February, and there was little he could do except make the necessary financial arrangements. In May, Bambridge returned to England from Madrid; in October he and Elsie were married, and left for the house Kipling had bought for them in Brussels, where Bambridge had recently been posted. It was only a small consolation that in November Baldwin was again asked to form a government, this time with a huge majority.

The next few months were filled with a round of social visits, to compensate for Elsie's absence. In February they spent a week in Brussels, to find her and George enjoying 'any amount of receptions, balls and functions, in the diplomatic line . . . and unlimited calling and visiting between'. It was hardly the principled life Kipling had recommended to the students at St Andrews – 'At any price that I can pay, let me own myself' – but Elsie appeared happy, and they made themselves content with that.[47] They saw her again in March, on a shopping trip to Paris, as he and Carrie motored down to the Hotel du Palais in Biarritz – 'pure Philistia', he admitted to Haggard, 'and wealth and comforts accumulated on fatted comforts' – stopping on their way to visit the cathedrals at Rouen and Chartres, and as usual to inspect the war graves. It was in the cemetery at Rouen that the sight of an elderly Frenchwoman tending one of the graves moved Rudyard 'almost to tears': only 'almost', and he told Haggard that she was probably 'an old maid', but later that day he began 'The Gardener', in which a middle-aged spinster is miraculously helped to find the grave of her illegitimate son.[48]

In May they left again for Brussels, only to return almost at once on hearing of the death of Lord Milner. Rider Haggard, Kipling's closest friend for more than a decade, died only days later, followed in the same month by Louisa Baldwin. Of the Macdonald sisters, only Edith remained; she had lived so long with the Baldwin family that she seemed to inherit her sister's determined invalidism, and now took to her bed. The funerals over, the Kiplings kept up the social round though the summer, including a garden party at Buckingham Palace, but in November they were back in Brussels to see Elsie. A week after their return, however, Rudyard fell ill with pneumonia. For a time he was thought close to death, and the Bambridges were summoned to Bateman's. The worst was over by mid-December, but his sixtieth birthday passed almost unmarked, and the year ended bleakly. Carrie's last entry in her diary for 1925, written on her sixty-third birthday, was typically gloomy: 'George and Elsie leave about noon . . . Rud sits these last few days a little in his chair. So ends the year. A very sad year for me with nothing ahead for the other years but the job of living.'[49]

10
The Last Decade

The Kiplings spent their winter holiday in the south of France. They stayed longer than usual, to allow Rudyard to convalesce, and then found their plans to return in May disrupted by the General Strike. The strike had been called to show solidarity with the miners, who had refused to accept the reduced pay and longer hours demanded by the owners. It was essentially an industrial dispute, though Kipling and other hard-line Tories chose to regard it as the first act in a class war, including Churchill, who stigmatised the strikers as subversives in the *British Gazette* – produced, with Gwynne's assistance, on the presses of the *Morning Post* – and the Home Secretary, William Joynson-Hicks, who was to become one of Kipling's ministerial friends. The strike ceased to be general after only nine days, and the miners were left to fight on alone, unsuccessfully, into the autumn. In Italy, Rudyard noted approvingly, Mussolini had succeeded in reducing the number of stoppages.

Kipling's illness over the winter had obliged him to resign from the committee examining the structure of what was to become the British Broadcasting Corporation, though not before he had taken a dislike to its future Director-General, John Reith, whose missionary approach to broadcasting he found irritatingly high-minded. In August 1926, however, the Empire Marketing Board sought his advice on how to publicise its activities. He suggested the production of a propaganda film, and he and Walter Creighton worked together to develop a scenario. Creighton knew little about film, and their plans were overtaken by the arrival of the new talking pictures; the EMB later brought in John Grierson, the pioneer of documentary film-making in Britain. Despite this setback, Kipling studied the movie industry closely, and sold the rights to a number of his books, including options on *Captains Courageous* and

Kim, but it was not until after his death that Hollywood began to take a serious interest in his work.

In July 1926, in a speech given to thank the Royal Literary Society for awarding him its Gold Medal, Kipling told his audience that there was no human mood the writer of fiction was forbidden to explore, though since readers would accept only what they required 'the true nature and intention . . . of a writer's work does not lie within his own knowledge'.[1] In writing the speech, he must have had in mind the volume of stories he was about to publish in October. *Debits and Credits* makes few concessions to the reader. The two opening stories are 'The Enemies to Each Other', a study of marital discord written as a pastiche of Arabic literature, and 'Sea Constables: A Tale of '15', a story about the wartime pursuit of a neutral vessel which even the sympathetic Charles Carrington found morally deplorable;[2] the third, ' "In the Interests of the Brethren" ', is rather a pageant of war-damaged men than a narrative; and few readers can have been excited to discover two new 'Stalky' tales. Yet this only adds to the sense that *Debits and Credits* can be taken as a summation of Kipling's later work. 'The Eye of Allah' is another historical fantasy, stripped of the frame it might have had in the Puck stories, 'The Bull that Thought' another parable about the imperatives of art, 'The Prophet and the Country' another farce, while at the heart of the book is a series of meditations on the key theme of his late fiction: how men and women can put their lives back together after everything they believe in has been 'knocked out' of them, by war, by illness, or by the torment of an illicit or disappointed love.[3]

The two finest of the stories succeed in different ways. The opening sentence of 'The Gardener' declares that 'Everyone in the village knew' that Helen Turrell had done her duty by bringing up her illegitimate nephew under her own roof, but there are several clues to suggest that what everyone in fact knows, but agrees not to say, is that Michael Turrell is Helen's child. The only person not to know is Michael himself; he is allowed to call her 'Mummy', but only as a petname between themselves. With the outbreak of war he proposes to enlist, rather than wait for a commission, because, he tells Helen, 'it's in the family'. This is a reference to what he has been told, that his mother was the daughter of a non-commissioned officer. Helen's shocked response seems to be a coded admission of the truth of their relationship: ' "You don't mean to tell me that you believed that old story all this time?" said Helen.' If Michael sees this, his reply is equally coded:

'Oh, *that* doesn't worry me. It never did,' he replied valiantly. 'What I meant was, I should have got into the show earlier if I'd enlisted – like my grandfather.'

The only clues here are in the word 'valiantly', which hints at suppressed feeling, and in the pause before 'like my grandfather', which might suggest that Michael intends to preserve his mother's fiction about his parentage – the fiction, after all, on which her place in the village depends. As J. M. S. Tompkins puts it, astutely, the narrative 'speaks through a mask, the candid-seeming mask that Helen had designed. . . . The skill lies in imparting to us what was under Helen's mask.'[4]

Michael is sent to France, 'to help make good the wastage of Loos', and killed by a shell. The village has 'evolved a ritual' for grief, and Helen follows it, just as she had obeyed its rules for dealing with scandal; she takes refuge in a 'blessed passivity', and learns to 'incline her head at the proper angle, at the proper murmur of sympathy'. Like Rudyard and Carrie after John's death, she goes through 'an inevitable series of unprofitable emotions' before reconciling herself to the fact that 'missing' means 'dead'. Again like them, she comes slowly back to life after the armistice, and prepares to visit Michael's grave at Hagenzeele Third Military Cemetery, gathering the necessary information about rail and boat timetables, and 'a comfortable little hotel . . . where one could spend quite a comfortable night and see one's grave next morning'. The language is nicely adjusted to the stifled world in which she lives, and the dulled state of her own feelings. Only the uncontrolled grief of another bereaved woman suggests what she is holding back, and invites the question whether she gains or loses by her reticence.

On her journey Helen meets a Mrs Scarsworth, who at first insists that she has come to take photographs for friends unable to travel, but then breaks down and confesses that she has come to see the grave of her lover. The narrator offers no explanation of why Mrs Scarsworth chooses to tell Helen of a love she has kept hidden for thirteen years; the reader is left to guess that she recognises instinctively that Helen has had a similar experience. Nor does the narrator explain how we should understand Helen's 'murmured' response, 'Oh, my dear! My dear!':

Mrs Scarsworth stepped back, her face all mottled.
'My God!' said she. 'Is *that* how you take it?'
Helen could not speak, and the woman went out; but it was a long while before Helen was able to sleep.

Mrs Scarsworth's confession has not unlocked Helen's self-restraint; whatever she feels, she is unable to express more than 'the proper murmur of sympathy'. The following day she goes alone to the cemetery, where she stands lost and helpless amidst 'a merciless sea of black crosses', until a gardener asks who she is looking for. She gives the answer she has given many times before: 'Lieutenant Michael Turrell – my nephew.' The gardener replies 'with infinite compassion':

'Come with me,' he said, 'and I will show you where your son lies.'

The reader recognises the gardener as a figure of Christ, but Helen does not; there is a break in the text, and then she leaves the cemetery, 'still supposing him to be the gardener'. The direct allusion to John's account of Mary Magdalene at Jesus's grave has been found tactless, an instance of Kipling's tendency to give the screw a last unnecessary turn, but even so the ending remains equivocal. For one moment Helen is accepted as a mother, and the burden of secrecy is lifted; but she also turns away without identifying the gardener as Christ, and without the implied hope of her son's resurrection. If she finds any release, it is hidden in the blank space Kipling leaves on the page between the gardener's words and her departure.[5]

'The Gardener' is a gentle as well as a reticent story. 'The Wish House' also deals with illicit love, but in an altogether more bruising fashion. Two elderly women, knowing that they are talking together for the last time – Grace Ashcroft, a Sussex cook, is dying, her friend Liz Fettley is going blind – exchange stories of lost or bitter love. Grace's story is of her continuing love for a man who had grown tired of her, and then fell ill. Little Sophy Ellis, who has a crush on Grace, tells her how it is possible to go to the Wish House, and there ask the 'Token' who inhabits it to allow her to take on herself all her man's pain. This Grace has done, and her action is – she believes – the origin of the cancer which is killing her. Her love is at once self-sacrificing and relentlessly possessive; only at the last, when she whispers to her friend, 'It *do* count, don't it – de pain?', does she admit any weakness.

Kipling uses the Sussex dialect to help establish Grace as a convincing figure. The story begins in the twentieth-century world of the Saturday shopping 'bus and the tourist traffic through the village, but as the two women talk they slip into 'easy, ancient Sussex'. The dialect works in two ways. First, it provides a point of entry into an unfamiliar world, closed to the Church Visitor or the Nurse, to whom Grace speaks in standard English. Little by little the story takes on a different accent:

the dropping of final 'g', 'shruck' rather than 'shrank', 'gran'chiller' for 'grandchildren', and the use of dialect words. Some of these Kipling may have learned from Wright's *English Dialect Dictionary*: to 'stub' hens, for example, meaning to pluck the feathers from young fowls, or 'spang', used here to mean the prong of a pitchfork. If Wright is taken as a definitive guide – and this might not be appropriate in dealing with words existing mainly in spoken form – Kipling makes some errors. Grace's 'to scutchel up' seems to mean 'to gather', or perhaps 'to scrounge'; Wright gives 'scutchel' as a substantive, meaning a footpath between two houses, and 'to scutch', meaning 'to catch hold of', but not 'to scutchel' as a verb. When Grace loses weight, she becomes 'poochy' under the eyes; Wright explains 'poochy' as 'protruding', as of someone with full lips, which seems not to be the sense needed. No doubt Kipling caught up the words he heard, and sometimes misheard. Despite these slips, if that is what they are, the dialect succeeds in its first task, which is to edge the reader, unobtrusively, away from the known towards the unknown, from the modern urban world towards a rural traditional one.

But simultaneously the dialect works to imply a firmer purchase on the realities of daily life: the world of stubbing hens, and jabbing with fork spangs. Like the quietly suggested context of seasonal work, it serves to root the events Grace recounts so laconically in the known world. There is a fine moment when Sophy has been to the Wish House to take away Grace's headache, and is now suffering it herself. Grace takes her on her lap 'till it come time to light de gas, an' a liddle after that, 'er 'eddick – mine, I suppose – took off, an' she got down an' played with the cat.' Sophy is both a child with access to a secret knowledge, and a little girl who wants to play with a cat. The scene is imagined so powerfully that the carefully rendered detail passes beyond the literal: as Randall Jarrell puts it, 'the pressure of the imagination has forced facts over into the supernatural'.[6]

Grace herself is entirely credible, both as an individual and as a representative of a world passing into history, dislodged by urbanisation and the motor-car. Sandra Kemp links her wish to take away Harry's pain to the Catholic tradition of the 'Way of Exchange', which holds that vicarious suffering, freely chosen, both imitates and re-enacts Christ's sufferings on the Cross. This is persuasive, but the thought does nothing to soften Grace's character.[7] When she wants an excuse to keep off work to stay with Harry, she tips scalding water over her arm; when she knows he is preparing to leave her, she hears him out in silence:

At the last, I took off a liddle brooch which he'd give me an' I says: 'Dat'll do. *I* ain't askin' na'un'.' An' I turned me round an' walked off to me own sufferin's.

She accepts her suffering willingly, but she is determined to exact all the satisfaction she can: ' "I've got ye now, my man," I says. "You'll take your good from me 'thout knowin' it till my life's end." ' Like 'The Gardener' and 'A Madonna of the Trenches', the story reaches out to suggest the redemptive possibilities of sexual love, but it does so without making any direct allusion to Christian teaching. Whatever value attaches to Grace's love is fully earned, not underwritten by a biblical text.[8]

Much the most perceptive review of *Debits and Credits* was that by Edmund Wilson. Kipling, he argued, invented 'the whole genre of vernacular stories', in which the comedy or tragedy is revealed through 'the half-obscuring veil of the special slang and technical vocabulary of the person who is telling it'. He also applauded what he called Kipling's 'unrivalled collection of . . . marvellous language exhibits: the kitchen chatter of a Sussex cook, the eloquence of a Middle Western realtor and several varieties of war slang.' The point is well taken, as is his conclusion: 'I cannot believe that James Joyce . . . would ever have written the Cyclops chapter of *Ulysses*, if he had never read Kipling.'[9] Kipling was not a modernist – whatever Joyce made of him the traffic was all one-way – but Wilson's essay suggests significant affiliations between his work and theirs: notably, in this volume, an extreme literary self-consciousness, evident in the frequent allusions to other writers, the intercutting of 'high' and 'low' culture, and the subtle verbal links between different stories. But there is a strong personal note too. It is not by chance that 'The Gardener', the final story in *Debits and Credits*, makes its climax out of the long-delayed use of the word 'son', the word Kipling had forbidden himself in his history of the Irish Guards. Apis, the bull in 'The Bull that Thought', with 'a breadth of technique that comes of reasoned art', has learned to achieve his finest effects by cunning and indirection. So too, in *Debits and Credits*, does Kipling.

The following year, 1927, began badly, with the death of Perceval Landon. He had been a friend since the early days of the war in South Africa, and one of the few people Carrie seemed to trust. Kipling's commemorative poem, 'A Song in the Desert', recalls him as an inveterate traveller, 'his shadow in front of him, / Ceaselessly eating the distances': an alter ego, who had never forsaken 'The Gipsy Trail'. Kipling had, however, and even as the funeral was taking place he and Carrie were on their way to Brazil in search of warm weather. Rudyard was lionised more than he wished in Rio, and called on to address the Brazilian Academy of Letters, but they enjoyed the visit:

> The Cocoa-palms were real, and the Southern Cross was true:
> And the Fireflies were dancing – and I danced too![10]

On their return to Europe they stopped to see Elsie, before going to stay with Peter Stanley, a friend of Bland-Sutton's, and his wife Frances, the daughter of their friend Julia Taufflieb. Wealthy and intellectual, the Stanleys were good company, and the two families began to meet frequently. Kipling drew on Peter's experience of a front-line field hospital in 'The Tender Achilles', one of a number of late stories about psychosomatic or hysterical illness. His outward life was comfortable, even luxurious, but his fiction continued to explore the need to build 'a bulkhead 'twixt Despair and the Edge of Nothing'.[11]

The year brought one tribute which Kipling would rather have forgone, with the establishment of a Kipling Society. Dunsterville became its first president, and in 1928 brought out a memoir, *Stalky's Reminiscences*, largely concerned with his memories of Kipling and the United Services College. Rudyard kept his distance from the Society, as he tried to do with the bibliographers and collectors who were increasingly drawn to his work.[12] The perils of becoming an institution, rather than, as Eliot had put it, a neglected celebrity, were underlined with the death of Thomas Hardy in January 1928. Hardy had wanted to be buried at Stinsford in Dorset, alongside his first wife and his parents, but Sydney Cockerell, his literary executor, together with James Barrrie, insisted on a funeral in Westminster Abbey. In a macabre compromise, Hardy's heart was removed and laid in the grave at Stinsford, while at the same time his ashes were buried in the Abbey. Kipling was one of the pallbearers, and to his dismay found himself paired with the much taller Bernard Shaw. The difference in their heights was as nothing to that in their politics; according to Shaw's secretary, Blanche Patch, Kipling shook hands 'hurriedly, and at once turned away as if from the Evil One'.[13] It was a good enough story to be told more than once (in Shaw's version, he had to follow Kipling, and was in danger of tripping over his heels), but the double funeral was a vivid illustration of public intrusiveness. Kipling and Carrie could only stiffen their defences.[14]

The year continued with the usual round of holidays and visits, beginning with Taormina in Sicily, which had become a fashionable resort for the English. From Naples they made an uncomfortable voyage to Gibraltar, before travelling to Madrid to see Elsie, and then into France. The Mediterranean background found its way into two stories written in this summer. In 'The Manner of Men', a sea-captain of the first century AD recalls the impression made on him by one of his passengers, Paul of Tarsus, during a shipwreck. Kipling's Paul is a complex figure: partly a tough-minded administrator, determined that men should at the least obey Caesar's law, and partly a version of Keats's chameleon poet, with 'the woman's trick' of losing himself in imaginative identification with others. There is a similar dichotomy between the external and the inner world in 'The Church that was at Antioch', where Paul's insistence on forms and observances is suddenly rebuked by St Peter, a man whose moral authority has grown from the recognition of his own weakness. Both stories deal with the relation between the Law and the Spirit, the male and the female; both admit that the Spirit is more than the Law. There is a self-reflexive aspect to both stories (Paul is 'a small hard man with eyebrows', like Kipling in one of Beerbohm's caricatures), and though neither writer would have liked the comparison, it is tempting to link them with the idea of the androgynous writer that Virginia Woolf was to explore a year later in *A Room of One's Own*.

Kipling and Woolf were more predictably on opposite sides in the prosecution of Radclyffe Hall's novel of lesbian love, *The Well of Loneliness*. Hall's publisher, Jonathan Cape, had withdrawn the novel in response to official threats, but it had been distributed from Paris, and in November 1928 author and publisher were convicted of publishing an obscene book. Kipling had contacted Joynson-Hicks at the Home Office after receiving a promotion addressed to 'Miss Kipling', which he took as evidence that the novel was proselytising for female homosexuality.[15] He had agreed to speak for the Crown when the case came to appeal; Woolf and E. M. Forster were among more than forty writers and public figures who offered to speak for the defence, though in the event none of them was called. Kipling's disaffection from the society of the 1920s can be measured by his willingness to make common cause with social-purity enthusiasts like Archibald Bodkin, the Director of Public Prosecutions, who had acted for the National Vigilance Association in its campaigns against the music-halls. Bodkin was no friend to Tommy Atkins.

The Kiplings' spring tour in 1929 was to Egypt and Palestine. In Egypt they followed much the same route as they had done in 1913, except where they stopped to visit the cemeteries of Allenby's army. Egypt had been granted a limited independence in 1922, since when nationalist

demands for greater autonomy had been met initially with force, latter-
ly with efforts at conciliation. Kipling lamented the loosening of the
British hold as a portent of things to come, but he enjoyed meeting
A. E. W. Mason, whose best-selling adventure story, *The Four Feathers*,
had some slight affinities to *The Light that Failed*. Born like Kipling in
1865, Mason remained a dashing figure. In the intervals between yacht-
ing and Alpine climbing, he had appeared in the first production of
Shaw's *Arms and the Man*, collaborated with Andrew Lang on a novel,
been a Liberal MP, served during the war with the Royal Marine Light
Infantry, and thereafter as a spy in Spain, Morocco and Mexico. Kipling
continued to read widely, but among modern books he preferred adventure stories and the literature of travel, and he found Mason a sympathetic companion.

The political situation in Palestine was still more fraught than in
Egypt. Balfour had intended his wartime declaration in favour of a
Jewish homeland to win the support of Russian and American Jews, but
many British imperialists had genuine Zionist sympathies: not, however, those who had served their time in India, who were more likely to
be pro-Arab. The Kiplings arrived in Jerusalem in 1929 at a time of
mounting tension, with Arabs protesting at the levels of Jewish immi-
gration, and Zionists at British proposals to limit the number of immigrants. Rudyard hardly needed persuading that Zionism could be a
destabilising force, but as ever he was eager to see events at close hand;
Jerusalem, he wrote to Elsie, was 'an indescribable muck heap, but it's
the most interesting muck heap in the world'.[16]

The return to power of a Labour government in May 1929 intensified
his fears for Britain's imperial future, though the issue which caused
him most concern, the promise to give Dominion status to India, was
not really a party matter: Lord Irwin, the Viceroy, had been appointed
during Baldwin's premiership. The next steps were far from smooth.
The Indian National Congress demanded full independence, and in
April 1930 Gandhi started a new campaign of civil disobedience. He
was imprisoned, as were thousands of his supporters, but the Round
Table conference on India's future could not progress without him, and
he had to be released, prompting Churchill's sneer that the representative of the King-Emperor had been forced to pay court to a 'half-naked
fakir'. Churchill was now the politician closest to Kipling on imperial
matters, though this did nothing to reconcile the two personally, and
neither of them could hinder the progress of the Government of India
bill; that it was Baldwin who in 1935 saw it on to the statute books only
added to Rudyard's sense of betrayal. The India he had left in 1889 was

long gone, recoverable if at all only in print, in the pages of *Something of Myself.*

A more immediate concern was Carrie's worsening health. She had suffered for years from rheumatism and diabetes, and her eyesight was failing; then, in February 1930, during their holiday visit to Jamaica, she fell ill with appendicitis. Rather than trust to the island's medical facilities they made their way to Bermuda, where she was kept in hospital until May; determined not to set foot in America, they returned via Montreal. When she was not in pain, Carrie was prone to hysterical tantrums, including threats of self-harm if Rudyard suggested spending time away from Bateman's. He acceded quietly to her demands; in Elsie's words, 'his kindly nature, patience, and utter loyalty to her prevented his ever questioning this bondage, and they were seldom apart.'[17] There is no need, as some have done, to belittle as weakness what his daughter saw as kindness; both may have been present, but the one does not invalidate the other.

There was further emotional strain for them both in August, when they were in France for the inauguration of the Loos Memorial, where John's name was to be commemorated. They were forgivably angry when foreign dignitaries were told that they need not feel obliged to lay wreaths at the Cenotaph or on the Tomb of the Unknown Warrior, because, in the words Kipling quoted at the head of his poem 'Memories', the Labour government aspired to 'the eradication of memories of the Great War'. Kipling interpreted this as an attempt to 'filch' the honour due to the dead, 'through the power / Of small corroding words'. In this, at least, he and Carrie felt as one.[18]

With the Labour government in power, Baldwin had come under attack from the most powerful of the press barons, Beaverbrook and Rothermere, who tried to force him from the Tory leadership. In March 1931, Baldwin countered by accusing newspaper proprietors of seeking 'power without responsibility – the prerogative of the harlot throughout the ages'. Rudyard had recently used the phrase 'power without responsibility' in a letter to his aunt Edith, and either he or she probably offered it to Baldwin. Kipling had some sympathy with Beaverbrook's programme, which included free trade within an Empire protected by a high tariff wall, but more loyalty to his cousin; though this was to be tested later in the year, when Baldwin took the Tories into the National Government under Ramsay MacDonald. Rudyard could never shake off a suspicion that Baldwin was 'a Socialist at heart', yet he himself had anticipated the style and values Baldwin brought into politics in his story of 1905, 'An Habitation Enforced'. As George Chapin comes to understand: 'It's not our land. . . . We belong to it, and it belongs to the people – our people they call 'em.' Kipling's politics had since become less accommodating, but it was Baldwin's reputation as an honest countryman, forced by his sense of duty to become a servant of a people wiser than himself, that kept him at the centre of British political life in the inter-war years.

In 1931 the Kiplings again voyaged to Egypt, in the hope that the climate would bring some ease for Carrie's rheumatic pains; she now had gout to add to her other troubles. Rudyard too was threatened with another operation, though in the end his doctors decided against it, and as usual recommended that he cut down on his smoking. His mood was, he admitted, increasingly sour. He raged against the taxation policy which took away 40 per cent of his income, and spent it on projects he disliked: popular education, for example, which did not teach a milkmaid to milk or a ploughman to plough.[19] Whether or not the British had acquired their empire in a fit of absence of mind, he could not stand to see it given away in a mood of indifference. Worst of all, the politicians were still unprepared to meet the threat from Germany. British policy in favour of disarmament, hitherto mainly theoretical, had become a reality in response to the economic crises of the early 1930s, when arms estimates dropped to their lowest levels between the wars. In June 1931 the *Morning Post* reprinted Kipling's poem of 1909, 'The City of Brass', with its attack on leaders who 'disbanded in face of their foemen'. The National Government was making the mistakes the Liberals had made more than twenty years before; the warnings too were the same. It was easy to come close to despair.

Limits and Renewals

The Kiplings were resting in Monte Carlo when Rudyard's last collection of stories, *Limits and Renewals*, was published in April 1932. Eleven of the fourteen stories had previously appeared in the magazines. Only one, 'The Tie', an unpalatable tale from 1915, had been written before 1924, and this is in some respects an old man's book, preoccupied with disease and healing, revenge and forgiveness, lives saved or wasted. Four of the stories deal with shell-shock – or war neurosis; what the condition was to be called was still the subject of debate.[20] Kipling treats these victims with sympathy. Wollin, in 'Fairy-Kist', is 'burned out – all his wrinkles gashes, and his eyes readjustin' 'emselves after looking into Hell'; Wilkett, in 'The Tender Achilles', is guilty of 'bleedin' vanity', but it is the vanity of a man who accuses himself of the deaths of those he was unable to save during his service in a field-hospital. The weakness of these stories is if anything an excess of compassion, the need to believe that there is some agency, human or divine, which can wholly banish pain. In 'The Miracle of Saint Jubanus', the gentlest of Kipling's farces, the healing of Martin Ballart, left blasted and dumb by the war, is claimed as a miracle by the priest who tells the story. In 'Fairy-Kist' Wollin's pain is removed by a piece of detective work: 'as soon as he got the explanation it evaporated like ether and didn't leave a stink'. This is to diminish the reality of suffering, as if it were an aching tooth to be extracted. In these stories one hears Kipling murmuring, like Grace Ashcroft, 'It *do* count, don't it – de pain?'

This sympathy extends beyond the victims of war. 'Uncovenanted Mercies' is a fable of the after-life in which Satan himself is constrained to pity the unnamed man and woman who have endured the test for Ultimate Breaking Strain. In 'Unprofessional' Mrs Berners's doctors use astrological forces to help avert her death from cancer, though even as her surgeon congratulates himself on leaving a beautiful scar, we are reminded that she can no longer hope to bear children, and that she, and the men who have saved her, are still 'astray' in a difficult world. Except in the two revenge stories, 'The Tie' and 'Beauty Spots', Kipling reaches out, in *Limits and Renewals*, towards tolerance and forgiveness.

Forgiveness, or at least the fading away of the desire for revenge, is the subject of 'Dayspring Mishandled', one of the most complex of Kipling's stories. Two hack writers, Alured Castorley and James Manallace, become rivals in love. Castorley later gives up writing fiction to construct a reputation as a Chaucer scholar, while Manallace nurses the woman they had loved, named only as "Dal's mother', through a fatal illness. Soon after the two men meet again, when in some way connected with 'Dal's mother, a woman 'who suffered and died because she loved one unworthy', Castorley triggers in Manallace a desire to destroy his position. To do so, he makes an elaborate forgery of a 'Chaucer' manuscript, and arranges for Castorley to proclaim its authenticity; the plan is to reveal it as a forgery when Castorley's fame seems assured. The plot is heading for success, but then Manallace pulls back; Castorley falls ill, and eventually dies, without discovering that he has been duped, and Manallace agrees to act as his literary executor. How he will present Castorley's 'Chaucer' fragment is left unresolved at the end of the story.

Kipling weaves three further texts into this already complicated story. There is an epigraph, taken from a poem by Charles Nodier, in which 'la fille des beaux jours' proclaims 'Je suis la Mandragore'. There is a frame story, which involves a narrator who appears initially as a disinterested observer of events. And following the story proper there is a poem, described as 'Modernized from the "Chaucer" of Manallace', called 'Gertrude's Prayer', which asserts the futility of all hopes of renewal: 'Dayspring mishandled cometh not againe.' The three texts work subtly to shape our reading.

Kipling refuses to guide the reader on two key points in the story: Manallace's reasons for devising the plot, and his reasons for aborting it. The second of these is perhaps to be explained by Castorley's illness. Near the end of his life, delirious with 'the hideous, helpless panic of the sick', he begs to be allowed to see 'Dal's mother again because there is 'an urgent matter to be set right'. This suggests that his illness derives from a sense of guilt, or at least that Manallace comes to think so; it would be one of many symmetries in the story if Manallace, having nursed 'Dal's mother while her eyes sought for the 'one unworthy', should find himself comforting the dying Castorley as he called for her. A further reason for Manallace not to bring his plot to completion must be his suspicion that the unpleasant Lady Castorley has guessed his intentions, and now urges him on in order to be rid of a husband she despises. In her, Manallace sees the image of what he is, or might become, and is appalled.

It is more difficult to guess why he embarks on the plot. Craig Raine suggests that Castorley was the 'one unworthy' for love of whom 'Dal's mother died.[21] There is a parenthetical 'it was said' attached to the story that Castorley had proposed to her, as if to cast doubt on this version of events, perhaps even to hint that he ought to have proposed but failed to do so. This would then be the 'urgent matter to be set right'. But this is not fully convincing. Some of Raine's clues work equally well for the supposition that Castorley said something insulting which the narrator, who knows from Manallace the cause of his anger, is too courteous to repeat. For example, the epigraph from Nodier's poem, which Raine takes to refer to a love affair between Castorley and 'Dal's mother, applies as well or better to Manallace: in his own words, he has been 'dead' since the month of her death, and the plot against Castorley has become a consuming passion; 'Dal's mother', 'la fille des beaux jours', has indeed been 'la Mandragore' in his life, slowly poisoning his existence. The urgent matter Castorley wants to set right may be no more than his refusal earlier to help fund new treatment for her during her illness. Similarly, the Latin words Manallace inserts into the Chaucer fragment, incorporating an anagram of his name – a text within a text within a text – may describe his rather than Castorley's position, with

'Dal's mother as the 'alma Mater', and he himself 'the accepted one', in whose arms she died.

Like the stories of illness and shell-shock elsewhere in *Limits and Renewals*, 'Dayspring Mishandled' confronts the reader with the waste of human energy and talent: 'Dal's mother's capacity for love, Castorley's scholarship, which is genuine as well as self-preening, Manallace's dedicated pursuit of a revenge he is unable to take. The pivotal irony of the tale is that Manallace has considered punishing Castorley by telling him the real provenance of the Chaucer fragment, and then obliging him to continue to assert its authenticity, but at the last finds himself in exactly this position, since only by maintaining the forgery as genuine can he uphold Castorley's good name, and thus make it more difficult for Lady Castorley to remarry. Typically, Kipling's plotters assume their own immunity, becoming the authors of other people's lives; Kit and Jem, in the last sentence of 'Beauty Spots', do not even turn round to watch their victim's discomfiture. Manallace finds himself instead entangled in the complexities of a situation he expected to control. No less than Castorley, he comes to feel that life is 'one long innuendo', and not the manipulable thing he had supposed.

This also becomes the position of the narrator, who begins the tale very much in the smart, confident manner of the young Kipling, looking back to 'the days beyond compare'. But as the narrative develops he finds himself caught up in Manallace's plot. Like Manallace, he wraps himself 'loving and leisurely' around the task of planning Castorley's downfall, fully aware that the shock of exposure might kill him, only to discover, as Manallace loses conviction, that he is called upon instead to humour him through the last stages of his illness. Rather than enclose the story, the frame begins to slip into it, as we discover that the unnamed man who once put the drunken Manallace to bed, 'in the days beyond compare', was in fact the narrator. Gradually his role as Manallace's confidant and accomplice comes to parallel that of Gleeag, Lady Castorley's adulterous partner, with each left uneasily loyal to one of the two main actors as they compete over Castorley's posthumous reputation. The final scene, at Castorley's funeral, holds the four in a restless tableau: Manallace watching Lady Castorley, Lady Castorley watching Gleeag, the narrator observing all three. No longer nonchalantly superior to the other characters, exempt from the doubt and uncertainty which are the normal human condition, he is like them bound into the story he has to tell.

This impression is reinforced by the poem which follows. It stands both within and outside the story proper: partly Manallace's 'Chaucer', as modernised by Kipling, but also a poem which is included in the *Definitive Edition*. The speaker who mourns over lost chances and the vulnerability of human life is at once the heroine of the forged Chaucer story, Manallace the forger, and Kipling the author:

> That which is marred at birth Time shall not mend,
>   Nor water out of bitter well make clean;
> All evil thing returneth at the end,
>   Or elseway walketh in our blood unseen.

Placed at the beginning of his final volume of stories, 'Dayspring Mishandled' gives Kipling's verdict, that the artist owns no special immunity from suffering, and must take his place, like those he creates, in the wider plots of the world.

It was in a discussion of *Limits and Renewals* that Edmund Wilson made his remark about Kipling 'losing his hatred' in his later years, and allowing the 'big talk of the world, of the mission to command of the British' to fade away.[22] Kipling never ceased to attend to the big world, but there were, from 1932, some more relaxed moments in his life. There was a visit to Bateman's from Trix, at long last free of the depressive illness which had plagued her for more than thirty years. In May he was in Cambridge, to become an honorary fellow of Magdalene College. Later in the year he helped to write the King's Christmas Day broadcast to the Empire, and listening to it on the radio moved him deeply: here was 'the circling word' passing from East to West, of which he had written in 'The Song of the Cities' forty years before.

There is, too, a sense of stock-taking and retrospection in his work after *Limits and Renewals*. 'Proofs of Holy Writ', in which Ben Jonson and Shakespeare discuss the Authorised Version of the Bible, is essentially a master-class in rhythm and diction, in which Shakespeare, like Kipling, waits on and trusts to his 'Demon'.[23] ' "Teem": a Treasure-Hunter', narrated by a truffle-hunting dog, is a fable about art. 'Teem' knows of 'precious things' hidden underground, which he alone can bring to light: stories waiting to be unearthed, if only the artist can find an audience ready to receive them.[24] *Souvenirs of France* is a collection of travel sketches previously published in the newspapers, given extra point by Kipling's conviction that France and England would soon be allies in another war. In Monte Carlo, in the spring of 1933, he spent much of his time revising the proofs for his *Collected Verse, 1885–1932*, indexing and arranging the poems. This was a considerable burden of work, which probably caused his collapse with stomach pains during his return journey through Paris. Here at last the problem was correctly diagnosed as a duodenal ulcer. He was given another new diet, and apart from a bad spell in August 1934 he had less pain in the last two years of his life than in most of the previous fifteen.

There were still family worries to attend to. George and Elsie Bambridge were back in England, but unsettled, moving from one rented mansion to another. Whether through choice or not, Elsie remained childless; George was no longer with the Foreign Office, and they were living beyond their means. Rudyard and Carrie were concerned enough to send them on a cruise to Jamaica, and to offer to pay £300 towards their rent. Bambridge flirted with politics – Rudyard warned him off Oswald Mosley, whom he regarded as an opportunist – and he tried and failed to win adoption as a Conservative candidate for the 1935 election, but his heart was not in it, and his political career was abandoned before it had begun. It was only after Rudyard's death, when Elsie's inheritance financed the purchase of Wimpole Hall in Cambridgeshire, a Georgian house set in 2400 acres of parkland, that he found an occupation as a landowner.[25]

Rudyard and Carrie continued to spend time in the south of France, in search of warmer weather and medical advice. Back in England, there were further discussions with film companies who bought options for films they would never make – though Alexander Korda, who paid £5000 for the rights to 'Toomai of the Elephants', did make *The Jungle Book* in 1942, albeit the 'jungle' was in California, and the animals from a menagerie. But while his dealings with the film world amused and occasionally exasperated him, political questions were never far from his mind.[26] 'The Storm-Cone', published in May 1932, was a warning that the nation was not free from crisis, but in the lull between storms:

> If we have cleared the expectant reef,
> Let no man look for his relief.
> Only the darkness hides the shape
> Of further peril to escape.

The peril that worried him came from Germany. The issue of reparations had rumbled on ever since the Treaty of Versailles; twice the French had occupied the Ruhr after Germany had defaulted, and each time Kipling had applauded their action. He could see no reason to allow Germany to re-enter the international community. The Germans had based their national life and ideals 'on a cult – a religion as it now appears – of War'; at any moment the German Wehr-Wolf would abandon the human form it had adopted for the past decade, and reappear in its true, monstrous form.[27] Kipling was wiser than many of his contemporaries in prophesying war, but he refused to admit that the attempt made at Versailles to reduce Germany to a second-class power might have prepared the ground for Hitler's National Socialist party. His predictions were based on race, not on politics or history.

In November 1933, as the German people voted to support Hitler's decision to withdraw Germany from the League of Nations, Kipling published his poem 'Bonfires on the Ice' in the *Morning Post*:[28]

> We know the Fenris Wolf is loose.
>> We know what Fight has not been fought.
>> We know the Father to the Thought
> Which argues Babe and Cockatrice
>> Would play together, were they taught.
> We know *that* Bonfire on the Ice.

His target was the ideal of 'collective security' through disarmament, which seemed to him merely naive. The attack was timely, though his contempt for democracy did little to support his case; the 'We' invoked here is not the nation, but only a small part of it, calling ever more loudly to an audience it despises for its blindness. But Kipling knew from his connections with the General Staff that the service chiefs shared his fears, even if the government did not – or at least, would not admit that it did – and one can hardly blame him for raising his voice. In 1934 he told Gwynne that Britain would be lucky to be granted another three years before Germany attacked, and urged him to run a campaign to demand the building of air-raid shelters.

There were some signs that the case for rearmament was beginning to be heard. In March 1935 a government White Paper announced that the British would no longer put their trust in collective security through the League of Nations, but begin to rebuild their armed forces. Two months later, in a speech to mark the Jubilee celebrations for King George V, Kipling returned to the attack. The government, he argued, had sought to improve living standards, without first providing 'that reasonable margin of external safety, without which even the lowest standard of life cannot be maintained'. The predictable result had been the resurgence of German militarism, and the domination across much of the eastern hemisphere of 'State-controlled murder and torture, open and secret . . . State-engineered famine, starvation and slavery [and] . . . State-imposed Godlessness'.[29]

It was a strong performance, but there was still nothing like a consensus for the level of rearmament Kipling and the service chiefs were demanding. It was barely an issue in the November election, which saw Baldwin returned to power at the head of the National government. The uncertainty in British foreign policy was exposed when Italy invaded Abyssinia in October. Kipling was ready to accept Italian militarism in Africa while Mussolini was a potential ally in Europe. This was more or less the position taken by the government, but it felt bound to support Abyssinia, as a fellow-member of the League of Nations. It was now facing two ways at once: supporting the economic sanctions imposed by the League, while at the same time seeking a compromise which would give Mussolini most of what he wanted. The public mood, however, was with the League and against the compromise, and Baldwin was forced to withdraw it. In December, in the midst of the debate, Kipling sent off some verses to *The Times*, and then hastily recalled them, perhaps because they were too intemperate. His considered view however was clear: in attempting to support the League, Britain risked breaking with an ally, at the expense of her own national interest.

In March 1936, as the League dithered over Abyssinia, Hitler ordered his troops into the demilitarised Rhineland. Kipling did not live to see it, but he would not have been surprised. The next European war, in his view, had been in preparation since 11 November 1918; its coming hung like a shadow over the last year of his life. Yet his last months were not wholly gloomy. Elsie and George, whatever their problems, were at least in England. With the improvement in his health he was able to spend more time attending to the Bateman's estate, which was thriving under a new bailiff. He had agreed to invest some money in the *Civil & Military Gazette*, which had run into financial difficulties, and the renewed involvement with his first paper kept him busy, and happy.

He was also, from August 1935, at work on his autobiography. This was not an attempt to forestall other biographers, as Hardy's third-person autobiography had been, but like Hardy's *Life* it manages to be at once tight-lipped and oddly suggestive. To use his own words about *Rewards and Fairies*, the material is 'worked . . . in three or four overlaid tints and textures', which might or might not reveal themselves to the reader (*SM* 111). By the middle of the month he was already sufficiently engrossed to take the manuscript with him on a visit to Marienbad.

He would no doubt have revised it. Carrie did so, with Gwynne's assistance; she certainly cut some passages, but one can only guess how freely she interpreted her role as Rudyard's editor.[30] The last day on which he is known to have been working on it is 26 December, four days before his seventieth birthday. It ends, as logically an autobiography should, with the words 'my death': a last flash of writerly cunning. His death was in fact to come soon after. On 12 January, in London to visit George and Elsie, he was taken ill at Brown's Hotel, when his ulcer burst; he died in the Middlesex Hospital just after midnight on 18 January. It was his forty-fourth wedding anniversary, and as she had been throughout, Carrie was with him when he died.

His ashes were buried in Westminster Abbey on 23 January. There were eight pallbearers: Stanley Baldwin, Sir Fabian Ware from the War Graves Commission, Field Marshal Sir Archibald Montgomery-Massingberd, the Admiral of the Fleet Sir Roger Keyes, A. B. Ramsay from Magdalen College, Howell Gwynne, A. S. Watt and J. W. Mackail. James Barrie, the only writer who had been asked to take part, was ill. Virginia Woolf wrote about it in her diary, 'forced by a sense of what is expected by the public, to remark that Kipling died yesterday; & that the King (George 5th) is probably dying today. The death of Kipling has set the old war horses of the press padding round their stalls.'[31] It seemed that Kipling's death was a national event, not a literary one. He would not much have minded that; nor would he have been much impressed that in the next few years, critics on both sides of the Atlantic, among them T. S. Eliot, Edmund Wilson, George Orwell, W. H. Auden and Lionel Trilling, would feel impelled to re-examine his work. He might have reflected that in literature as in the history of empires, 'The Captains and the Kings depart.' It remains for his admirers to add that when the tumult and the shouting die away, he remains our greatest writer of the short story.

Notes

1 Childhood and Youth

1 *Something of Myself, and Other Autobiographical Writings*, ed. Thomas Pinney (Cambridge, 1990), p. 112; subsequent references are given parenthetically in the text as (*SM* 112).

2 Charles Carrington, *Rudyard Kipling: His Life and Work* (1955; Harmondsworth, 1970), p. 577.

3 Lord Birkenhead was told by Trix that 'it was a grievous blow' to her parents when they read the story, and that they tried to make her admit that it was exaggerated. She was unable to do so; *Rudyard Kipling* (London, 1978), pp. 27–8.

4 One story, that he was forced to go to school wearing a placard with the word 'LIAR', has sometimes been discounted because it echoes an episode in *David Copperfield*; but perhaps Mrs Holloway borrowed the idea from Dickens.

5 See 'Values in Life', in *A Book of Words* (1928), p. 20.

6 'The Blue Closet'; see Ina Taylor, *Victorian Sisters* (London, 1987), p. 42.

7 Kipling was more comfortable with his Yorkshire than his Celtic background; when in 1919 he thanked God for his 'Scotch blood', it was the 'granite-gutted, self-sufficient' Presbyterian tradition he admired, and not a romantic Jacobite one (*Letters* IV.599).

8 Hannah bore eleven children in eighteen years; three died in infancy, and another in her teens.

9 Harry had left for America in 1858, and died there in 1891. Fred married on the day after the double wedding of Agnes and Louisa in 1866.

10 F. W. Macdonald, *As a Tale that is Told* (London, 1919), p. 333.

11 Trix married John Fleming, an officer in the Survey Department, in 1889, at the age of twenty-one. Her novel, *The Heart of a Maid* (1890), records their unhappiness.

12 His poem 'En-Dor' warns that 'the road to En-Dor is the oldest road / And the craziest road of all!' The subject of automatic writing is taken up in several stories, including '"The Finest Story in the World"' and '"Wireless"'.

13 See Angus Wilson, *The Strange Ride of Rudyard Kipling* (London, 1977), p. 43.

14 In 'The Impressionists'.

15 *The Letters of Rudyard Kipling*, ed. Thomas Pinney (London, 1990), volume I, p. 45. Subsequent references to the four volumes published to date are given in the text, in the form (*Letters*, I.45).

16 G. C. Beresford, *Schooldays with Kipling* (London, 1936), p. 113.

17 In 1919 he told André Chevrillon that the poem 'seems to set the key for the rest of my writings' (*Letters*, IV.573).

18 'Les Amours Faciles', in *Early Verse by Rudyard Kipling*, ed. Andrew Rutherford (Oxford, 1986), p. 116.

19 *Early Verse*, p. 10.

2   Seven Years' Hard: Kipling in India

1   *Egypt of the Magicians*, in *Letters of Travel (1892–1913)*, p. 222.
2   Quoted from Bernard Porter, *The Lion's Share: A Short History of British Imperialism, 1850–1983*, 2nd edition (London and New York, 1984), p. 20.
3   'The City of Evil Countenances', in Thomas Pinney, ed., *Kipling's India: Uncollected Sketches, 1884–88* (London, 1986), p. 85.
4   The manuscript has not survived.
5   Three items were by Lockwood, four by Alice and one by Trix; among the eight by Rudyard were 'The Strange Ride of Morrowbie Jukes' and 'The Phantom 'Rickshaw'.
6   Kipling, too, broke down during the summer; in the autobiography he writes that Walter Besant's novel, *All in a Garden Fair* (1883), helped him through 'the horror of a great darkness' (*SM* 39).
7   For the changes to the paper, see *Kipling's India*, pp. 243–6.
8   'Typhoid at Home', *Kipling's India*, pp. 69–77.
9   'Anglo-Indian Society', *Kipling's India*, p. 187.
10   E. Kay Robinson, 'Kipling in India' (1896), in Harold Orel, ed., *Kipling: Interviews and Recollections*, 2 vols (London, 1983), I.74
11   Kipling's monthly salary when he joined the *Pioneer* was 600 rupees.
12   *Kipling: the Critical Heritage*, ed. Roger Lancelyn Green (London, 1971), pp. 34–5.
13   *Critical Heritage*, pp. 38–41.
14   They were unattributed; at least one was written by his sister.
15   For the Sussex edition (1937) Kipling reinstated two stories from the *CMG* series, 'Bitters Neat' and 'Haunted Subalterns'.
16   *Critical Heritage*, pp. 47–8.
17   See Sandra Kemp, *Kipling's Hidden Narratives* (Oxford, 1988), p. 18.
18   In 'The Education of Otis Yeere' (*Wee Willie Winkie*).
19   The Native States were self-governing territories which while officially independent acknowledged the authority of the British in India.
20   Harry Ricketts links this passage to E. M. Forster's account of the Marabar Caves in *A Passage to India*. Both scenes convey the same atmosphere of existential panic. See *The Unforgiving Minute: A Life of Rudyard Kipling* (London, 1999), p. 106.
21   Edmonia Hill, 'The Young Kipling' (1936), in Orel, ed., *Kipling: Interviews and Recollections*, I.103.
22   Ricketts, pp. 71–4, interprets passages in Kipling's diary for 1885 – the only one to have survived – to mean that he thought he might have contracted a venereal disease following a visit to a brothel.
23   The eighth volume in the series was Trix's *The Heart of a Maid* (1890).
24   Compare 'The Bronkhurst Divorce Case' in *Plain Tales*, where one character is said to be 'quietly' cutting another to pieces with a whip. To protest at 'quietly' is to identify oneself as an outsider, unable to see the justice of the action.
25   George Orwell, 'Rudyard Kipling' (1942), in *Collected Essays* (London, 1961), p. 179.
26   *Critical Heritage*, p. 46.
27   Carrington, *Rudyard Kipling*, p. 152.

28　In 1937 Shirley Temple starred in a version of 'Wee Willie Winkie' directed by John Ford. In the magazine *Night and Day* Graham Greene accused the star's management of exploiting her sexual appeal. The producers sued for libel; the magazine closed down, and Greene left America to write a travel book about Mexico and, three years later, *The Power and the Glory*.

29　Henry James, Introduction to *Mine Own People* (1891), *Critical Heritage*, pp. 159–67.

30　Patrick Brantlinger, *Rule of Darkness: British Literature and Imperialism, 1830–1914* (Ithaca and London, 1988), pp. 227–53.

31　*The Letters of Joseph Conrad, Vol. I: 1861–97*, ed. Frederick B. Karl and Lawrence Davies (Cambridge, 1983), pp. 422–3.

32　Louis Cornell describes Dravot and Carnehan sympathetically as 'tragic figures', in his *Kipling in India* (London, 1966), pp. 162–3. For a severer view, see among others Benita Parry, *Delusions and Discoveries: Studies on India in the British Imagination, 1880–1930* (Berkeley and London, 1972).

3　The Conquest of London

1　Margaret Burne-Jones had married J. W. Mackail. Kipling disapproved of his liberal politics, and though they kept in touch the friendship became less close.

2　*From Sea to Sea*, 2 vols (London, 1900), I, pp. 304–6.

3　*From Sea to Sea*, I, p. 376, p. 275.

4　*From Sea to Sea*, I, p. 253, p. 472.

5　*From Sea to Sea*, II, pp. 131–2, p. 167.

6　*From Sea to Sea*, II, p. 178.

7　'The Comet of a Season' (uncollected); see *Letters*, I.360.

8　See Peter Keating, *The Haunted Study: A Social History of the English Novel, 1875–1914* (London, 1989), pp. 32–4.

9　In December 1890 Kipling complained to Besant that his 'pig of a (Indian) publisher [Thacker, Spink and Co.] . . . hasn't submitted any statement of acc[oun]ts for near 2 years' (*Letters*, II.29).

10　*Henry James Letters*, ed. Leon Edel, 4 vols (Cambridge, Mass., and London, 1974–84), III. 284. In later years, perhaps because he resented Carrie's influence over Kipling, Gosse spoke less generously of Wolcott; see Ann Thwaite, *Edmund Gosse: a Literary Landscape 1849–1928* (London, 1984), pp. 332–3.

11　Depending on one's interests, Kipling's work is either a nightmare or a godsend for bibliographers. The standard work is James McG. Stewart's *Rudyard Kipling: A Bibliographical Catalogue*, edited by A. W. Yeats (Toronto, 1959).

12　The argument has been put moderately by Angus Wilson, in *The Strange Ride of Rudyard Kipling*, pp. 277–8, and with finger-jabbing insistence by Martin Seymour-Smith, in his *Rudyard Kipling* (London, 1989).

13　*The Life and Work of Thomas Hardy, by Thomas Hardy*, ed. Michael Millgate (London, 1984), p. 236.

14　Lockwood brought with him the manuscript of a book, *Beast and Man in India*, which was published by Macmillan towards the end of the year.

15　*Critical Heritage*, p. 109.

16   Kipling's plan to visit Stevenson in Samoa proved unworkable; they never met.

17   Ann Thwaite, *Edmund Gosse*, p. 332.

18   Quoted from Ricketts, *The Unforgiving Minute*, p. 169.

19   In his autobiography, he wrote: 'When your Daemon is in charge, do not try to think consciously. Drift, wait, and obey.' (*SM* 123)

20   'Mr Kipling's Stories', *Contemporary Review*, Vol. LIX (March 1891); *Critical Heritage*, pp. 85–6.

21   In 1887 Eadward Muybridge's photographic studies of horses at the gallop gave a new impetus to the representation of movement. The imperial conflicts of the 1880s and 1890s were the last to give a prominent role to the war artist as a reporter; by the time of the Boer War the press had turned to photo-reproduction.

22   The quotations in this paragraph are from *Critical Heritage*, pp. 104 (Wilde), 48 (Lang), 41–2 (*Spectator*), and 51 (Ward).

23   Anthony Trollope, *An Autobiography* (London, 1883), 2 vols, I. 195.

24   The terms realism and naturalism, though occasionally distinguished, were more often used interchangeably.

25   There were at least 500 in London alone by the 1890s.

26   The word dialect is contentious. In 1909 a conference on the teaching of English described Cockney as not a dialect but 'a modern corruption . . . unworthy of being the speech of any person in the capital city of the Empire'; Peter Keating, *The Working Classes in Victorian Fiction* (London, 1971), p. 286 n.5.

27   *The Working-Classes in Victorian Fiction*, p. 166.

28   The remark is made about Mrs Yule, in chapter 7 of the novel.

29   George Orwell, 'Rudyard Kipling', in *Collected Essays*, pp. 185–6. Forster's comments are in an unpublished lecture now in the Library of King's College, Cambridge.

30   Craig Raine claims Kipling as 'our greatest practitioner of dialect'; *A Choice of Kipling's Prose* (London, 1987), p. 1.

31   See the 'General Explanations', p. xvii in the first volume of the *OED*.

32   *Letters*, II.256.

33   'The Story-teller at Large', *Fortnightly Review*, New Series, LXIII (April 1898), p. 652.

34   *Partial Portraits* (London, 1888), p. 264.

35   Introduction to *Mine Own People* (1891); *Critical Heritage*, p. 167.

36   G. K. Chesterton, *Charles Dickens* (London, 1906), p. 85.

37   See Clare Hanson, *Short Stories and Short Fictions, 1880–1980* (London, 1985).

38   Quoted from Derek Standord, ed., *Short Stories of the '90s* (London, 1968), pp. 13–14.

39   *Heart of Darkness*, ed. Robert Kimbrough, 2nd edition (New York, 1971), pp. 29, 34.

40   Alan Sandison has argued that the core of Kipling's artistic vision is the belief that 'Man is alone'. Society helps to shelter us from that terrible truth; it is 'an illusion created by the individual to establish, identify and protect the self'. See his 'Kipling: the Artist and the Empire', in Andrew Rutherford, ed., *Kipling's Mind and Art*, pp. 164, 166.

41 Benita Parry, *Delusions and Discoveries*, p. 206.
42 'Rudyard Kipling', *Fortnightly Review*, Vol. LVI, pp. 686–700.

4 Citizens of America

1 'From Tideway to Tideway', in *Letters of Travel, 1892–1913* (London, 1920), pp. 11, 13.
2 *Letters of Travel*, p. 16
3 Carrington, *Rudyard Kipling*, p. 592.
4 *Mark Twain – Howells Letters*, eds H. N. Smith and W. G. Gibson (Harvard, 1960), II.641.
5 *The Strange Ride*, p. 166.
6 In a review of *The Seven Seas* in March 1897; *Critical Heritage*, p. 193.
7 The last native Tasmanian was reported to have died in 1876.
8 The Outward Bound Edition began publication in 1897; in the same year Doubleday left to form a new company with Samuel McClure, which published all Kipling's new American material, beginning with *The Day's Work* in 1898.
9 *Letters*, II, pp. 104, 204, 117.
10 In this case the price was £1200.
11 See *Letters*, II.181: 'Don't believe a grandmother is infallible . . . they forget things or get 'em mixed up and the results are apt to be disastrous for the Kid.'
12 *Selected Letters of Henry James to Edmund Gosse*, p. 113.
13 'Values in Life', in *A Book of Words* (London, 1928), p. 20.
14 Shamsul Islam, *Kipling's Law: a Study of his Philosophy of Life* (London, 1975), p. 143.
15 Mark Paffard, *Kipling's Indian Fiction* (London, 1989), p. 92, sees Mowgli as 'undoubtedly the young "sahib" of the jungle', hated as well as revered because of his superiority.
16 Alan Sandison, *The Wheel of Empire* (New York, 1967).
17 Kipling wrote that he drew on Jameson's character for 'If' (*SM* 111), but it is difficult to take a man who collapsed into tears on the failure of the Raid as a model of equanimity; the poem's place in *Rewards and Fairies* suggests that he had Washington in mind.
18 Letter to Norton, 8 January 1896; *Letters*, II.225–6.
19 This was the first of Kipling's poems to appear in *The Times*.
20 Kipling told Norton that he intended Cheyne's attitudes to be seen as 'flagrantly un-moral not to say heathen' (*Letters*, II.323).

5 The Song of the English

1 Serial publication in England, in *Pearson's Magazine*, began a month later.
2 Twenty years later the poem evolved into a silent movie, *A Fool There Was*, with Theda Bara starring as the original 'vamp'.
3 Sir John Seeley, *The Expansion of England* (1883; London, 1914), p. 10.
4 Quoted in R. Faber, *The Vision and the Need* (London, 1966), p. 64.
5 *Critical Heritage*, pp. 187, 195.

6   J. H. Millar, 'The Works of Mr. Kipling'; *Critical Heritage*, p. 201.
7   Not only soldiers: one of the best of the poems, 'Mary, Pity Women!', a pre-echo of Brecht, has a female speaker.
8   Conrad writes that 'the main characteristic of the British . . . is not the spirit of adventure so much as the spirit of service': 'The mere love of adventure . . . lays a man under no obligation to faithfulness to an idea and even to his own self.' 'Well Done', in *Notes on Life and Letters* (London, 1921), pp. 254–6.
9   *Henry James Letters*, ed. Leon Edel, IV.40. James adds that it is 'masterly in its way, and full of the most insidious art'.
10   See Bernard Porter, *The Lion's Share*, p. 127.
11   Orwell, 'Rudyard Kipling', in *Collected Essays*, p. 180.
12   'Israel is a race to leave alone. It abets disorder' (*SM* 130).
13   Martin Seymour-Smith, p. 277. Similar discussion has been prompted by Kipling's 'The White Man's Burden'. White Men, he told a correspondent, are those who speak English and live quietly 'under Laws which are neither bought nor sold' (*Letters*, II.309).
14   Quoted in Porter, *The Lion's Share*, pp. 130–1.
15   Henley's *New Review* ceased publication in December 1897. He was awarded a civil-list pension of £225.
16   They also took Carrie's maid, a nursemaid and a governess.
17   Burne-Jones to Dr Jessop, quoted from Penelope Fitzgerald, *Edward Burne-Jones: a Biography* (London, 1975), where the date given is 21 April 1897; Kipling was in South Africa in 1898, not 1897.
18   In fact the British were too busy with the Delhi Durbar to provide much help in 1877, when India's worst famine led to more than 5 million deaths.
19   In *Past and Present*, III.4, Carlyle writes that 'All work, even cotton-spinning, is noble; work is alone noble', but elsewhere that '*all* human work is transitory, small, in itself contemptible; only the worker thereof and the spirit that dwelt in him is significant' (*Reminiscences*, (London, 1971), p. 3). This dual position – work as both the source of human dignity, and as ultimately meaningless – has clear affinities with Kipling's.
20   For a less sympathetic account, see Sullivan, *Narratives of Empire*, pp. 119–27.
21   *A Fleet in Being*, p. 5.
22   *A Fleet in Being*, pp. 34–5.
23   Doubleday's move from Scribner's in 1897 had slowed the progress of the Outward Bound edition. This gave G. H. Putnam the opportunity to bring out a rival edition, made up of unbound sheets of American editions already in circulation. Putnam paid the publishers for the material, thus allowing Kipling to receive a royalty. Nonetheless, Kipling sued Putnam, seeking to enjoin publication; the decision, upheld on appeal, went against him. He then tried to undercut Putnam by publishing the 'Swastika Edition' with Doubleday and McClure (see *Letters*, II.373–4 and notes). In November 1900 he undertook a similar, and similarly unsuccessful, action against R. F. Fenner & Co. of New York; see *Letters*, III.49–50.
24   Among those who sent messages of support was the German Kaiser.
25   Quoted from Lord Birkenhead, *Rudyard Kipling* (London, 1978), p. 198.
26   Wilson, *Strange Ride*, pp. 195–6; Carrington, *Rudyard Kipling*, p. 350.

27 This includes Elsie's recollections in the Epilogue to Carrington, *Rudyard Kipling*.

28 Carrington, p. 352.

29 P. W. Musgrave, *From Brown to Bunter: the Life and Death of the School Story* (London and Boston, 1985), p. 130.

30 See David Newsome, *Godliness and Good Learning: Four Studies on a Victorian Ideal* (London, 1961), for a fuller discussion.

31 Robert Buchanan, 'The Voice of the Hooligan', *Contemporary Review* (December 1899); *Critical Heritage*, pp. 233–49. Kipling wrote of Buchanan, 'I expect something we know nothing of is bothering him' (*Letters*, III.8); in fact he never fully recovered from a stroke in 1890, and was to die in June 1901.

32 See *The Outline of History*, p. 522; *Critical Heritage* p. 307. The italics are Wells's.

33 It appears in the Definitive Edition above the date 'October 9, 1899', when Kruger issued his ultimatum.

34 The others were H. A. Gwynne, future editor of the *Morning Post*, and Perceval Landon of *The Times*, who both became lifelong friends, Julian Ralph, 'the very best of Americans' (*SM* 90), and F. W. Buxton of the *Johannesburg Star*.

35 Her death of typhoid, only a few months later, is remembered in Kipling's poem 'Dirge of Dead Sisters'.

36 Andrew Rutherford, 'Some Aspects of Kipling's Verse', in *Critical Essays on Rudyard Kipling*, ed. H. Orel (Boston, 1989), p. 43. For Kipling's defence of Milner, see *Letters*, III. 31.

37 The reference is to General Sherman's destructive march through Georgia in the closing stages of the American Civil War, November–December 1864.

38 In a later story, Mary Postgate deliberately violates this code, though she knows that Wynn, whose death she is avenging, was a 'sportsman', and would not have approved.

39 Martin Seymour-Smith, *Rudyard Kipling*, p. 310.

40 The reference is to 1 Kings 21, where, after Jezebel has arranged for the murder of Naboth and the king her husband has claimed his vineyard, Elijah demands: 'Thus saith the Lord, Hast thou killed and also taken possession?'

6 *Kim*

1 The New York edition includes a third tale about Taffy, 'The Tabu Tale'.

2 The preamble mentions Effie five times by name, once for each year of her life.

3 Angela Mackail, later Thirkell; Orel, ed., *Interviews and Recollections*, II. 312.

4 *The Strange Ride*, pp. 228–31.

5 It had been in his mind as early as 1892; he returned to it in earnest in the autumn of 1898.

6 *Letters of Henry James*, vol. IV, ed. Leon Edel, pp. 209–12.

7 As other Sahibs more literally take possession of other aspects of Indian culture, such as the 'fragments of statues and slabs crowded with figures' in the Lahore Museum.

8   Edward W. Said, *Culture and Imperialism* (London, 1994), p. 188.
9   Kipling of course refers to the 'Mutiny'.
10   Edmund Wilson, 'The Kipling that Nobody Read', in *The Wound and the Bow* (1941; London, 1961), pp. 110–11.

7   In a Hidden Kingdom

1   In Kipling's view the old guard included much of the army, which 'even now . . . is looked upon as the perquisite of the aristocracy, who do not take the trouble to learn their job' (*Letters*, III.108–9).
2   Nearly 6000 soldiers died in action, and 16,000 of disease. The Boers lost some 7000 fighters, as well as those who died in the camps; losses among black Africans are estimated at around 14,000.
3   After the election, the new Under-Secretary at the Colonial Office, Winston Churchill, famously declared that 'slavery' was 'a terminological inexactitude'.
4   Britain, Australia, New Zealand, Canada and South Africa – though Kipling continued to regard America as essentially Anglo-Saxon.
5   *Rudyard Kipling to Rider Haggard: the Record of a Friendship*, ed. Morton Cohen (New Jersey, 1965), p. 42.
6   Lycett, *Rudyard Kipling*, p. 364.
7   Ford Madox Ford, *The Spirit of the People: An Analysis of the English Mind* (London, 1907), p. 34. On the conflict between 'place' and 'race' see Ian Baucom, *Out of Place: Englishness, Empire, and the Locations of Identity* (Princeton, N.J., 1999).
8   'Feminized', because the deepest vision of the regenerative powers of rural England is held in Kipling's story by Sophie Chapin, and in Forster's by Margaret Schlegel.
9   Huret was accompanied by Coudurier de Chassaigne, who wanted permission for a dramatic adaptation in French of 'The Man Who Was'. An English dramatisation by Kinsey Peile had already proved a successful vehicle for Beerbohm Tree; another, of *The Light that Failed*, by Constance Fletcher, was a success for Forbes-Robertson.
10   See *Letters*, III.297–8.
11   Three ministers, Lloyd George, Alexander Murray and Rufus Isaacs, secretly bought shares in the American Marconi Company, a month after Godfrey Isaacs, MD of the company in Britain, had secured a major government contract. Kipling refused to tone down the poem, in which Isaacs is portrayed not merely as a liar but a leper: 'It's meant for that Jew-boy on the bench and one day – please the lord – I may get it in' (*Letters*, IV.208). It had to wait until 1919 to be published in *The Years Between*.
12   Charles Morgan gives a blow-by-blow account in *The House of Macmillan (1843–1943)* (London, 1943), pp. 193–297.
13   John Bayley, *The Uses of Division: Unity and Disharmony in Literature* (London, 1976), p. 65.
14   See David Lodge, ' "Mrs Bathurst": Indeterminacy in Modern Narrative', in Phillip Mallett, ed., *Kipling Considered* (London, 1989).
15   *A Choice of Kipling's Prose*, p. 16.

16   The same can be said of readings by C. A. Bodelsen, *Aspects of Kipling's Art* (Manchester, 1964) and Elliot Gilbert, in *The Good Kipling* (Manchester, 1972). Nora Crook, in *Kipling's Myths of Love and Death* (London, 1989), offers an astute reading, but reaches the baffling conclusion that the narrators come to believe that Mrs Bathurst's spirit has sent Boy Niven to meet with Vickery, and that there has been a homosexual relationship between them.

17   In both stories the Shakespearean quotation is used to suggest that humble people may have tragic experiences.

18   *Rudyard Kipling to Rider Haggard*, p. 100.

19   Elsie was to write later, after John too had died, 'The two great sorrows of their lives, my parents bore bravely and silently, perhaps too silently for their own good.' Carrie never spoke of them to her; her father sometimes did. See Carrington, *Rudyard Kipling*, p. 595.

20   Under the pseudonym 'Mrs Holland', Trix was experimenting with automatic writing for the Society for Psychical Research.

21   The best of the stories, however, ' "Dymchurch Flit" ', with which Kipling himself was 'unashamedly content' (*SM* 110), has little to do with the imperial theme, while 'Brother Square-Toes' and ' "A Priest in Spite of Himself" ' concern Talleyrand and Washington.

22   See 'A Doctor of Medicine', in *Rewards and Fairies*.

23   See J. W. Burrow, *A Liberal Descent: Victorian Historians and the English Past* (Cambridge, 1983), p. 211–13. Freeman's fear of racial dilution led him to become a Little Englander.

24   One of the best known statements of the 'Southern metaphor' ('To me, England is the country, and the country is England') was made by Kipling's cousin, Stanley Baldwin, in *On England* (London, 1926); see especially pp. 1–9.

25   In 1910 Kipling wrote in a letter of 'the spirit of the land', 'the queer unchangeable force that persists at the back of everything'; see *Letters*, III.430.

26   In 1906, the year of *Puck of Pook's Hill*, Kipling drew up a mock charter, in a calligraphic hand, assigning part of his land to his children; it is given in facsimile in *'O Beloved Kids': Rudyard Kipling's Letters to his Children*, ed. Elliot L. Gilbert (London, 1983), p. 9.

8   Towards Armageddon

1   Most of the letters are to John; Elsie was educated at home.

2   Edmund Gosse, *Father and Son* (Harmondsworth, 1989), p. 251.

3   *Letters of Travel (1892–1913)*, pp. 135, 202, 204.

4   In addition to the honour, the prize was valued at around £7700.

5   Letter of 23 December 1915, quoted from Hugh Brogan, *Mowgli's Sons: Kipling and Baden-Powell's Boy Scouts* (London, 1987), p. 39.

6   See *Letters*, IV.390, and note.

7   *Letters*, III.250–1. The same year, 1907, saw the publication of a *Collected Verse* and the thin-paper English Pocket Edition.

8   Joyce M. S. Tompkins, *The Art of Rudyard Kipling* (London, 1959), p. 158.

9   The *Definitive Edition* adds a reference to II Samuel 14: our lives 'are as water spilt upon the ground', but a loving God has devised means 'that his banished be not expelled from him'.

10 *Letters*, IV.592. Kipling makes Einstein, 'nominally a Swiss, certainly a Hebrew', an illustration of 'the Boche's mental workings': 'When you come to reflect on a race that made the world Hell, you see how just and right it is that they should decide that space *is* warped.'

11 'The Playmate' accompanies another farce, 'Aunt Ellen', in *Limits and Renewals*.

12 *TLS*, 7 October, quoted in *Letters*, III.393n; *Athenaeum*, 16 October, p. 453; *Academy*, 30 October, p. 681.

13 Including 'Conversation Galante', the earliest poem in his *Collected Poems 1909–1962*.

14 Louisa's husband, Alfred Baldwin, had died the previous year; Agnes Poynter, her sister and Kipling's aunt, had died in 1906.

15 *Letters*, III.422–3. Among the authors who did join were Hardy, James, Conrad and Yeats.

16 Published in *The Times* as well as the *Morning Post*, Kipling's first appearance in the former for some years.

17 See 'The Roman Centurion's Song', 'The Anvil' and 'The Dutch in the Medway'.

18 *The Times*, 28 March 1912; Kipling owned a copy of his *The Unexpurgated Case Against Woman Suffrage* (1913).

19 His parents looked the school over first, and assured themselves that it was 'awfully jolly', 'quite like an Oxford College in miniature'; '*O Beloved Kids*', p. 114.

20 References in this paragraph are to *Egypt of the Magicians*, in *Letters of Travel (1892–1913)*, pp. 284, 269, 231, and 278–9.

21 '*O Beloved Kids*', p. 165.

22 The Welsh solicitor is Lloyd George; Jack Johnson was the black heavyweight boxing champion.

23 The poem was first published in *The Covenanter*, and two days later in *The Times* and the *Daily Telegraph*.

9   The Great War and After

1 Bernard Bergonzi, *Heroes' Twilight* (London, 1965), p. 33; Jon Silkin, *Out of Battle: The Poetry of the Great War* (Oxford, 1972), p. 65.

2 'The Outlaws' (1914). Kipling came to believe that Germany had planned 'a very cleverly worked' campaign to discredit him personally; *Letters*, IV.532.

3 *Letters*, IV.256: 'with England out of it, Germany holds the U.S. in the hollow of her hand.'

4 *The New Army in Training* (1915), pp. 14–15. Sections IV and V deal with 'Canadians in Camp' and 'Indian Troops'.

5 *O Beloved Kids*, p. 181.

6 Published in the *Daily Telegraph* and the *New York Sun*, and in volume form in 1915 as *France at War on the Frontier of Civilization*.

7 *France at War*, pp. 26, 63, 25, 40, 73.

8 *O Beloved Kids*, p. 221, pp. 211–13.

9 *O Beloved Kids*, p. 222.

10 *Rudyard Kipling to Rider Haggard*, pp. 84–7.

11 The Commonwealth War Graves Commission reported in 1992 that his grave had been found. This has been questioned; see Tonie and Valmai Holt, *My Boy Jack? The Search for John Kipling* (Barnsley, 1998).

12 First published in the *Daily Telegraph* in October 1916.

13 *The Fringes of the Fleet*, in *Sea Warfare* (1916), p. 7.

14 *Tales of 'The Trade'*, in *Sea Warfare*, p. 123.

15 *Sea Warfare*, p. 143.

16 *Destroyers at Jutland*, in *Sea Warfare*, pp. 153, 217.

17 The government had no coherent propaganda policy until Aitken, now Lord Beaverbrook, took charge of a new Ministry of Information in 1917. Kipling refused an official post.

18 Kipling regarded Churchill as an incurable 'political prostitute', vacillating between the Liberal and Conservative parties (*Letters*, IV.218).

19 Apart from 'In the Interests of the Brethren' (1918), Kipling effectively abandoned fiction between 1917 and 1924.

20 *Critical Heritage*, pp. 319–21. The reviewer also dismisses 'The Children', the poem in which Kipling comes closest to the mood of Owen and Sassoon.

21 Two speeches to American men and officers were published in pamphlet form in July 1918, as *To Fighting Americans, by Rudyard Kipling*.

22 Kipling's articles about the tour were published in the *Daily Telegraph* as *The War in the Mountains*; they remained uncollected until the Sussex edition.

23 First published in *The Years Between*, in 1919.

24 In April 1918 the Roman Catholic hierarchy denounced the proposal to extend conscription to Ireland as 'an oppressive and inhumane law'.

25 *Rudyard Kipling to Rider Haggard*, p. 101.

26 In 1924, he refused the Order of Merit. Lord Birkenhead, *Rudyard Kipling*, Appendix B, details the honours Kipling was offered, but refused to accept.

27 He suggested to Doubleday that 'the word hun be set up *lower case always*', and that a German be referred to as 'it' (*Letters*, IV.507).

28 See *Letters*, IV.510–12, and notes.

29 Montagu himself thought his easy relationship with Indians owed something to the fact that he was an 'Oriental'.

30 *Rudyard Kipling to Rider Haggard*, p. 110. One outcome of their discussion was the short-lived Liberty League, formed to fight Bolshevism; it was announced in *The Times* on 3 March 1920, and wound up on 14 May the same year.

31 Wondering why 'the Hun was let off', he answered his own question: 'I suppose it was the Jews' (*Letters*, IV.520).

32 'England and the English', *A Book of Words*, p. 182.

33 *Rudyard Kipling to Rider Haggard*, p. 101.

34 *Critical Heritage*, p. 322.

35 *Critical Heritage*, p. 323.

36 A three-volume 'Inclusive Edition' of his verse was published by Hodder & Stoughton in December 1919.

37 *A Book of Words*, pp. 181, 186. According to Rider Haggard, Kipling's speech 'took no hold' of the audience; *Rudyard Kipling to Rider Haggard*, p. 114.

38 Quoted from Philip Longworth, *The Unending Vigil: A History of the Commonwealth War Graves Commission 1917–1967* (London, 1967), p. 52.

39 Quoted from Longworth, *The Unending Vigil*, p. 79.

40   According to Julia Taufflieb, formerly Caitlin; see Orel, ed., *Interviews and Recollections*, II. 318.
41   'A Thesis', in *A Book of Words*, pp. 201, 204. Kipling shared French dismay at Lloyd George's refusal to approve an independent buffer state in the Rhineland.
42   Longworth, *The Unending Vigil*, p. 80.
43   Orel, ed., *Interviews and Recollections*, II. 337. Dorothy Ponton had been Elsie's governess before the war.
44   *The Irish Guards in the Great War: The Second Battalion*, p. 28; *Critical Heritage*, p. 332. Paul Fussell, *The Great War and Modern Memory* (Oxford, 1975) is more sympathetic.
45   First published in *Debits and Credits*.
46   *Rudyard Kipling to Rider Haggard*, pp. 122–3.
47   'Independence', in *A Book of Words*, p. 247.
48   *Rudyard Kipling to Rider Haggard*, pp. 131, 152, 159.
49   Lord Birkenhead, *Rudyard Kipling*, p. 299.

10   The Last Decade

1   'Fiction', in *A Book of Words*, pp. 283–4.
2   Carrington, *Rudyard Kipling*, p. 500.
3   'A Madonna of the Trenches': 'it knocked out everything I'd believed in. I 'ad nothing to lay 'old of, d'ye see?'
4   J. M. S. Tompkins, *The Art of Rudyard Kipling*, p. 116. It is equally possible that the 'old story' is simply that Michael's supposed parents, the dead George Turrell and the daughter of the NCO, were not married.
5   It is more fully expressed in 'The Burden', the poem which accompanies the story (and closes the volume): 'But God looked down from Heaven / And rolled the Stone away!'
6   Randall Jarrell, *Kipling, Auden & Co.: Essays and Reviews 1935–64* (New York, 1980), p. 358.
7   In a note to her edition of *Debits and Credits* (Harmondsworth, 1987), p. 297.
8   There are biblical echoes in the two poems added when the story was published in volume form, ' "Late Came the God" ' and 'Rahere', in each case wrenched out of context.
9   *New Republic*, 6 October 1926, pp. 194–5. Wilson does not comment that 'The Gardener' too employs a 'special slang', albeit that of respectable people in a Hampshire village.
10   'The Friends', one of the 'Brazilian Verses'; Kipling wrote up the visit for the *Morning Post* under the title *Brazilian Sketches*.
11   'The Supports' (1919), which suggests that such a bulkhead might be built from 'the everyday affair of business, meals, and clothing'.
12   Two of the more scholarly, Admiral L. H. Chandler and Flora Livingston, did eventually win his confidence.
13   James Gibson, *Thomas Hardy: Interviews and Recollections* (London, 1999), p. 243.

14 Hardy's accessibility to younger writers contrasts with Kipling's reserve. Kipling could not have written, as Hardy did, of having 'quite a paternal feeling, or grandpaternal', towards, among others, Siegfried Sassoon, Walter de la Mare, John Masefield, and Edmund Blunden (*Collected Letters of Thomas Hardy*, ed. R. L. Purdy and Michael Millgate, 7 vols (Oxford, 1978–88), VI.93).

15 Hugh Walpole reported Kipling's comments in his journal: 'No, he doesn't approve of the book. Too much of the abnormal in us all to play about with. Hates opening up reserves. All the same he'd had friends once and again he'd done more for than any woman' (Rupert Hart-Davis, *Hugh Walpole*, p. 296). Seymour-Smith, pp. 118–19, uses these remarks to support his thesis about Kipling's homosexuality, but Walpole may have recorded what he wanted to hear; it is hardly credible that having so often inveighed against 'beastliness' Kipling would now come close to an admission of it.

16 Lycett, *Rudyard Kipling*, p. 554.

17 Carrington, *Rudyard Kipling*, pp. 592–3.

18 There was a lighter side to his writing, with the publication of *Thy Servant a Dog*, which sold 100,000 copies between October and Christmas. Since Elsie's departure, the family dogs had helped to ease some of the tension at Bateman's.

19 Lord Birkenhead, *Rudyard Kipling*, p. 342.

20 'Shell-shock' implied a physical aetiology; this did not explain why the numbers suffering continued to increase for more than a decade after the shells had stopped.

21 *A Choice of Kipling's Prose*, pp. 18–22.

22 'The Kipling that Nobody Read', in Rutherford, ed., *Kipling's Mind and Art*, pp. 66, 69.

23 *Strand Magazine*, April 1934; not collected until the Sussex Edition.

24 *Strand Magazine*, January 1936.

25 Bambridge died in 1943, of pneumonia, leaving Elsie to live on alone at Wimpole Hall until her own death in 1976.

26 Discussing the absence of sex appeal in *Captains Courageous* with the MGM studio, Kipling helpfully explained that 'a happily married lady cod-fish lays about three million eggs at one confinement' (*SM* 77).

27 From Kipling's speech to the Royal Society of St George, 6 May 1935.

28 'The Bonfires', in the *Definitive Edition*. The Fenris wolf is a beast from Norse mythology.

29 *Morning Post*, 7 May 1935.

30 Thomas Pinney discusses the issues in the introduction to his edition of *Something of Myself*, pp. xix–xxi.

31 *The Diary of Virginia Woolf*, ed. Anne Olivier Bell, 5 vols (London, 1979–85), V.8.

Bibliography

A full Kipling bibliography would fill a fair-sized volume. Most of the items listed below have a biographical emphasis; those which are mainly critical have been selected to suggest the range of discussion of Kipling's work. In addition to the works listed, the eight volumes and 5000 pages of *The Reader's Guide to Rudyard Kipling's Work*, prepared by Roger Lancelyn Green, Alec Mason and R. E. Harbord (1961–72), provide a mass of useful material.

Beresford, G. C., *Schooldays with Kipling* (London, 1936)

Lord Birkenhead, *Rudyard Kipling* (London, 1978)

Bodelsen, C. A., *Aspects of Kipling's Art* (London, 1978)

Brogan, Hugh, *Mowgli's Sons: Kipling and Baden-Powell's Scouts* (London, 1987)

Carrington, Charles, *Rudyard Kipling: His Life and Work* (1955; Harmondsworth, 1970)

Chevrillon, André, *Rudyard Kipling* (Paris, 1936)

Cohen, Morton, ed., *Rudyard Kipling to Rider Haggard: The Record of a Friendship* (Cranbury, N.J., 1965)

Cornell, Louis, *Kipling in India* (London, 1966)

Crook, Nora, *Kipling's Myths of Love and Death* (London, 1989)

Dobrée, Bonamy, *Rudyard Kipling: Realist and Fabulist* (London, 1972)

Dunsterville, Lionel Charles, *Stalky's Reminiscences* (London, 1928)

Eliot, T. S., ed., *A Choice of Kipling's Verse* (London, 1941)

Flanders, Judith, *A Circle of Sisters* (London, 2001)

Gilbert, Elliott L., *The Good Kipling* (Athens, Ohio, 1972)

——— , ed., *Kipling and the Critics* (New York, 1965)

——— , ed., *'O Beloved Kids': Rudyard Kipling's Letters to his Children (1906–1915)* (London, 1983)

Gilmour, David, *The Long Recessional: The Imperial Life of Rudyard Kipling* (London, 2002)

Green, Roger Lancelyn, *Kipling and the Children* (London, 1965)

——— , ed., *Kipling: the Critical Heritage* (London, 1971)

Harrison, Albert, *The Years Between: Kipling's Art from the Beginning of the South African War to the End of the Great War*, unpublished PhD thesis, University of Strathclyde, 1998

Islam, Shamsul, *Kipling's Law: a Study of his Philosophy of Life* (London, 1975)

Kemp, Sandra, *Kipling's Hidden Narratives* (Oxford, 1988)

Le Gallienne, Richard, *Rudyard Kipling: A Criticism* (London, 1900)

Lycett, Andrew, *Rudyard Kipling* (London, 1999)

Macdonald, Edith, *Annals of the Macdonald Family* (London, 1923)

Macdonald, F. W., *As a Tale that is Told* (London, 1919)

Mallett, Phillip, ed., *Kipling Considered* (London, 1989)

Mason, Philip, *Kipling: The Glass, the Shadow, and the Fire* (London, 1975)

McClure, John A., *Kipling and Conrad* (Cambridge, Mass., 1981)

Moore, Gilbert, B. J., *Kipling and 'Orientalism'* (London, 1986)

Nicolson, Adam, *The Hated Wife: Carrie Kipling, 1862–1939* (London, 2001)

Orel, Harold, ed., *Kipling: Interviews and Recollections*, 2 vols (London, 1983)

——, ed., *Critical Essays on Rudyard Kipling* (Boston, 1989)

——, *A Kipling Chronology* (London, 1990)

Paffard, Mark, *Kipling's Indian Fiction* (London, 1989)

Page, Norman, *A Kipling Companion* (London, 1984)

Pinney, Thomas, ed., *Rudyard Kipling: Something of Myself, and Other Autobiographical Writings* (Cambridge, 1990)

——, *Kipling's India: Uncollected Sketches, 1884–88* (London, 1986)

——, ed., *The Letters of Rudyard Kipling*, vols 1 and 2 (London, 1990)

——, ed., *The Letters of Rudyard Kipling*, vols 3 and 4 (Iowa, 1996)

Rao, K. Baskara, *Rudyard Kipling's India* (Norman, Okla, 1967)

Ricketts, Harry, *The Unforgiving Minute: A Life of Rudyard Kipling* (London, 1999)

Rutherford, Andrew, ed., *Kipling's Mind and Art* (Edinburgh and London, 1964)

——, ed., *Early Verse by Rudyard Kipling, 1879–1889* (London, 1986)

Sandison, Alan, *The Wheel of Empire* (New York, 1967)

Seymour-Smith, Martin, *Rudyard Kipling* (London, 1989)

Stewart, James McG., *Rudyard Kipling: A Bibliographical Catalogue*, ed. A. W. Yeats (Toronto, 1959).

Sullivan, Zohreh T., *Narratives of Empire: the Fictions of Rudyard Kipling* (Cambridge, 1993)

Taylor, Ina, *Victorian Sisters* (London, 1987)

Tompkins, J. M. S., *The Art of Rudyard Kipling* (London, 1959)

Wilson, Angus, *The Strange Ride of Rudyard Kipling* (London, 1977)

Wilson, Edmund, *The Wound and the Bow* (1941; London, 1961)

Wurgaft, Lewis D., *The Imperial Imagination: Magic and Myth in Kipling's India* (Middletown, Ct., 1983)

Index

Printed in the United States
103023LV00001B/212/A